Why Do People Get Ill?

DARIAN LEADER AND
DAVID CORFIELD

HAMISH HAMILTON
an imprint of
PENGUIN BOOKS

HAMISH HAMILTON

Published by the Penguin Group
Penguin Books Ltd, 80 Strand, London WC2R 0RL, England
Penguin Group (USA) Inc., 375 Hudson Street, New York, New York 10014, USA
Penguin Group (Canada), 90 Eglinton Avenue East, Suite 700, Toronto, Ontario, Canada M4P 2Y3
(a division of Pearson Penguin Canada Inc.)
Penguin Ireland, 25 St Stephen's Green, Dublin 2, Ireland (a division of Penguin Books Ltd)
Penguin Group (Australia), 250 Camberwell Road,
Camberwell, Victoria 3124, Australia (a division of Pearson Australia Group Pty Ltd)
Penguin Books India Pvt Ltd, 11 Community Centre,
Panchsheel Park, New Delhi – 110 017, India
Penguin Group (NZ), 67 Apollo Drive, Mairangi Bay, Auckland 1310, New Zealand
(a division of Pearson New Zealand Ltd)
Penguin Books (South Africa) (Pty) Ltd, 24 Sturdee Avenue,
Rosebank, Johannesburg 2196, South Africa

Penguin Books Ltd, Registered Offices: 80 Strand, London WC2R 0RL, England

www.penguin.com

First published 2007
1

Set in 12/14.75pt Bembo
Typeset by Palimpsest Book Production Limited, Grangemouth, Stirlingshire
Printed in Great Britain by Clays Ltd, St Ives plc

A CIP catalogue record for this book is available from the British Library

ISBN: 978-0-241-14316-2

Why Do People Get Ill?

For Ed

Contents

Introduction

If two men of the same age have heart attacks resulting in equal damage to their hearts, why is the man who is single and depressed more likely to die of heart disease within the following year than the man who is married and not depressed? If a woman suffers from rheumatoid arthritis, why might the condition be relatively stable when her life is calm, but flare up when she has a conflict with her grown child? Why do people with little decision-making power in their jobs have more heart attacks and gastrointestinal disorders than their supervisors? How is it possible that asthma sufferers will have better lung functioning after they start writing about troubling experiences in their lives? And why is social isolation just as hazardous to one's health as smoking, obesity and lack of exercise?

These questions, adapted from an American Psychosomatic Society brochure, may seem surprising. We are all familiar with information about the dangers of smoking, poor diet and a sedentary lifestyle, but what about the psychological factors that may affect our lives? When we speak casually of an illness being 'psychosomatic', it is usually to indicate a transitory condition that isn't very serious: a stomach ache before a job interview, a headache before going on a date or a weak bladder before an exam. But the examples listed above refer to life-threatening illnesses like heart disease and chronic, debilitating conditions such as rheumatoid arthritis and asthma. Could what's going on in our heads actually have an impact on these ailments? And if so, how?

Three out of every four people in the UK and the US experience symptoms in any given month which they will try to relieve in specific ways, such as taking medication, resting or visiting their GP. Anxieties about health are fuelled by media stories that present readers with an increasing number of illnesses and conditions which they can suspect themselves of suffering from. Indeed, it has been estimated that between 25 and 50 per cent of GP visits are for medically inexplicable complaints, and the most common diagnosis in general-practice medicine today is non-illness. How can we account for this increase in the worried well? Is the body being used as a loudspeaker to signal some other kind of distress?

This is a fascinating question, but what about the remaining 50–75 per cent of cases – the ones where the patient's complaints *do* receive a medical diagnosis of illness, such as heart disease, diabetes and cancer? Could it be possible that thoughts and feelings might play a part in making our bodies ill with medically recognizable diseases? Would some of us be more prone to fall ill than others? And if so, would that mean susceptibility to specific illnesses or just to ill-health in general?

We will argue in this book that it isn't *what* we worry about that can make us ill, but the *ways* in which we worry. Research from several different traditions converges on the idea that what matters is how we are able – or unable – to process our experiences. Human beings are processing creatures: from the hunt tallies found on the walls of prehistoric caverns to the notches on the wall of a prison cell, we need ways to register what happens to us. Speaking and writing are the most obvious examples of how we make sense of the events in our lives, but what happens when these modes of communication are unavailable? Is it possible that, in some cases, a bodily illness could take their place?

As we explore these questions, we reach a number of conclusions. First of all, that there is no such thing as a psychosomatic illness. No single major illness is exclusively caused by the mind, just as few illnesses will always be completely exempt from the mind's influence. What matters are the *potential* connections between mind and body. If a study showed that several hundred women experienced no change in the state of their rheumatoid arthritis after a conflict with their children, but that one woman did, we might still learn something from this one case. It could suggest how the bodily mechanisms at work in arthritis can be linked to mental processes. These might be more or less dormant in some cases and active in others, or dormant and active at different moments in the same person's life. But the fact that there are routes between mental experience and the body means that the possibility of their interaction is never absent.

If one person blushes in an embarrassing situation, another may experience no comparable physical change. In the first case, the sense of embarrassment is the reason for the increased dilation of blood vessels in the cheeks. The other person may feel embarrassed but not blush, just as blushing can be caused by states other than embarrassment, such as excitement or pleasure. This simple example should warn us of the dangers of generalizing and of positing exclusive mechanisms to link mind and body. The same physical symptom can have a variety of causes, sometimes weighted psychologically, sometimes not. Likewise, the same psychological pressures will not produce the same physical symptoms. Everything depends on the particular combination of factors in each particular case.

Despite this, there may be times when the body is left more open to ill-health. Moments of separation and loss are especially significant here. When a vital relationship is broken, we will be left in a difficult, even impossible, situation. If we are unable to find ways of processing the loss, some of the body's internal systems may be compromised. This will weaken our resistance to disease. Ill-health will be more likely, though by no means definite. One of the interesting points made by psychoanalysis here is that separation and loss can apply to many different things: not just other human beings, but also jobs, activities and even hobbies. What matters is the central place they have in our lives. If an observer searches for more obvious types of loss, such as bereavement, they may well miss these other more subtle factors in a person's life.

Thinking about loss brought us to another conclusion. It has often been noticed that a bereaved person will identify with their lost loved one. They might adopt the same tone of voice or the same way of walking, or start to wear an article of clothing or scent linked to the loved one. These *identifications* frequently take place outside conscious awareness. And they may play a part in physical illness. A symptom may be a way of identifying with someone else, either to express a common bond or simply because the mechanisms for making sense of the relationship with that person, or with their loss, are not available. Today's vogue for stressing genetic factors masks these unconscious processes. If a symptom is found in two generations of a family, it will all too often be ascribed to genetic determinants rather than to unconscious identifications. This is not to say that an unconscious identification might not rely on genetic factors to emerge. But the interplay of the two is far more interesting to consider than the banishment of psychological factors favoured by some currents of contemporary medicine.

Keeping an open mind about this interplay means that rather than using the word 'psychosomatic' to refer to an illness, it should be used to designate an *approach* to illness. Instead of labelling asthma or hyperthyroidism or hypertension psychosomatic illnesses, *any* disorder could be approached psychosomatically, from the common cold to malaria, to heart disease or cancer. Psychosomatic medicine would not be a speciality, like ophthalmology or cardiology, but simply a term to indicate a *way of cooperating* between different practitioners. We hope that this book will encourage that kind of cooperation.

We start our book by looking at some common misconceptions about illness. It is often assumed that each illness is a well-defined entity, with a single specific cause and a single specific cure. This model might seem applicable to a case of bacterial infection to be treated by antibiotics, but it fails to account for most known illnesses. As we will see, it is in fact not even accurate when applied to a bacterial infection, since several other contributing factors can enter the picture. Psychological pressures can play a part in something as simple as an everyday viral infection like the common cold.

Trying neatly to compartmentalize the causes of illness can eclipse the bigger picture. The more an illness is studied within the context of a patient's life as a whole, the less reliable the standard explanations become. Today's emphasis on what can be counted and measured is inadequate for exploring the role played by psychological factors. When stress is evoked as an all-embracing explanation, the specificity of an individual case is lost. In place of the details of a unique life there is a vague catch-all concept. Individual case histories rather than large-scale statistical studies about stress are crucial for illuminating how psychological factors operate.

Yet the popularity of concepts such as stress and bacterial models of illness can in fact give us a vital clue to a better understanding of both health and disease. The more distanced we are from the events in our lives, the more likely it is they will appear as external influences that we have no control over. This distancing may be the result of a difficulty in processing what happens to us. When we are unable to think something through, the body may suffer the consequences. It is thus less what happens to us that matters than whether we are equipped to symbolize important changes in our lives.

An attention to these moments of change and transition can suggest why some people get ill when they do. Chapter 4 focuses on the timing of illness. If it is possible for someone to fall ill or even die at a symbolically significant or emotionally charged moment, it follows that there are very real routes from mental experience to the body. Hearing bad news, for example, has been shown in some cases to herald heart problems or exacerbate autoimmune disorders. If this can happen, it means that the words we hear can affect us deeply, in the very tissue of our bodies.

In Chapters 5–7 we explore the power of words. Words can shape our experience of the body and of medicine, and certain physical symptoms may even be made from words encoded in the body. Careful listening and interpretation may remove these symptoms, but there are many physical ailments that are not made from words yet still seem to have a link to mental processes. If someone hears that a loved one has just died of a heart attack, and then succumbs to the same fate themselves, should we assume that the specificity of the first death may have a link to the specificity of the second? Was it an accident that in both instances there was a heart attack, or should we assume that the news of the bereavement weakened the second person and so they fell ill at their most vulnerable point, which just happened to be the heart?

This brings us to the question of the different ways in which words can influence symptoms. We will see how some physical symptoms can be encoded questions or appeals for a response. They might be asking something about our identity or sexuality: 'Is there something inside me?', 'Am I a man or a woman?' or 'Am I at risk of losing part of myself?' But other symptoms may result from an arrest in the questioning process. Like a stamp or seal on the body, they emerge at the points where the possibilities of human dialogue and mental elaboration are curtailed. Unable to articulate distress, we fall ill at a symbolically charged moment.

Exploring the timing and course of certain illnesses shows how much we are bound up with other people. Friction, turbulence and disappointment in our relations with others can have very real effects in the body. How we react will depend to a large extent on our early relations with our caregivers. Chapters 9 and 10 examine some aspects of these relations and their consequences for illness and health. We will see how most of these reactions take place at an unconscious level, distanced from our conscious awareness.

If relations with other people can affect our bodies, how do they do it? How can mental experience change our physiology? Research on the immune system offers some clues here. It was believed until quite recently that the immune system was autonomous, independent of the brain and nervous system. New research suggests that the immune system is in fact in constant dialogue with the brain. Psychological difficulties can have a direct effect on how our immune systems respond to threats. It is one of the pathways by which mental experience can open up the body to illness.

Chapter 12 explores one example of this process. Cancer has been the subject of passionate debate in the area of mind–body medicine: can the mind affect the course or even the inception of cancer? We look at some of the evidence and suggest new ways of thinking about the mind–body connection here. Are some people more susceptible to cancer than others due to their psychological make-up? We question the concept of the cancer-prone personality, and the association often made between poor emotional expressivity and cancer.

The idea that the more problems we have expressing ourselves, the more likely we are to fall ill is discussed in Chapter 13. It raises the important question of how we process experience. What mechanisms do we need to make sense of the world? And could the absence of such mechanisms make us ill? Researchers from several countries have proposed that a defensive distancing from one's emotional life can set the ground for physical illness. The coolest, most well-adapted people would be most at risk. How robust is this theory? And if there's anything to it, what would be the effects on a person's physiology?

We argue that although these ideas can be helpful and illuminating, they tend to put too much emphasis on the expression of emotions. Perhaps it is less acute emotional experiences that can prepare the ground for illness than the absence of a mental framework for processing them. This would explain why people so often fall ill when they find themselves called to occupy a new symbolic place: a death, a birth, a marriage, retirement, for example, all introduce vital changes in our lives. They involve shifts in the position we occupy in the world, and so demand that we make sense of the new configuration we find ourselves in. If we are unable to do this, we may in some cases fall ill.

Chapter 14 draws out some conclusions here. A theory of why people get ill is not the same thing as a treatment plan. We believe that psychoanalytic ideas may be helpful in understanding the details of how someone becomes ill, but it is not psychoanalysis as such that will cure the disease. Unconscious mental forces may have powerful effects on the body, but talking therapies are rarely the unique answer to bodily illness. Rather, they may work in conjunction with sensitive medical treatments that are alert to the importance of human dialogue and recognition. Psychoanalytic theories are also useful here to demonstrate why some non-psychoanalytic treatments actually work.

Our final chapter raises the delicate issue of the psychology of doctors. What impact will the doctor's mental processes have on their understanding of and response to illness in a patient? This is a question that could of course be raised about any profession: how does the sea captain's psychology affect the way he steers his ship and handles his crew? How does the barrister's mental life shape the way she relates to her clients and then argues their case? The breadth of these examples doesn't lessen the relevance of this enquiry in the context of medicine, and we examine some of the problems that our question raises.

Throughout the book, we hope to revive an interest in psychosomatic medicine: not as a way of labelling certain illnesses and segregating them from others, but of approaching *any* illness. This project seems all the more vital today given the progressive disillusionment with conventional medicine. More and more patients are seeking alternative or complementary treatments. Orthodox medicine has both attacked and, at times, embraced such treatments, but has by now recognized that they are here to stay. While debate continues as to the medical benefits of practices such as homeopathy and acupuncture, they clearly offer a more holistic approach than the average GP consultation. In contrast to the reduction of the body to its parts implicit in much of conventional medicine, they provide a space where a patient can feel recognized and listened to. Rather than let this split widen, it is surely imperative for medicine to rethink some of its assumptions and widen the scope of its interests.

This perspective faces many difficulties, however. Medicine has moved in a direction to a large part determined by economic interests. Payment methods in insurance-based systems tend to reward costly technical procedures, not listening processes. In some parts of America, a physician will only get reimbursed for a consultation if it results in a prescription. The power of drug companies has likewise grown exponentially. They now fund about two-thirds of clinical studies, and medical journals have increasingly become marketing devices for new products and diagnoses. After thirteen years editing the *British Medical Journal*, Richard Smith concluded that the studies funded by industry are subtly manipulated to give positive results. The same research will be published again and again in different journals, with minor variations, to give the impression of a unanimous acceptance and weight of evidence. Studies funded by industry, he observed, are four times more likely to have positive results than those funded by other sources.

Companies may then pay for and distribute thousands of reprints of articles detailing these positive results. These are sent to doctors or come in the form of supplements to medical journals. All in all, the whole field is swayed by economic self-interest. Pharmaceutical companies generally have little to gain from psychological perspectives on illness. If a drug is found that can apparently extend the lives of breast-cancer sufferers by two years, this would make the newspapers. But when forms of group therapy have claimed the same results, this has not happened. Group therapies and support groups don't fit well into the marketplace. They won't make anyone millions, and most forms cannot be patented.

There has predictably been a growing trend in recent years to package such therapies like drugs. Some of them claim to target specific aspects of illness. They are supposed to be administered like a pill or injection, and this no doubt makes them attractive to health-service providers. But this has left aside the question of how patients participate and contribute to all forms of therapy. The more that market forces exert their pressure on the field of therapy, the more such treatments will become distorted and reframe their aims and results in the terms required by a market which sees human interactions in terms of goods to be bought and sold.

This presents a rather bleak picture of the future. Psychological therapies will aim to do without the psychology. The human factor will be progressively emptied out of the equation, and the unconscious forces at play in therapies will just be reduced to the level of other external factors. If the market looks for specific interventions that can be packaged and sold, what place is there for research which does not lead to a conventional product? Psychoanalytic theory, for example, does not necessarily provide a treatment method for a physical illness, but it may well illuminate some aspects of the illness which have remained obscure. Yet what agency would fund further research in the knowledge that there may be no specific, marketable outcome?

If it is possible to generate a dialogue around some of the themes we discuss in this book, perhaps this situation can change. An openness to different and perhaps unfamiliar ways of thinking can foster a more humane approach to illness. Once we acknowledge the part played by our unconscious mental life, illness is no longer an isolated physical problem but something that concerns the whole person and the networks of our relationships to others.

*

We would like to thank many people for their involvement in our book. First of all, the patients and doctors who told their stories to us and, in some cases, allowed us to accompany them on medical visits. Their insights have been tremendously important for us, and their generosity in sharing their experiences has been invaluable. Others have helped to form this book in a variety of different ways and we are grateful to the diverse contributions of Maria Alvarez, Pat Blackett, Ed Cohen, Antony Gormley, Anouchka Grose, Andrew Hodgkiss, Hanif Kureishi, Janet Low, Michael Kennedy, Bridget Macdonald, Kate Parker, Vicken Parsons and Sophie Pathan. Georgina Capel at Capel-Land was as ever the perfect agent, and Simon Prosser at Hamish Hamilton was as candid as every editor aspires to be and every writer dreads. His comments, advice and suggestions have been crucial in shaping this book and we would like to thank him for his commitment to our project and the perspicacity of his input. Finally, where would we have been without the patience, support and advice of our partners, Mary and Ros, and their ability to see us through our book-induced hypochondria?

1. What Causes Illness?

In her first term at boarding school, a fifteen-year-old girl is taken ill with fever and vomiting. The fever quickly subsides, yet the vomiting continues and, as it worsens, her mother is called. She takes her daughter home and arranges private medical help. A round of visits and tests ensues, yet medical opinion differs. The mother is keen to find a name for her daughter's malady, and has more confidence in those doctors who will provide one. It is important to her that the vomiting can be explained by a known, classifiable medical cause such as infection.

The patient, in contrast, wants something different. As she says when she finally has the opportunity to see a psychotherapist, her world has not been the same since her separation from her family to attend the new school. These events, it turns out, have been precipitated by the divorce of her parents. Her father had left the family home some months before her own departure to the school. And significantly, one of the first details about the father she mentions is the fact that he suffers from habitual acid reflux. Although she wants relief from the vomiting, she senses that there is something more that needs to be said beyond a purely medical diagnosis – something that is at odds with her mother's refusal to see that her symptoms are in any way linked to her experience of the family upheavals.

In this case mother and daughter each wanted something different from their encounter with medicine. The mother's wish for a neat diagnosis was felt by her daughter to be her way of refusing to recognize the pain caused by the break-up of the family. The daughter's insistence that the doctors weren't understanding her was felt by the mother to be sheer self-indulgence on the girl's part which she should just snap out of. The mother wanted a medical label and a pill to cure her daughter. The daughter wanted more than a label. She wanted to be able to voice her feelings, even if she wasn't sure how exactly she should do so or what exactly she should say.

This example brings into focus some of the problems that can emerge when we ask what has made us ill. The vomiting must have an explanation in terms of the body. Since it is a somatic or bodily phenomenon, it can't fail to have a bodily description. And this is probably what the mother was searching for. But in its particular context, it also has a meaning in terms of the patient's life. It could be seen as a way of articulating distress, a response to the family break-up and the exile to the new school. On another level, it could be seen as an identification with the father, the vomiting mimicking the symptoms of acid reflux. But which of these explanations would be the truest? Are they mutually exclusive or can they coexist?

How these questions are answered reveals a great deal about our presuppositions and what we expect by way of an explanation. Where one individual would seek an answer couched in medical terms, another would find it alienating to see their body's functioning reduced to the cellular or molecular level. But it isn't just about choosing mind or body here, since what matters is the sort of link we expect them to have. For the mother, the explanation she sought effectively ruled out the psychological factor, while the daughter was interested in how the body was expressing something. The answers to our questions will thus partly depend on how we experience our physical symptoms and what place we have given them in our lives – and this, in turn, will have an effect on what we want from medicine.

Although people may have very different views here, don't we all want to know about causes, whatever terms they are phrased in? If we go to our GP with chest pains or nausea or a cough, we will want an explanation as to why we have the symptoms and what they might be signs of. We probably won't ask why we have flu, but will simply want a prescription for the medication that works best. But many of the problems we might see a GP about are more complicated than this. If we have a cough, it might be reassuring to learn that it's due to air pollution or pollen or diet or an air-borne bacterium. We might be angry because the air isn't clean or frustrated because there's too much pollen around, but at least there's a definite and concrete explanation for why we're coughing.

But what if the GP were to list five or six causal factors? Wouldn't the confusion this gives rise to only add to the problem? And if all we had was a common cold, would we really want to know that several factors are involved in getting one? Most people will have 2–5 colds a year, the incidence among schoolchildren increasing to 7–10. A cold might only be a minor nuisance, but should this impede curiosity about its origins? A number of experiments have tested people's stress levels and then exposed them to rhinovirus, the germ generally linked to the common cold. Years of this kind of work at the Common Cold Unit of the Medical Research Council in Salisbury have shown that rhinovirus on its own isn't enough to produce this everyday malady.

The Common Cold Unit operated between 1946 and 1989, and was promoted to volunteers as a holiday opportunity. Housed in a large property and paid a fee for their troubles, the human guinea pigs were allowed to enjoy walks on Salisbury Plain but forbidden from entering the local town. Rhinovirus or a placebo would be squirted up their nostrils every day, and they would have to blow their noses regularly into collection tubs. Despite being inconvenienced in this way, the volunteers nonetheless found these enforced 'get away from it all' conditions so attractive that many were keen to go back, and one couple even visited the unit twenty-one times. There would always be a waiting list, and couples met, married and even honeymooned there.

Thanks to the enthusiasm of these volunteers, the researchers reached a number of conclusions. They found that emotional distress is linked to a greater risk of infection, and difficult life events increase the chances of actually catching a cold, with chronic problems like unemployment or friction within a relationship proving particularly significant. We might think it obvious that the more run down we are, the more likely we'll come down with a cold, but results like these are important to show how it isn't just the single isolated factor of exposure to a germ that will make us ill.

Surprisingly, the idea that one unique entity, such as a germ, causes another, such as a cold, is relatively new in medical thinking. One of the landmark moments in the development of this paradigm was the discovery by Robert Koch in 1882 that there was a link between *Mycobacterium tuberculosis* and the disease itself. He isolated a tubercle bacillus from a patient and injected it into a guinea pig. A fortnight later, enlarged lymph nodes appeared adjacent to the site of the injection and the infection spread. This infection model of disease is probably the one that most people subscribe to today: an external agent comes into contact with an organism, infects it, and the organism falls ill. And from here it's an easy step to the assumption that, given one external agent and one organism, there will also be one cure.

The discovery of tissue changes caused by an external agent that could be captured under a microscope created a universal template for causality in medical thinking. And when a cure is found that will counter the effects of these changes, it produces a certain kind of awe. There is indeed something wondrous when we witness the effect of antibiotics on bacteria, or insulin therapy in diabetes, or L-Dopa in the management of Parkinson's. But these amazing and sometimes life-saving developments are not the same thing as a proof of the single-cause or 'bacterial' model of illness. In reality many more factors play a part in the recovery of a patient.

The discovery of the tubercle bacillus and the demise of TB seem one and the same phenomenon. Yet when medical historians studied the evolution of the disease, they made an equally intriguing discovery: TB was on the wane many years before a vaccine became available. Environmental changes in people's lives, such as better hygiene and nutrition, were key factors here. And this doesn't apply just to TB. Historians have shown repeatedly that the decline of deaths from infectious disease has generally preceded the introduction of antibiotics and immunization by several decades. One study has even claimed that only 3.5 per cent of the decline in mortality due to infectious disease since 1900 can be attributed to pharmacological intervention. There is thus a mismatch between our beliefs about disease and the curative power of medicine, and the facts.

But do these findings really contradict the single-cause model? Wouldn't improved social conditions just mean decreased exposure to a bacillus, less chance of coming into contact with a sick person due to less crowded accommodation and better food hygiene due to pasteurizing procedures? The social argument might still support the single-cause model. And yet, in the case of TB, although every known case of the disease is a result of exposure to the bacillus, only a minority of those exposed to it will actually go on to develop the disease. Rather than a single cause, there have to be many factors at play here.

The idea of a single cause for a single illness may be more a belief system than a rational perspective. If the tubercle bacillus is a necessary cause of TB, not everyone harbouring it will get TB, just as *Streptococcus pneumoniae* may cause pneumonia, yet many people play host to this creature in their mouths without developing the illness. In fact, 5–10 per cent of healthy adults and 20–40 per cent of healthy children carry it. Malaria, likewise, is caused by a parasite of the genus *Plasmodium* which is transmitted by the anopheles mosquito. What is less well publicized is that, as army studies in the 1940s found, development of the disease is affected by psychological pressures, such as the threat of air raids. Similarly it has also long been known that diseases like typhus and dysentery will flourish with greater success in defeated armies rather than victorious ones.

Clinical studies have shown again and again how an individual's response to the risk of infection is determined by several different factors. This is crucial even in a common illness like influenza. Although it is often pointed out that specific antibody responses, and hence resistance to disease, decline with age, they are also affected by our relations with other people. For instance, antibody responses to the flu vaccine are much lower in elderly people who look after someone else than in those who don't have a caregiving role. This becomes all the more significant when we realize that, in the United States alone, there are an estimated 24 million homes where a chronically ill person is being cared for. There are thus other factors besides simple infection that account for the development and course of illnesses. We can be exposed to many different infections, yet not become ill in any real sense.

Take a well-known problem like ulcers. In the early 1980s it was famously demonstrated that, after years of searching for psychological causes such as stress at work, a bacterial cause had at last been found. Ulcers were caused by the presence of *Helicobacter pylori* in the stomach. This idea was apparently scoffed at when it was first aired in 1983, since it seemed so obvious that factors like diet and stress were intimately linked to the illness, and that bacteria wouldn't thrive in the acidic environment of the stomach. Yet after Barry Marshall publicly swallowed a petri dish of the stuff and succumbed, as predicted, to gastritis, it seemed as if cause and effect had finally been found. Bacteria did matter. And soon enough the single-cause model captured everyone's imagination: *Helicobacter pylori* caused ulcers and antibiotics could then be used to treat them.

However, it soon became clear that between a third and two-thirds of the world's population carried *Helicobacter pylori* in their stomachs, yet clearly not all of them developed gastritis or an ulcer. And furthermore, about 15 per cent of ulcer cases turned out not to have these bacteria in the gut at all. Just as intriguing was the fact that when Marshall received the Nobel Prize for his work on ulcer causation in 2005, the many accounts of the discovery that filled the newspapers depicted him as having been a desperate man back in the 1980s. People hadn't been listening to him, and so he swallowed the *Helicobacter* as a last resort – to the horror of his wife and family. Doesn't this suggest that he was a little bit tense and anxious to start with? The fact that the bacteria gave him gastritis, then, was perhaps just as much a proof that mental strain had to be present for the bacteria to take effect.

What happens to the single-cause model of illness in a case like this? The picture is quite complex, and becomes even more so when issues like immunity, predisposition and resistance are factored in. How many other possible contributing causes should we add? And where should we stop? Since the suicide rate goes up when newspaper and television stories about a suicide are broadcast, should media reports be included in the list of 'causes' of suicide? Or should talk of 'causes' be dropped altogether and replaced by 'correlations' between events?

Yet however often we attest to recognizing these complex pictures, it seems we're forever drawn to single causes. We can accept complexity rationally, but in reality we want something less confusing. Strange as it may seem, this reinforces beliefs and superstitions that supposedly characterized the time before the rise of scientific medicine. The bacterial model, after all, conceives illness as a single, discrete entity, and this is suspiciously close to the ancient idea of illness as an autonomous entity which is visited upon one, like a demon. The discovery of microscopic organisms and infection processes did not dispel these archaic fears but rather gave them a new, scientific veneer. In the words of physician and psychosomatic researcher Alberto Seguin, 'The germ was the scientific form of the demon who attacks and kills.'

Many of the seemingly miraculous discoveries of bacterial medicine made these old belief systems even more concrete. Personalizing the enemy had finally become scientific, and there was a new vocabulary to name the agencies trying to destroy us. Everyday ways of speaking about illness illustrate this: we 'battle' illness or 'fight' against it, just as we can 'surrender' to it or be 'beaten' by it. Television adverts and media articles tell us we have to distinguish between 'good' and 'bad' bacteria, eradicating the latter and nourishing the former. These ways of personalizing micro-organisms rely on child-like divisions into good and bad, benign and evil, and they also invite us to make a much sharper distinction between the inside and the outside of our bodies than rationality might suggest. Picturing and describing the body along these lines actually reinforces the bacterial single-cause model of illness.

Today's popular emphasis on genetics has a similar effect. Genetic factors are referred to as if they were external agents entirely responsible for illness. One gene problem is supposed to cause one illness or behaviour pattern. But we must remember that there are very few disorders that can be attributed to a single gene. How a gene manufactures – or 'expresses' – proteins is highly dependent on its biochemical milieu, and how these proteins then function is again highly contextual. As David Weatherall, director of the Institute of Molecular Medicine at Oxford University, has pointed out: 'When scientists announce that they have discovered a "gene" for heart disease or asthma, what they really mean is that they have identified one of a number of genes that may, under certain circumstances, make an individual more or less susceptible to the action of a variety of environmental agents, some of which are known to be involved in our common intractable diseases.'

Although each of the stem cells of an embryo contains the whole genome, it will be the complex history of its interactions which determines whether it becomes a bone, skin, blood or gut cell. Likewise, organs require the contributions of many genes. In a humble creature such as the fruit fly, three-quarters of its genes contribute to the formation of its eye. The workings of any single gene are dependent on many variables. In the cells of an adult human, whether the C282Y gene will express itself, exposing that person to the risk of developing the iron-absorption disorder haemochromatosis, will depend on sex, age, diet, alcohol consumption, whether they are menstruating, whether they've had hepatitis C, and other possible factors.

Nonetheless, in the face of such extreme complexity, almost every aspect of the human condition has now been linked simply to genetic propensities, from alcoholism to celibacy to sexual orientation. Genes are portrayed as distinct causal agents – like germs – rather than as parts of dynamic systems in which they won't act all the time, but only in response to a complicated range of other factors. Very few illnesses are reducible to pure genetic inheritance, but let's just assume for a moment that they were. If one of the reasons some people wish to dismiss psychological factors as a cause of illness is to shield themselves or their loved ones from blame, wouldn't this just redistribute it?

Belief in genetic inheritance already introduces the vast psychological problem of inter-generational blame and guilt, and there is a growing literature now on the specific psychological problems encountered in areas like genetic oncology. If one family member is afflicted with an illness linked to strict genetic inheritance, it is quite common to witness the rise of debilitating guilt in those sharing the same genetic stock but who escaped the disease. This can even lead to self-destructive behaviour and oddly coincidental 'accidents' in those who have escaped, as if to draw punishment on themselves.

A 39-year-old woman began psychotherapy faced with the terrible problem of having to decide on whether to go ahead with the double mastectomy her doctors had advised. There had been six deaths from breast cancer in three generations of her family, and genetic tests had shown the high probability of her developing the disease. The patient's acutely anxious state led the therapist to believe that the medical advice must have been received recently, yet it turned out that this had occurred more than three years previously, after her older sister had herself been diagnosed with breast cancer. What, then, had happened in the interim?

After the sister's biopsy proved positive, the patient had left her stable job in the Civil Service to drift from one part-time job to another. 'I had no energy,' she said. 'I couldn't focus on anything.' During this time, it was as if she had abandoned herself. She would put herself in increasingly dangerous situations, going home with random men she met in dodgy clubs and having unprotected sex, hitching lifts home late at night and repeatedly driving while drunk. Over the three years, she had four accidents, two of them serious. As she described these remarkable changes in her behaviour, it became clear that her sister had always envied her safe Civil Service job, and that the dissolute night-life had been a feature of the sister's, and not her own, adolescence.

Following her sister's diagnosis, the patient had asked herself why it had not been her instead. She had known about the other deaths in the family, and had a sense of a fate or destiny that lay waiting for them. When the terrible disease struck her sister and not her, her behaviour showed that she was putting herself in the sister's place, giving up her job and drifting around clubs as the sister had once done. The dangerous situations she created were punishments for her guilt at having escaped. Interestingly, during this time she experienced very little conscious anxiety. This appeared at a precise moment: after she had met a man who wanted to have children with her. It was this, rather than the medical opinion, which upset the unconscious equilibrium she had maintained.

The assumption of genetic determinism can remove blame from one person only to displace it on to another. As for the person afflicted with the illness, how would they deal with their rage at their parents or grandparents for transmitting a disease to them? Would that rage have any effect on the actual course and outcome of the disease in question? If such troubling feelings remained unarticulated, would they then risk making the person even more unwell? If the rage conflicted with feelings of love, how would the body bear the brunt of this unresolvable tension?

Even a highly simplified view of genetics swiftly unravels into this more complicated picture. Likewise, as medical research finds more and more interconnections between the many systems of the human body, causal models are forced to take into account a host of links and communicating pathways. This complexity is augmented by the fact that there are often problems in defining and differentiating between quite common disorders. Take rheumatoid arthritis, for example. This is often diagnosed by the presence of IgM rheumatoid factor in the blood, yet there are plenty of people who have IgM without showing the symptoms of arthritis, just as there are those who show the symptoms yet have less than significant rheumatoid factor in their bloodstream. Other patients may have rheumatoid arthritis due to the fact that they suffer from a particular protein deficiency.

While medicine acknowledges this complexity, popular images of medical research often disregard it. Clear correlations between an illness and a unique cause make better media stories. Yet this can work the other way round: medical research can be pushed in the direction of easy compartmentalization and over-simplification. Highly complex models may conceal a string of single-cause models. When the *Helicobacter* thesis about ulcers was shown to be limited, rather than searching to include psychological factors, some researchers just looked for a more specific kind of *Helicobacter*. The discovery of new strains featuring a syringe-like structure that can inject a protein into cell walls to produce an inflammatory response makes this theory look more precise. But there is still the question of what other factors determine the strength of the inflammatory response and how some people can carry the bacteria without becoming ill. The precision of a fine-tuned piece of research here risks obscuring the bigger picture.

Likewise, sub-forms of diseases are still being found. Researchers have discovered nine different mechanisms which result in the formation of peptic ulcers, and whereas it was once assumed that secretion of high levels of hydrochloric acid and pepsin was necessary, some patients turn out to have normal secretory levels. Gout was once associated with high levels of uric acid in the blood, yet some gout patients have relatively normal levels. The factors that allow a diagnosis of disease to be made will be clearer in some cases than in others. Hepatitis B, for example, can be linked to chronic or acute liver disease, hepatic carcinoma or may cause no symptoms at all. The more supposedly homogeneous diseases are studied, the more it seems that different mechanisms may produce the same lesions and physiological disturbances, just as the same mechanisms may produce different lesions or physiological responses.

This might not be true all of the time, but if we accept the possibility that it will be so in some cases, there will be an impact on how disease is thought about. A single elusive mechanism will not necessarily be the culprit when we fall ill. And likewise, a strong psychological factor in one case would not necessarily be present in another. This point was made many years ago by the surgeon David Kissen, who ran the Psychosomatic Research Unit at Glasgow University in the 1960s. To find a plausible mechanism in one case and not in another does not automatically rule out the mechanism, if we have recognized that a disease is not always a homogeneous entity. And so, as Kissen suggests, it would make little sense to ask a question like 'Which psychological factors give rise to which illnesses?'

The quest for simplicity should not become an obstacle here. The Plato scholar Seth Bernadete once told an illuminating story about a conversation he had one day with the philosopher Willard Quine. Bernadete was telling him about an interesting new book which analysed the differences between habit and understanding, a theme that Quine was working on. As he explained some of the arguments, Quine said, 'Yes, that's true, but it's too complicated.' He wanted simplicity. Rather than a proper analysis of what was happening, his wish for a simple model got in the way of proper thinking.

Quine claimed to have a love of desert landscapes, perhaps reflecting this same desire for simplicity and lack of clutter. Yet the more we look, the more we find, and it turns out that the kind of ecosystems that deserts support are of an astonishing complexity. In fact, the bacteria found in desert soil is typically far richer than that found in the Amazonian rainforest. And why should a human being be treated as any less complex than a desert landscape? If we stick to the simplistic bacterial model of illness, we will, like Quine, block out the many other more subtle sets of relations involved in human health and disease. And this will stop us from seeing the bigger picture. As the psychoanalyst and medical researcher Franz

Alexander lamented as early as 1939, the great (bacterial) discoveries of the past in medicine were in danger of becoming obstacles to the discoveries of the future.

This brings us to another problem. The bacterial model of causation seemed attractive where infectious diseases were concerned, yet these are no longer the most common cause of death in industrialized countries. They have been replaced by chronic conditions, which are the most frequent source of complaint in general-practice medicine today, as well as being the most frequent cause of death. In America, it is estimated that almost 100 million people suffer from chronic diseases like arthritis, diabetes, Alzheimer's and coronary heart disease.

This trend towards mortality due to chronic disease was already apparent in the US by 1950. Heart disease was a particular concern, but it clearly could not be attributed to a single cause. So medical researchers decided to pursue a number of long-term studies. In one of the most famous, over 5,000 residents of the town of Framingham in Massachusetts were assessed using a range of behavioural and physiological measures, before coronary heart disease had set in. Vast amounts of data were collected, requiring sophisticated statistical analysis. Complex mathematical techniques were used to sift through the figures in search of the most significant risk factors, such as family history, weight, exercise, personality type and cholesterol levels.

This certainly seemed like progress beyond the single-cause models. But as professor of medicine Robert Aronowitz points out, the new multi-causal models that came out of studies like the one at Framingham had a number of flaws. For one, they left out any in-depth investigation of cause: Why did someone become overweight? Why did they eat high-cholesterol foods? What effect did the death of a loved one have on them? The distinction between cause and effect seemed blurred here. Secondly, the risk-factor approach saw the individual as the one who had to take responsibility for him or herself. It implied that the levels of risk they exposed themselves to were their own choice. The responsibility for health is then confined to conscious decision-making by the individual, leaving no place for the consideration of the effects of unconscious processes or of a wider social framework.

Chronic illnesses pose a special problem to simplistic views of causality. Long-standing illnesses tend to generate advice from physicians to sufferers as to how to reduce symptoms or the chances of future flare-ups. These may involve modifications to the individual's behaviour, environment and lifestyle, such as regular exercise, relaxation techniques or the avoidance of particular foods. It has been estimated that up to 50 per cent of the commonest causes of death in the US are linked to modifiable behaviours. The rise of chronic disease means that the ways in which a patient will respond to medical advice become more visible than ever. So would the decision to keep on enjoying a high-cholesterol diet after a diagnosis of heart disease count as a cause of mortality?

Given the massive prevalence of chronic conditions and the recognized importance of social factors in treating them, it has often been argued that GPs should be taught how to persuade people to alter their lifestyles, and that advertising consultants should be brought in to advise on how best to exert influence on the public. Hence doctors and advertising companies are both encouraged – and paid – to spread the message in the most effective ways possible. So why is it that, out of the seven to eight thousand hours of training a medical student receives, the mean number of hours devoted to teaching medics how to get a patient to stop smoking is precisely one?

It might seem obvious that techniques of persuasion should occupy a central place in medical education, like the schools of rhetoric of classical and mediaeval times. Persuasion would not only be confined to risk-reducing behaviours, but also to the vast problem of so-called non-compliance. This rather sinister term refers to the habit patients have of failing to follow a prescribed medical regime. The word 'compliance' is now often replaced by 'adherence', to avoid the Big Brother-like nuance of the older term. The Royal Pharmaceutical Society has even suggested 'concordance', to imply a relationship between partners of equal standing.

Whatever term we use, this is a major problem. It is estimated that non-compliance amounts to around 30 per cent of health costs in Great Britain, while in the States it has been called 'America's second drug problem' by the US National Council on Patient Information and Education. Surprising as it may seem, it represents a high-risk factor in cases where the patient knows full well what the consequences of non-compliance may be. A quarter of cancer patients don't take medication as it is prescribed or miss chemotherapy appointments. And several studies have shown the high rate of non-compliance after organ transplant, which is reckoned to account for 25 per cent of post-transplant deaths. In kidney-transplant patients the rate of non-compliance is between 20 and nearly 50 per cent, and around 30 per cent for heart-transplant cases. This does not concern just the rather obvious variables like diet and smoking, but also the taking of immunosuppressive medication, the monitoring of blood pressure and attending medical appointments.

Since the reasons for non-compliance will vary from person to person, one could object that persuasion is too simplistic a technique to be relied on here. In one case, an eighteen-year-old diabetic girl had refused to follow the treatments her doctors advised. She would neglect to take her insulin injections and induce states of total exhaustion through physical hyperactivity and eating binges. This dangerous behaviour led on several occasions to diabetic coma. Exploring her history and questioning her attitude to her illness with an analyst revealed some of the threads that lay behind it.

Her parents had separated some months before her birth, the father having refused to accept a monogamous relationship with the mother. Disgraced and defamed, his name was not to be mentioned, and he was completely excluded from the family's discourse. Curiously, her descriptions of her diabetic condition matched word for word her descriptions of her father: in each case, she would say, 'I decided not to think about it.' Just as her father was not allowed to exist for her mother and her family, so the existence of the diabetes was blanked out. And just as speaking about her father would make her cry, so speaking about the illness would produce tears – a reason for her to speak about neither. As these associations continued, it became clear that she had linked the idea of her father firmly to that of her illness. She had diabetes because she didn't have a father.

By this logic, not only should the treatment of her diabetes be neglected but the disease itself *should endure*. If her diabetes was no longer visible, thanks to proper use of the medication, it would be as if she had relinquished her father. As the analyst observed, her illness was both a marker of her father's absence – she had diabetes because she didn't have a father – *and* the guarantee of his existence: through not being talked about, he was there. She had constructed a complex, contradictory knot of her father and the diabetes. Having one meant having the other. This was reinforced by the mother's decision not to mention her daughter's illness in the same way that she had obliterated all reference to the father. Complying with her medical regime would thus mean for her abandoning the idea of her father and her link to him.

It was the detailed exploration of the patient's psychological life rather than persuasion that allowed her to rethink her refusal to take medication carefully. The fact that these same factors will be involved not only in compliance behaviour but in illness itself receives just as little attention. Mind–body connections were once a popular theme in medical education, and the textbook for students *Psychosomatic Medicine* by Weiss and English went through endless reprints in the 1940s. By the 1970s, however, this would be found only in second-hand bookshops. No equivalent textbook replaced it, and the study of psychological factors in illness declined rapidly. About half of the medical schools polled in a recent survey reported that they offered less than forty hours of teaching in psychosomatic-behavioura medicine, which represents less than half of 1 per cent of their curricular work. This is worrying, given even the most obvious problems claimed to stem from how people behave, be it smoking or failure to exercise or some other self-destructive activity. It might even make sense for physicians to leave all this to the advertising experts. Indeed, the estimated 70 per cent decrease in sudden infant death syndrome in the US is supposed to be the result of Procter & Gamble's decision to put the words 'Back to sleep' on disposable nappies, teaching mothers to put babies to sleep on their backs.

Even if some fields of medicine choose to ignore the role of psychological factors in physical illness, it would be difficult to deny the part played by these same factors in patients' lifestyle choices and patterns of compliance. If the way to affect these behaviours is not only through advertising and education but, as we saw in the case of the diabetic girl, through listening and speaking, it might seem logical that the way in which these practices work would be a major topic of interest for medicine; how words and images can change people's behaviour – or not, as the case may be. The power of words and images would thus deserve a special place in medical education, and not just in the humanities where it currently resides. And this, we might guess, would bring into focus the role of speaking and listening in the medical encounter.

2. Why Listening Matters

Patients today often complain of feeling that they are merely peripheral phenomena in the busy schedule of a GP or consultant. One study found that hospital patients were less satisfied with the way medical staff communicated with them than they were with the food they were served. The rising use of computers in general practice means that doctors are often typing in data as they speak with patients, sometimes reducing eye contact to a bare minimum. In the US, the average time a patient is allowed to speak in a first consultation before being interrupted by their physician is twenty-three seconds.

Primary-care medicine today is generally directed at the management of patients. They should be kept as healthy as possible, and the frequency of their visits kept to an ideal minimum. It is important to recognize that although no doctor would be averse to curing a patient, this is not always the cardinal aim, especially given the prevalence of chronic illnesses like heart disease and diabetes which can be managed but not cured. Most doctors have to cope with a staggering workload and ever-increasing bureaucracy, so it is hardly surprising that there is less and less time to listen to the individual. Given that the average length of a consultation in a city like London is between six and eight minutes, who would have the time required to take a thorough history – to explore the patient's biography, the details of recent life events, their aspirations, difficulties or any challenges they may be facing?

Yet without careful listening, can more than a partial aspect of illness ever be grasped? Many patients complain of not being properly listened to and of receiving hasty advice. They are often left feeling literally unrecognized. One survey even found that in 50 per cent of medical encounters, the patient and the doctor disagreed as to what the main presenting problem was. If today's hospital has become what one physician has called 'a mosaic of specialities', patients are turning elsewhere to find different forms of recognition and receptiveness. Doctors before the Second World War were already lamenting how the study of disease had begun to overshadow the study of the patient. Commenting on the changes he had witnessed in the first decades of the twentieth century, the Austrian writer Stefan Zweig said that 'disease meant now no longer what happens to the whole man but what happens to his organs'.

This movement away from biography and particularity towards fragmentation inevitably encourages a wide range of alternative and complementary therapies. In America the number of visits to alternative practitioners exceeds the number of all visits to primary-care physicians. Today, more than a third of the American population use so-called alternative therapies. And significantly, more than 70 per cent of these people don't tell their conventional doctors about these treatments. One might wonder what effect this has on assessments of the efficacy of conventional treatments.

The expansion of alternative practices is sometimes explained as a consequence of the medical profession's unwillingness to listen to its patients. For much of the medicine practised today, the body is merely the sum of its parts and little more. In a 1,400-page best-selling textbook for medical students, lip service is paid in the first chapter to the doctor–patient relationship, before the book gets down to the real business of the human organism. Doctors are told to show empathy by indicating to the patient that their experiences are recognized and accepted, yet the suggested phrasing of questions and responses to patients reads like extracts from a bad foreign-language primer. Likewise, scare quotes around phrases like 'treat the whole patient' seem to imply that they shouldn't be taken too seriously.

When it comes to explaining the rationale of showing the patient that they have been heard properly, we learn that this will allow the patient to feel that their ideas have been incorporated into the clinician's interpretation of their condition. Why will this matter? Since 'otherwise the patient may tend to believe that the clinician has not got things right, which increases the risk of the patient not adhering to the recommendations that follow'. The reason, then, is to make it more likely that the doctor will be obeyed. Medical bodies of course acknowledge the importance of factors like stress, lifestyle, behaviour and psychology, and public-awareness campaigns will often do their best to disseminate the relevant information. But this is sadly not reflected in the curriculum of many medical schools.

This is not to say that obeying a doctor may not be an important, even life-saving thing. The failure to do so in many cases will have tragic consequences. But it should encourage us to question the role of knowledge in the medical encounter. When we visit a doctor, we hope to be able to rely on their experience and learning. Yet this will naturally enough have its limitations. Doctors in general practice will rarely get to see cases of certain diseases (like some forms of cancer) and so it is quite natural that their diagnostic skills may not be as sharp as those of the specialist. GPs are more likely to be stuck with problems like lower-back pain, asthma and chronic-illness management. For other kinds of serious organic pathology, patients are sent off to consultants, and here again there may be problems. Aside from the fact that being shunted from one physician to the next can be an alienating experience for the patient, the consultant occupies a peculiar space.

Revered by doctors, who during their training come to look up to consultants as significant sources of authority and knowledge, their horizons may be quite different from those of the GP. They may complain that they sometimes feel obliged by their position to pretend to know more than they actually do. They often have little experience of the average GP's client population, and they are usually unable to follow a patient for a significant amount of time. This removes any possibility of building up a degree of personal intimacy with patients, and hence of learning more about their own individual ways of coping, reacting, responding and dealing with their lives. To object that the consultant's job is simply to bring expertise to the specific, localized area of the patient's body that is diseased takes us back to square one. The patient becomes a body part, and any chances of studying the relationship between illness and the person considered as a whole have been lost.

Illness management often has the unfortunate consequence of putting the patient on a conveyor belt, with stops at various destinations to produce little packets of localized knowledge. This problem is echoed in the specificity of the medications themselves. One drug may be prescribed for a particular symptom, generating side-effects which require a further drug, and then, in many cases, yet another drug is recommended to deal with the unwanted effects of the latter. One effect of these processes is that responsibility is made anonymous, as the patient is alienated in a chain of inter-linked medical procedures. Lost in all of this is the place from which the many variables could be considered together.

Let's take an everyday example. A young woman complains to her GP of feelings of 'fuzziness' in her head and a noticeable swelling in her neck, which she takes to be at the site of a lymph node. The GP examines her carefully, takes a blood sample and arranges for her to have an ultrasound of her neck. He explains to her that her symptoms may well be caused by a thyroid problem. Next stop is the consultant who carries out the ultrasound. As she prepares the patient for the procedure, they chat about her symptoms, and the patient mentions not only that her sister had been diagnosed with an underactive thyroid but that their father had died of a cancer in his neck. The consultant finds nothing on the ultrasound and reassures the patient that everything is all right.

The patient then meets with the GP to discuss the results of her blood test. He also finds nothing. Now, both the GP and the consultant have done their job professionally and courteously. Nothing is diagnosed and the patient is dispatched back to everyday life. But what if the GP and consultant had actually spoken to each other? The patient had not told the GP about either her father or her sister, yet had brought this up with the consultant. The consultant, although privy to the information, had not asked any further questions. Yet she could have asked when the father had died, or what the sister's thyroid problem had meant to the patient. If she had, she might have found out that the date of the father's death matched the date of the appearance of the young woman's symptoms. Instead, what happened was that the patient became the object of a series of pieces of localized expertise. After the round of medical visits, we might wonder what further physical symptoms the problems which had led her to the initial consultation might generate.

The way in which the medical chain operated here blocked any possibility of learning more about the case. At the end of the process, if the patient is considered well, what will their fate be? If they feel the need to talk to someone, whom should they address? It is a fact that many patients become depressed and unwell after the completion of apparently successful courses of treatment. This pattern is often observable after surgical operations, and also after recovery from serious illness. Which of the many doctors they have seen should they now contact? And if they return to their GP, how long will they remain on a waiting list before being able to see some kind of therapist?

Localized knowledge in medicine and the reduction of the body to the sum of its parts has other consequences. Dentistry is a perfect example here. Up until the mid 1950s, it was not uncommon for a psychotherapist or psychiatrist to receive referrals from a dentist, yet today this would be a newsworthy event. So what happened? Psychological factors were proven long ago to be able to bring about changes in the saliva and gums that might encourage bacterial activity. Medical students, for example, have far higher rates of dental erosion and decay after exam time than at other less tense moments, due to the altered composition of their saliva. Other problems like bruxism, the night-time gnashing of teeth, are not only clearly linked to the psychological state of the person but have been proven to be so by literally hundreds of studies. The term 'dental health' was once used to chime with 'mental health', yet today teeth problems simply mean a trip to the dentist. Case closed.

Does the patient lose out here? To give one example, a dentist informed his patient of what he diagnosed as a constant clamping of the jaw at night, and advised on what dental procedures would have to be done about it. Since he was a dentist and not a therapist, he didn't ask any further questions, and so was unaware, as was the patient for a time, that the symptoms had started when she knew that a painting she had been working on for a considerable time, and was particularly attached to, was going to be sold. Once she realized the link between this wish not to part with what she had produced and her jaw clamping, the nocturnal symptoms disappeared.

The health of one's teeth and gums in a very general sense will be largely affected by one's behaviour. Brushing and flossing may be important, but it is interesting to consider that whereas activities that evolve in the early relation of an infant to its caregivers, such as eating, drinking and looking, may all be sources of pleasure, dental care seems to escape this. Few people enjoy brushing their teeth, and presumably this has something to do with when and how this activity was imposed on us. Thus, our attitude to this health-related activity and our 'compliance' or 'non-compliance' is linked to the history of our interactions with our caregivers. Trivial as it may seem, teeth and gums do matter. When elderly people were asked what they regretted most in life, the commonest answer was not that they hadn't been more debauched, had more sex, bungee-jumped or visited some exotic country, but that they had not taken greater care of their teeth!

Ophthalmology is a similarly isolated branch of medicine. Again, analysts and psychiatrists once received many referrals from ophthalmologists, yet today this would be seen as bizarre. Despite the many hundreds of papers written and the detailed case reports which show the rationale and efficacy of such treatments, their usefulness has been forgotten. In 1960, it was reckoned that between 40 and 100 per cent of recorded eye disorders were influenced by psychological factors. Intraocular pressure, for example, can be clearly associated with states of anxiety and emotional conflict, and so may affect conditions such as glaucoma. This has never been disproved, but advances in medical technology have drawn attention away from it. Whereas in the past talking therapies have been successfully used in conjunction with medication to reduce pressure within the eye, today drug treatments are applied almost automatically. Textbooks like Schlaegel and Hoyt's once popular *Psychosomatic Ophthalmology* have become historical curiosities. The amazing and detailed knowledge now available about the eye and its structure must seem much more appealing than psychological theories about the unconscious factors underlying eye problems. And who can blame ophthalmologists for this?

Yet here again the patient is being compromised. The emergence of corneal ulcers, styes, glaucoma, optic neuritis and many other disorders have all been linked to our unconscious mental life. In one case, a man consulted an ophthalmologist for an inflammation of the iris of his right eye. A detailed examination of the iris revealed traces of previous attacks, the patient confirming that twelve years previously, on Good Friday, he had been woken at night by a severe pain in his eyes. The explanation offered for this earlier attack had been syphilis, yet although this was soon disproved, it had sown a seed of doubt in the man's mind. It turned out that the second and third attacks had also occurred on Good Friday, the day on which Christians are obliged to remember their misdeeds. Whatever cause we posit for the first attack, it is surely more than coincidence that the subsequent episodes of iritis all chose the same highly significant date, as if the symptom of – and perhaps punishment for – his imagined sexual fault was being visited upon him. A treatment that focused solely on reducing the inflammation could hardly be said, then, to be responding to the patient's problem. The iritis here seems to be more a way of articulating distress than the cause of distress itself.

Other kinds of fragmentation exist throughout the medical profession. As in so many disciplines today, it is no longer possible for anyone to keep up to date with developments outside their own speciality. The sheer number of medical journals alone is staggering, with over 3,000 published world-wide, and web articles and new research appear so swiftly that it is remarkable anyone can keep up even in their own field. In immunology, for example, a new paper is published on average every twenty minutes. During our research for this book, we were surprised to find that some consultants were unaware of the existence of whole areas of contemporary medicine. It wasn't that they didn't read the literature, which they could hardly be chastised for, but that they didn't even know that the speciality existed. And given the vast workloads of most medical people today, where would they find the time to read or research anyway?

Even in the field of psychosomatic medicine, many contributions remain not just ignored but unavailable. Paris has one of the only psychosomatic hospitals in the world, a whole institution run on the principle of collaboration between medical specialists who take psychological factors seriously. Detailed case studies and theoretical works are published regularly, but our searches failed to find these publications in a single British medical library. Nearly thirty years ago, the American physician Richard Rahe complained of the 'aversion' US researchers had to reading European journals, and it would seem that little has changed today. It seems a great pity that these works, absent from the bibliographies of most English-language texts, do not form part of a dialogue around what are, after all, a shared set of clinical problems.

We found remarkable differences between the styles of the Anglo-American and European publications. It was quite a shock, after wading through pages and pages of mathematical equations used in statistical calculations, with not one single piece of reported speech from a patient, to come upon Swiss conference proceedings where there wasn't a single graph, chart or number in sight, just detailed case reports of individual patients. Such major differences in scientific style almost guarantee that the Swiss research would not be taken seriously, if read at all, by an Anglo-American audience. In a recent survey of psychosomatic literature on the popular topic of pain research in the field's premier journal *Psychosomatic Medicine*, it was found that after the publication of many case studies in the 1940s, and a handful in the '50s and early '60s, not a single clinical case had been published.

Within an Anglo-American context, it is the production of statistics that matters more than the individual patient and the listening process. In a recent cardiology study, we can read that 'one patient (0.7 per cent) developed somatic contraindications for a heart transplantation', but apart from knowing that they represented 0.7 per cent, we learn nothing more. Not who the patient was, not what they said, nor what the somatic contraindications were. It reminds us of the ironic comment made by a doctor in the mid 1950s: 'The patient recovered and lived to be a statistic in a published report.' The philosopher Henri Bergson once said that it is unlikely that anyone analysing thousands of buckets of water from the ocean will ever learn very much about the tides.

What one learns will depend on what one asks to begin with. And this will be determined to a large extent by what medicine sees as measurable. Measurable units in one form or another provide the framework for the majority of medical research projects. A study of heart disease, for example, might well examine data about exercise, blood pressure and diet. A big project might include these variables but make no enquiry about marital status. The next study will offer this as a criticism, and the whole thing will be done again with the new variable on board. But the key is that everything in the study can be measured. Whatever the researchers choose, it has measurability in common.

What about the possibility that factors that cannot be measured are playing a significant role in the development of illness? The prime example here could be speech itself. If a questionnaire is run through with a patient, what can be expected from the answers to questions like 'Would you rate your childhood as (a) unhappy, (b) fair, or (c) happy?' or 'Can you relax in your leisure time?' Aside from the fact that a framework of vocabulary is being imposed on the patient, thus preventing them from using their own words, why should it be assumed that people know what they are saying? A piece of uranium will emit particles that can be measured by a Geiger counter, but human speech is profoundly different. It can involve truth, lies and, most importantly, self-deception. All these questionnaires can really show is a specific style of responding. They are ill-equipped to assess how human beings repress, deny and rewrite aspects of their lives.

For example, if one study found that 54 per cent of city dwellers would donate a kidney to an unrelated stranger, should this really be understood as an objective piece of information about donation probabilities, or, on the contrary, about the way people wished to be perceived by the person interviewing them? People tend to want to be seen as nice or caring when they are put on the spot. No one could seriously believe that over half the urban population would go under the knife for someone they didn't even know. Cultural trends are significant here too. Surveys can tell us that Americans enjoy life more than the British, but all this shows is that there may be a greater cultural requirement in the US to put a positive gloss on life, especially to strangers. In any case, if we did believe that Americans enjoyed life more, how would one factor in the enjoyment, perhaps shown by the British, in not enjoying life?

Although we can certainly study the range of processes involved in responding to questionnaires and structured interviews, we cannot quantify it in the same way as we could, say, the radiation emitted by uranium. Today's methodologies of measurement are often inappropriate for the problems they aim to study. But how many funding bodies would look favourably on a proposal which dispensed with the usual batch of quantifying tests and measures? We could think here of G. K. Chesterton's story of the drunk found searching carefully on the ground beneath a street lamp. When asked what he is doing, he replies that he is looking for a lost coin. When the onlooker enquires where exactly he had lost it, it turns out that it had been in the next street, but since there were no streetlights there, he decided to look in this one.

Research tends to include only those measurable factors that have been chosen, and even mental states that would seem to defy quantification have been deemed fair game here. Today, many people believe that emotions can be measured, and a host of tests are available for experimental use. But how reliable can external ratings ever be? Self-ratings are problematic enough, but, as many studies show, so are external ones. When subjects were shown film footage of a baby crying and told it was a boy, the emotion ascribed to him would be 'anger', while if they were told it was a girl, she'd be 'sad'. The very same images would thus be inter-

preted in completely different ways depending on precon-
ceived ideas about the sexes. At this basic level, personal and
cultural preconceptions about behaviour influence our
understanding of the world around us and the feelings of
others.

We've used plenty of statistics in this book, although nearly
all of the studies we examined seemed flawed, especially the
more recent ones. We chose the statistics that seemed to us
interesting or thought-provoking or that supported or ran
against particular hypotheses. But whether the studies were
strictly biomedical or more psychologically biased, they all
had methodological flaws of the kind inherent in the statistical way of doing things. Psychological factors can never be
completely measured, and no manner of elaborate tests will
be able to provide international criteria that would allow
everyone to be assessed in the same way. Far more revealing
is the question of why anyone would wish to create such a
scale.

These studies, as we read through several hundred of them,
became tragicomic. However many thousands of people and
millions of dollars were involved, they always left something
out, some crucial variable to which they either admitted or
which was pointed out by the next article. The heart study
that included diet didn't find out if its subjects were married;
the next study did include marital status, but didn't ask if
the marriages were happy; and so on. Perhaps what can never
be pinned down is the 'psychical factor' as such, and so endless
variables are remembered, added and forgotten. This style of
research is strikingly similar to what Freud described as obsessional thinking. Obsessionals famously always add causes
they haven't taken into consideration before. Their symptom
(say, insomnia) must be based on X (say, alcohol intake), so
they might spend an evening without it and sleep nicely. But

then they realize that the beneficial effect could have been based on Y − say, the chocolate they had, unusually, eaten that day − and as they are in the process of giving up both X and Y to be sure, they realize it might be Z, so they give up Z, but then . . .

We can think here of Samuel Pepys and his distress at never being certain what was the cause of his bodily pains: was it 'my Hare's foot, or taking every morning of a pill of Turpentine, or of having left off the wearing of my gowne'? And never finding the true answer would only add to his suffering. This sort of circular thinking can continue for years until the person realizes that the reason the cause is so elusive is either that it has *already been considered but the significance ignored* or that *the cause cannot easily be represented*. It may, in fact, not be susceptible to representation at all, rather like the coin lying in the darkened alley.

Are we dealing here with two fundamentally different ways of viewing the world? One which favours statistics and does its best to remove all human subjectivity that cannot be tested or measured, and the other that gives priority to the non-quantifiable aspects of human life? These are complicated questions for the actual patient who consults a physician in a state of distress. How can the smoker with heart disease measure his craving for cigarettes? How can the migraine sufferer overly involved with her parents quantify her attachment to them? Wouldn't it be easier just to measure the amount of soya in their diet?

3. Is Stress the Culprit?

In a speech to open a new building at Harvard Medical School in 1883, Oliver Wendell Holmes set out an intriguing programme. 'I have often wished,' he said, 'that disease could be hunted by its professional antagonists in couples – a doctor and a doctor's quick-witted wife. Many a suicide would have been prevented if the doctor's wife had visited the victim the day before it happened. She would have seen in the merchant's face his impending bankruptcy, while her stupid husband was prescribing for his dyspepsia and endorsing his note. She would recognize the love-lorn maiden by an ill-adjusted ribbon – a line in the features – a droop in the attitude – a tone in the voice – which mean nothing to him.'

When a patient complains of a symptom, the first question that greets them is often 'How long have you had it?' rather than 'When did it start?' These two questions are quite different. The first requires an answer in terms of chronological time, which may or may not chime with medical knowledge about various illnesses obtained from a textbook or computer. But the other is about both chronological time and the subjective time valued by the doctor's wife in Wendell Holmes's fable. Asking 'When did it start?' opens up the perspective of the patient's unique history. The answer might be rich and detailed, or it might not be, but at least the question gives the patient the opportunity to provide some real information. It's the difference between saying 'I've had the symptom for three months' and 'the symptom started when my wife left me three months ago'.

It is easy for the seemingly obvious to be overlooked. In one reported case, the patient, a 36-year-old journalist, had consulted fifteen different physicians about palpitations, all of whom had taken electrocardiograms to measure the electrical activity of the heart. Finally, the sixteenth, by asking the right questions in the right way, found that the patient's symptoms had started three days after his father's death from coronary thrombosis. In another case, a patient had consulted a string of specialists about a gynaecological symptom, none of whom had been careful enough in their questioning to find out that it had appeared directly after she had kissed a boy for the first time.

Failure to obtain this kind of information is not always surprising. Even when questioned, a patient may not volunteer it, and if they do, it may be described quite flatly, or have no effect whatsoever on the treatment. Rather than taking the two questions about chronology literally, we might see them as bringing into focus two conflicting conceptions of illness: one that construes it as an independently existing entity whose natural history is described in the impersonal textbooks of medicine, and the other as something embedded in individual lives. This latter aspect is of course the subject of a doctor's clinical training, yet the strength of belief in an abstract model of disease is perhaps not to be underestimated.

This difference is echoed in the split between 'illness' – which refers to the patient's experiences, what they feel – and 'disease', which indicates an independently existing pathological process that the patient may or may not be aware of. Much medical consultation today centres on turning illness into disease, or at least seeing if it can be so transformed.

Historically, this has generated some major changes in the landscape of medicine. Angina, for example, was once defined by what the patient felt, but has since been turned into a sub-category of coronary heart disease with its own objective measures. This might be seen as progress, but it does leave the patient's pain as an unanswered question, even if it provides an apparent legitimization of many cases of angina. One can thus falsely believe one has heart disease today in a way that one couldn't falsely believe one had angina earlier in the twentieth century.

So what might a 'When did it start?'-type question reveal? If replies were forthcoming, the physician might learn that many patients with a particular illness or set of symptoms have experienced emotional difficulties suspiciously close to the onset of the illness. Let's take the case of a young man who saw his doctor due to a series of unexplained fits which resulted in loss of consciousness. The doctor was interested in the exact details of the attacks, and asked a number of questions. Had the patient had any forewarning of the attacks, did he pass any urine or bite his tongue? What the doctor did not ask was the very simple question: 'Was anyone else there?' If he had, he would have learned that the man's younger sibling had been in the room at the time of each attack, and this, perhaps, would have allowed him a more comprehensive understanding of the case.

Now, this does not mean necessarily that the presence of the younger sibling was the cause of the attack, but it would suggest that we should bear this information in mind and include it in our view of the best course of treatment. If a certain significant person was always around at the time of the attack, it would be difficult to imagine that a medication that blocked the fits would be enough to count as treatment. Other techniques would have to be used in parallel to explore

the question of the patient's relation to the person in question. One might find, perhaps, that the attack played out the
patient's murderous wishes towards the sibling which were
too disturbing to become conscious. Or that such feelings
had become redirected towards himself. Or, as is the case for
many kinds of symptom, that they only emerged when there
was someone particular there to address. A symptom can be
a form of language, an appeal which aims to make someone
else recognize one's distress.

The simplest example of this would be the symptom that
gets worse on the occasion of a visit to the doctor. Pain or
inflammation may flare up to coincide perfectly with a
medical appointment, as if to emphasize that the symptom
needs to be taken seriously. This means that the physical
complaint may be acting as a conduit for some other form
of unhappiness or malaise. What matters is that the doctor
listens and perceives that something is wrong. Often, demands
made to a doctor conceal this appeal for authentication: the
patient wants to be acknowledged as suffering, and it is obviously then a question of identifying in each case what kind
of suffering this is.

Physical symptoms are frequently signs that something is
being communicated, and this is perhaps clearest in skin and
gastrointestinal disorders. Changes and lesions to the body
surface will be noticed and usually responded to, in the same
way that gagging, vomiting and diarrhoea tend to be conspic-
uous and observable. When such problems occur in infancy,
they will initiate, in most instances, some form of treatment
by caregivers. *The very fact that they are observed confers on
them a communicative function*, which may become important
either then or at a later date. And this communicative function implies that there is someone there to register whatever
it is that the symptoms are articulating.

In the case of the young man who experienced un-explained fits, treatment might combine a course of medication with psychotherapy, to explore such questions as the relation to the younger sibling present during the attacks. If these had constituted an appeal to another person, or a concealed message being sent to them, preventing the fits, with their communicative function, might have its own particular dangers. The patient could live without the fits, but the wishes or worries that were seeking expression and an addressee would have to find another outlet, which could mean the emergence of a further physical symptom or a piece of dangerous behaviour. Or it could lead to non-compliance with a regime of medication.

The lack of interest in these aspects of a patient's suffering is reflected in a very simple observation made by the American physician James Gordon. He pointed out how absurd it is that medical forms leave only enough space for a single word under the rubric 'occupation'. What about the whole history of that person's relation to work, the work that has probably kept them occupied for the greater part of their waking life? What about the frustrations, aspirations and setbacks which it will have involved? What could be expected from a single word on a questionnaire, unless it is either to serve as a cue for further questioning by the physician or be used as a statistic? And if so, why not add a second box where the patient is asked whether they are satisfied or not in their occupation? A doctor would learn more from a patient's reporting whether they like their job than from actually knowing what job it is.

Suppose that from time to time the patient does mention an emotional event – a divorce, the loss of a job or a bereavement – which seems somehow linked to the time when the symptoms of illness first emerged. If, to give two rather extreme examples from medical literature, a woman develops symptoms of Raynaud's disease in her index finger as she is about to telephone her mother to admonish her, or if a man suddenly experiences arthritic symptoms as he is about to kick down the door of his girlfriend's apartment, what is the doctor to do? The average GP is not a psychotherapist, and so might acknowledge with the patient that they must have been very stressed at the time. And the doctor may even tentatively suggest, perhaps with the patient's agreement, that the symptoms could be stress-related. Surely this is progress?

But things are hardly so simple. Stress is a handy and ubiquitous concept, but what does it really mean? Diagnosing stress may ultimately be a way of avoiding a detailed analysis of a patient's history. It is a modern alibi to avoid listening. If the patient says, 'It started around the time my wife left me', and this is then glossed into 'It must have been a time of great stress', although the patient may benefit from the empathy and concern of the doctor, the specificity of what his wife's departure meant to him has been lost. The meaning of this event, and the associations and memories of the earlier separations it evokes, will be of the utmost importance. It should also be recognized that while a wife leaving might be a terrible blow for one husband, this could be a welcome relief for another. What matters is the way an event is registered in the particular and highly specific history of a unique person.

In one case, a woman was advised by her doctor to follow a stress-management course after work pressures seemed to bring about a marked aggravation of her symptoms of the autoimmune disease systemic lupus erythematosus. The demands made on her had been increasing since a new manager had arrived, which had coincided with her moving house. All in all, it seemed as if she had too much to cope with and this, together with the resulting depletion of her energy, was contributing to the exacerbation of her symptoms.

The course was helpful to her and she appreciated having the opportunity to think about her use of time and to meet other apparently stressed people. Yet although her symptoms became less acute when she was signed off work, they were soon to return with the same strength as before. The psychotherapy she began a year later clarified what lay behind her 'stress'. Her illness had first been diagnosed when she was in her early thirties following a significant sequence of events. Her parents had separated when she was eleven, and she had been brought up by her mother. A long-standing platonic friendship with a boy at school would finally become a marriage, and she moved out of the maternal home to a small flat with her husband. At this point, the father, who had shown no interest in her, only sending the rarest birth-day card from the city he had relocated to, suddenly announced that he intended to visit.

The woman had great difficulty in describing the subse-quent encounter. She had arranged that her father visit at supper time, so they could dine with her husband, yet he had shown up much earlier than expected. Alone with him in the flat, she felt awkward and stiff, not knowing what to say or how to behave. It was from this time onwards that she complained of odd sensations in her body, sensations that were later to be confirmed via immunological tests as lupus. When she spoke of her physical symptoms, she would often employ the same words that she had used to describe the scene with the father. It was as if her body had been struck at the point she was most aware of his proximity when alone with him in the flat.

It was exactly this sense of proximity that characterized her new work situation. The manager had reorganized the office, insisting that she stay on to help him after normal office hours. Once again, we have an obvious cause of 'stress': being forced to work longer hours against one's will. But the particularity here lies in the feeling of unbearable proximity. Being alone in the office with him evoked the scene with the father and the sense of enigmatic, inexplicable menace. Unable to make sense of this or to find a place to situate herself in relation to this impossible proximity, her body responded with an intensification of symptoms. It was in similar situations, especially when she had to stay on at the office, that her condition would worsen.

It was the exploration of these threads that shed light on the course of the patient's illness, rather than the vague notion of 'stress'. A diagnosis of stress, indeed, could be regarded as the modern way of not finding out more about a patient. It replaces the richness of an individual story with a blanket concept that can be used to explain just about anything, from anger to grief to frustration and depression. It's also good for patients who wish to keep their egos safe: undergoing 'stress management' allows someone to preserve their self-esteem more than they would if undergoing psychotherapy or psychoanalysis, forms of treatment which are sometimes stigmatized. This is similar to the replacement of the term 'war neurosis' with 'combat fatigue': it sounds less pathologizing, and takes the emphasis away from the idea of psychological conflict to the more everyday notion of weariness resulting from exertion.

The concept of stress was developed by the Harvard physiologist Walter Cannon in the 1920s. Cannon had been interested in the way an organism reacts to acute situations with bodily change. Animals would show increases in heart and respiratory rate, muscular tension, sweatiness and lower intestinal activity when in a high-pressure situation. He studied how the bodily processes involved were regulated by the autonomic nervous system, that part of the nervous system which is responsible for the control of smooth and cardiac muscles and glands, which are not under conscious control.

The autonomic nervous system governs the muscular contractions of breathing and the heart, and it is divided into the sympathetic and parasympathetic branches. The sympathetic nervous system is regulated by the hypothalamus, a highly important communication centre in the brain that orchestrates changes in the rest of the body. Sympathetic activity leads to the release of adrenaline and noradrenaline from the adrenal glands and nerve endings, and these hormones, together with direct neural signalling, will then affect heart and respiratory rates and other aspects of the body. The parasympathetic, on the other hand, mostly counteracts the sympathetic nervous system, and is associated with states of relaxation, slower heart rate, lower blood pressure and increased digestion. Cannon believed adrenaline to be the emergency hormone, and noradrenaline the everyday one, although this simplistic distinction has since been disproved.

Also in the 1920s, Hans Selye, still a teenager at the time, began to publish his ground-breaking work on what was to become known as general adaptation syndrome. Selye was curious as to why so many hospital patients had what he took to be the same downcast air about them despite suffering from different illnesses. He tried to find out if there was some single physiological change common to all of them. As he subjected animals to a wide range of unpleasant stimuli, such as heat, poison and electric shock, he found a biological pattern to their responses: an enlargement of the adrenal cortices, the outer parts of the adrenal glands, a shrinking of the thymus, spleen and lymph nodes, organs central to the body's immune system, and bleeding ulcers. Since these responses seemed to Selye to occur regardless of the specific stimulus, he used the term general adaptation syndrome. He argued that these responses were first of all the body's alarmed reaction to stimuli, but if these stressful stimuli – what he later called 'stressors' – continued for too long, then after a period of resistance, exhaustion would set in. If the stress was prolonged, the very mechanisms which ensured the organism's survival would be responsible for its demise and possible death.

The stress-response system Selye had discovered is known as the hypothalamus–pituitary–adrenal or HPA axis. When in a threatening situation, the hypothalamus in the brain stem releases hormones to stimulate the pea-sized pituitary gland, situated beneath it. The pituitary will in turn secrete a large number of hormones, including ACTH. This travels to the adrenal glands, above the kidneys, which release a different range of hormones, to act on various systems of the body. These will include a class of hormones known as the gluco-corticoids, which have been extensively studied in stress research. Cortisol is one of the most studied glucocorticoids, and its jobs include converting energy supplies into a form that can be used rapidly by the muscles. Whereas the sympathetic nervous system acts immediately during a stress response, the HPA axis takes a few minutes to start producing effects, and these may still be felt days or weeks after a stressful event. Generally, the presence of these hormones is used to determine whether a state of stress can be diagnosed.

Here, for Selye, was a very basic model of how one's experience of the world could produce illness. Feeling threatened or pressured would affect the HPA axis, and the longer this was sustained, the more hormones would be knocking around to flood the system, producing the symptoms he had observed. The physiological changes that Selye documented were of great interest, but his model of human situations was initially quite simplistic. The organism was seen as a closed unit, trying to maintain a low level of internal tension (known as homeostasis), and stressors would impinge from the external environment. These were modelled by Selye, perhaps not fully consciously, on wartime dangers. If we remember that this work took place in the interwar period, it is not surprising to see external stressors conceived as discrete, well-defined events, similar to the insults of bombs, gunfire and the other acute phenomena of wartime.

Many of the animal experiments used in stress research perpetuated this model, and the stressors introduced were very much unlike the kind that a human being – especially someone living in today's society – might have to deal with during the course of their life. Being suddenly confronted with a boa constrictor or receiving random electric shocks might have their parallels in human experience, but are still rather alien. Do they bear any relation to today's worker having to deal with a computer virus, or being unsure of their feelings towards someone close to them, or having a pressing deadline for a task that needed to be met in order to secure someone else's recognition? The animal-experiment type of model is more suited to the situation of army personnel under fire, and it is no accident that much of this research was in fact initially funded by the military. This model of uncomplicated external stressors is echoed in Cannon's pruning of the famous list of Darwinian terms in the title of his classic book *Bodily Changes in Pain, Hunger, Fear and Rage*, published in 1919. As the American physician James Lynch noticed, he had quietly dropped the fifth: love.

★

Later work came to separate acute stress from incremental or cumulative stress. If someone you love suddenly dies, this may be an acute stressor, whereas if you are continually undermined in your childhood by critical and negative comments from a parent, or later on by your boss or spouse, this is cumulative. Now, recognizing these factors might be very important to understand a particular case, but does the conceptual distinction really hold any water? All the complicated attempts to classify 'stressors' stem from the initial bias of seeing them as acute, localized, discrete events that are somehow external. Stress may be varied in its forms, but it always seems to come from the outside.

At the end of the day, what *doesn't* count as a stressor? Surely we could count the *absence* of many things in life as a cause of stress. Beyond the list of concrete events marshalled in stress research, it is also a distinctly human characteristic to respond physically in the ways described by Cannon to the experience of a void, as we see in cases of anxiety and depression. And ultimately, isn't reality itself a stressor? If heart disease might be brought about by daily, cumulative stress over many years, wouldn't the regime of regular exercise recommended by your doctor also count as a form of stress? Both of them involve types of 'stress' to the body, yet one is deemed positive and the other negative. And what about cases where the same physical activity is performed under some sort of additional pressure: the sport-shy schoolchild having to perform gymnastics, or the executive playing a 'friendly' tennis match with business rivals? Presumably, we need to take account of not just the activity as such, but the person's attitude towards it, *what it means to them*. Stressors will thus always involve a subjective factor.

Going to the gym may be stressful in a literal sense, in the same way as jogging, swimming or taking part in a lively scientific debate. Yet such activities are supposed to be healthy, and to prolong life. It is generally argued today that what matters is the *amount of control* we have over the activity and whether we can predict it. Stress then becomes just what we can't cope with: too many demands are placed on us and we have too little control over them. During the Second World War, sporadic bombing in the suburbs was correlated with a higher incidence of ulcers than regular bombing in central London. And army studies during the Vietnam War found that, in the same combat conditions, those who obeyed orders displayed fewer stress symptoms than those who had to make decisions and give orders.

The variables here are incredibly complex. How, for example, could one quantify the soldier's belief in the omnipotence of a commanding officer and compare it to the fear of the unknown timing of a missile assault? How could human relations be measured on a par with things like bullets and bombs? Similarly, if an experimental study can show how a monkey will secrete less of some stress hormone if it is prepared for the next electric shock it will receive by the ringing of a bell, what about the office worker who knows how awful each day is going to be? That is a predictable stress, but it doesn't improve the quality of life. A stress-free life is ultimately impossible, and Selye eventually concluded that absence of stress could only really occur after death, although he didn't specify exactly how long after.

One of the main problems with the early stress research was that it failed to account for what a particular event meant for a particular human being. To go back to our example, doing gymnastics might be a terrible ordeal for one child, but a welcome release for another. Events never just occur in a vacuum, but emerge in contexts laden with meaning for particular individuals. When researchers in the 1940s and

'50s started to come up with lists of stressors, they looked for events that could be graded in terms of stress-inducing potential. Long lists of stressful events were compiled, with numerical values accorded in terms of the perceived severity of the situation.

On one scale, death of spouse ranked number 1, with marriage at number 7 and a change in eating habits at 40. Two of the central figures in life-change scales were Thomas Holmes and Richard Rahe, who worked at the US Navy Medical Neuropsychiatric Research Unit. They believed that a consensus could be found on what constituted a life stress, and their research claimed to show an 80 per cent correlation of major life-change events and the onset of illness in a two-year period following the onset of stress. They also found a correlation between the number of life-change events and the severity of illness. The more of them that clustered around a particular time in the person's life, the more chance that they would become physically unwell.

Their life-event scale, it was claimed, provided very consistent results in cultures as apparently diverse as those of Sweden, the US and Japan. Several studies supported their thesis that health changes and life changes clustered together. The more that happened to you, the more likely you were to fall ill. People with the greatest number of life changes had the most signs of disease, and this was shown with illnesses as varied as myocardial infarction, psoriasis, tuberculosis and gastric cancer, as well as the exacerbation of diabetes and of post-operative symptoms following surgery for duodenal ulcer. The list went on and on.

But how enlightening is all this when trying to understand an individual case? Losing a job might be a catastrophe for one person, and a blessing for another, just as a marriage might be a joyous occasion for one person but a tragedy for another, if, for example, it was arranged against their will. A change in eating habits might occupy a lowly place on the scale, but not if the person has religious beliefs and is forced to eat something prohibited to them, or is trying to follow a particular diet. What counts as important will obviously depend on the person and their own unique history. The Canadian psychoanalyst Graeme Taylor reports the case of a transvestite who decided to give up cross-dressing. Each time he did so, however, he had a heart attack, and so it would be reasonable to assume that a change in clothing habits must be high on the life-event scale for this person.

Despite the manifest importance of personal meaning given to any life event, Holmes and Rahe came to a rather surprising conclusion. They argued that even if the same event could be a tragedy to one person and a minor mishap to another, the scale still worked. What mattered would be the degree of change from an existing, steady state during a one- to two-year period in the person's life. And this, they claimed, had greater predictive power than psychological meanings or emotions. *It was change as such that predicted illness*. This suggested that falling ill was really out of anyone's hands: even if all the changes were what society and the individual might deem positive, the person would still become unwell.

Here, it seemed, was confirmation of the old Hippocratic saying 'It is changes that are chiefly responsible for disease'. But what should we make of this surprising implication? At one level, it suggests that we're unaware of something being a problem. Changes may generate difficulties in our lives, even if we believe on a conscious level that things are going well. We could see the same sort of process operating in other aspects of life. If someone starts to overeat or drink too much, for instance, it may be because they feel psychologically threatened, though they are not aware of this. A man who felt no grief after the death of his mother noticed that this was when he began drinking heavily, yet made no connection between the two events. In another case, a teenage girl began binge-eating after her elder sister became involved with a boy for the first time. She dismissed the chronology here as mere coincidence, remarking that she couldn't care less what her sister got up to. A detailed exploration of the case showed, on the contrary, that the sister had always been an ideal for her, and that the new boyfriend had not only come between them but had introduced the question of sexuality. Unable to articulate this, she had fallen back on an auto-erotic form of enjoyment – the binge-eating – which short-circuited the question of her own relation to the opposite sex.

In both the above examples, the new activities were ways of reacting to a threat or loss without thinking it through. All the person felt consciously was the powerful need for the alcohol or food in question. The life-event scale is showing us here how we can have thoughts and feelings which do not enter our conscious minds, yet which still have serious effects on our bodies.

How reliable are such scales? By averaging out very different results and aggregating data, they certainly neglect specificity. But there is another factor here which the life-event scales obscure, and this brings us to a crucial issue. Why should any event count as a 'life' event? It might figure on a list of 'important' events and it might be subjectively important for the person in question. But surely the obvious point to make here is that something has to happen to *transform an experience into a life event*. If someone loses a loved one through death or separation, what will happen if no one else in their environment registers or acknowledges the significance of what has happened?

Let's take an example. A young couple fall in love and become engaged. The man goes to visit his family and tells them the good news of the engagement. As he is returning, he learns that his fiancée has been killed in a tragic accident. Yet when he expects to be able to share his grief with his friends and family, he realizes that none of them had ever actually met his lost loved one. He had only mentioned her to them very recently, and so he was faced with the problem of mourning someone who had not existed for those around him. No one else knew her. We see here a very particular situation. There had been a tragedy, but the young man felt the immense difficulty of *registering* this. When he went to meet her parents later on, he was in the strange situation of being the man she had been engaged to yet whom they had never met or heard of until then. And this, of course, created its own obstacles to the mourning process. It is difficult to see the string of health problems that followed as mere coincidence.

This might seem an extreme example. But there are plenty of cases where the person or those close to them will react to some major event as if nothing has happened. Life just goes on. A divorce, a death, a separation are treated as unfortunate but unavoidable, passed over in silence and never properly commemorated, mourned or remembered. There is no social registration that an event is, in fact, a life event. A life event must usually be made so by a social process, be it a form of ritual or simply a sharing of thoughts and memories between people. If this doesn't happen, how can we make sense of our lives? There is thus an important difference between events and life events. And isn't it likely that it is the very difference between these two sorts of event that may have consequences at the level of one's physical health?

★

An interesting question here is why anyone would want to remove the subjective dimension of life events in search of a set of numerical ratios. In a review of life-change scales many years later, Rahe lamented how his scale of choice could be 'contaminated' by the subjects' responses to the events. But why 'contaminated'? Why would one want to erase the individual's own input, if not to generate a questionable veneer of scientificity? All one could gain here would be an avoidance of the realities of an individual case and a failure to acknowledge the difference between human beings.

But this, perhaps, is exactly what the concept of stress had tried so hard to do. The bureaucratic systems of modern society, as the philosopher Alasdair MacIntyre pointed out, have no place within them for the individual narratives of a human life. And the concept of stress helps to get rid of narrative. Rather than speak about stress or an objective life-change scale, the particular factors that might have been relevant prior to a person falling ill should be explored. If the scale of life events can tell us that the death of a spouse scores highest, what should be accorded to the event 'giving up cross-dressing'? Knowing about this, and the details of the life that led to it, will reveal something about the particular case and why that particular person had his heart attacks. In the end, it is this particularity which matters.

A further problem with these scales is how swiftly life changes are forgotten. Paediatric studies have shown how parents consistently misreport health and behavioural changes in their children. Mothers tend to be able to remember accurately whether their child was breast- or bottle-fed, but beyond this the inaccuracies are astounding. After Dr Spock's popular child-rearing manual advised against thumb-sucking and encouraged the use of dummies, suddenly parents' memories of their children's thumb-sucking grew slimmer while memories of sucking on dummies became more numerous. Dating weaning or potty training also produces remarkable errors of up to a year on either side of the correct date. Our grasp of the chronological side of our own lives is equally unreliable. We forget about life changes steadily over time at a surprisingly rapid rate, and we are continually in the process of rewriting our own histories.

Similarly, the ways in which people discuss details about their lives are very different. One study of 463 patients with gastrointestinal problems found that those patients with irritable bowel syndrome tended to report readily the presence and significance of particular events preceding the onset of their symptoms, whereas those with inflammatory bowel disease tended to deny both. This may well depend on the atmosphere in which patients are asked questions, and the attitude that has been built up culturally around the representation of specific illnesses. Equally, if one believes one has a 'traumatic neurosis', it might invite the search for a trauma. But regardless of diagnosis, patients may often have no good reason to confront the meaning of life events that may have precipitated their symptoms, and frequently fail to mention them. This can be due to a basic failure to understand the effects of the situations we find ourselves in, and then to link these to health problems, or to other perhaps more obvious factors, as the following example shows.

The *New England Journal of Medicine* reported the case of a 22-year-old man who was examined after coughing up a cup of bright red blood. The authors noted that 'the initial history and physical examination were unrevealing', and the chest X-ray and blood tests were all normal. Further tests were then carried out with no clear result, which 'prompted additional questioning of the patient'. It turned out that he had drunk a whole bottle of Sambucca the night before, and had begun to choke and cough, with haemoptysis (the cough-ing up of blood) following soon after. Now, either the doctors didn't ask the right questions or, as seems more likely, the man had reason not to mention this unusual 'life event'.

This brings us to the crucial clue. We can criticize these simplistic models for their reliance on a vision of reality that presents everything according to the logic of response to a stimulus. Gunfire, electric shocks, boa constrictors or life events such as death or divorce are all construed as elements from the 'outside' that impinge on us as external dangers. But perhaps this criticism is actually the point: that for many people it is the very fact that the world cannot be seen in any other way that may play a role in their becoming ill.

When we hear again and again of a physical illness start-ing around the time of significant separations and losses yet with no link made between them, perhaps *this very absence of a link is the link*. In one case, a man could talk quite openly about many of the difficulties in his life and seemed eager to understand the frictions that plagued his marriage. He suffered from rheumatoid arthritis and would often complain about the pain this caused him, although this was not the manifest reason for his seeking help. The symptoms of this disease had first appeared not long after his forty-fourth birthday, and it was also in his forty-fourth year that the patient's father had been rendered immobile in an accident at work. Questioned about this curious coincidence, the patient, usually so communicative, just behaved as if there had been no question. During psychotherapy, flare-ups of the arthritis were clearly correlated with certain themes, yet the man consistently blanked any connection. The father's accident was always described as if it were an external event which had happened to some distant figure, rather than to an apparently loved family member. It was as if he were simply reporting some news item from a far-flung region of the world.

In another case, a diabetic man experienced a hypogly-caemic episode while speaking with a therapist. This dangerous deficiency of glucose in the bloodstream, which had often sent him into a diabetic coma in his past, had occurred while he was describing his son's first commun-ion. As he spoke, he became pale, trembling and confused. Reaching for the glucose he carried with him, he was unable to open the packet, fumbling and lacking the coordination necessary to handle it. Questioned later on about the communion gathering, he insisted that nothing had happened worth mentioning. As the therapist carefully probed further, it turned out that the man's father had chosen not to attend, spending the time with his new girlfriend instead. The sadness and anger this provoked had just been blanked out. Instead, his bodily illness became exacerbated.

Being able to view such emotionally charged episodes as unconnected external events means that very strong defence mechanisms must be at play. Things cannot be thought through mentally, so are kept 'outside'. This would explain why both apparently positive and negative life changes could be juxtaposed on the scales we have discussed. If it is change as such that matters, the key problem is *how to register* this change. This will involve mechanisms of mental elaboration and symbolization. An event, after all, must be turned into a 'life event'. It must be registered, processed, made sense of. This is going to be more difficult if there is no social network to help process the event and render it represented and recognized.

If processing breaks down, illness may be more likely. The event cannot be integrated psychically and so seems to impinge from the outside. It will be described as an external occurrence, something that happens *to* one rather than something one is involved *in*. This suggests that our very criticism of the concept of stress and life-event scales ***actually reveals*** a possible contributing factor to illness. As internal problems are refused and made external, this may be exactly what sets the ground for illness in some cases. The bacterial model of illness – in which something *external* threatens us – may in fact be a strange reflection of the actual process of falling ill.

4. The Timing of Illness

Since the earliest days of recorded medicine, physicians have noted that illness often appears at significant times. The symptoms might emerge after the experience of a traumatic event, and even the date and time of death may appear to have been carefully chosen. Contemporary doctors made much of the fact that the Virgin Queen, Elizabeth I, died on the vigil of the Annunciation of Our Lady, at the same place and day as her grandfather. More recently, it was widely observed that Churchill passed away on the anniversary of the death of his father who had so powerfully influenced him. Three of the first five US presidents died on 4 July, two of them who had signed the Declaration of Independence dying on its fiftieth anniversary. Stories of how American Indians can choose a time to die have become folklore, and many studies have claimed that people are more likely to die immediately after rather than before some significant event like a birthday or religious festival. Today, the single most likely time to die of a heart attack is between eight and nine on a Monday morning.

There are many reports in medical literature of death occurring during highly emotional moments. In one case, a woman said that she wanted to die while being interviewed by a doctor, and duly collapsed and died in front of him. In another case, a man suddenly died while celebrating his doctor's verdict that he was in good health. In yet another, a lawyer died while talking with police about the murder of one of her clients by her estranged husband. There are also many documented cases where a person dies on receiving news of the death of their spouse or of a close relative, or at happier times – the winning of a lottery jackpot, a long-awaited reunion or a release from prison.

There is a substantial literature now devoted to such cases, and where they were once grouped under the colourful term 'voodoo death', they are now called, more soberly, 'sudden death'. When Walter Cannon studied the phenomenon in 1942, he reviewed the testimonies of physicians and anthropologists who had documented deaths attributed to sorcery, spells, magic and bone pointing. He emphasized not only the beliefs of the person affected, but also those of the social group, who would sometimes ostracize the victim and treat them as if they were already dead. These social factors were assumed to play some role in the death itself.

Sudden death is usually defined as death occurring within six hours of the onset of symptoms. Although the examples above may seem unusual and remarkable, it is in fact the single most common type of death in the US, making up some 25 per cent of all fatalities. At autopsy, the most frequent findings are advanced atherosclerosis – a narrowing and stiffening of the arteries through scarring and fat deposits – and other cardiac pathology, although there are always some cases with no significant arterial or coronary damage. Ventricular fibrillation – an abnormal heartbeat producing ineffective contractions – is assumed to be the main process leading to death, since if medical help arrives before the person dies, rapid, irregular heartbeats known as ventricular tachycardia have often been found. More than a quarter of documented cases, however, show the opposite process – a slowing down of the heart known as bradycardia.

If emotional experiences can influence the timing of death or illness in some cases, there must be pathways that make this possible. It might appear extremely unlikely for someone just to decide when they want to die, but there may be subtle influences at work here beyond our conscious knowledge and control. The frequent occurrence of heart failure during sleep or rest has inclined some researchers to underplay the psychological angle, but there is plenty of data to suggest its importance. Surgeons, for example, know that patients who are sure they will die during surgery are often right, despite the actual nature of their medical condition. Some surgeons take these views so seriously that they will advise against operating. Such high-risk patients tend to avoid psychiatric scrutiny, since they are often so certain and so resigned to their imagined fate that they have none of the usual anxiety experienced by patients before surgery. Lack of pre-operative anxiety is frequently a negative sign in fact. When it comes to your post-operative health, it's actually better to be worried beforehand.

A recent study at the Department of Cardiology at the University of Heidelberg found that pre-operative depression in patients with ischaemic and dilated cardiomyopathy – dangerous narrowing and widening of the blood vessels feeding the heart – would predict higher mortality than the presence of pre-operative anxiety in a group of heart-transplant patients. Other studies have claimed to be able to predict with almost 90 per cent accuracy which patients would die during open-heart surgery based on purely psychological testing. A fairly simple battery of interviews and tests on pre-operative patients could show, it was claimed, who was more likely to survive the surgical procedures.

One of the most popular research areas in the early days of psychosomatic medicine was the study of peptic ulcers, and here again predictive studies yielded some interesting results. In one of the first systematic studies, Herbert Weiner and his colleagues subjected 2,073 military recruits to psychological tests to predict who would be the high and low acid secretors, to be indicated by pepsinogen levels. They were then able to predict who among the high-level secretors would be most likely to develop an ulcer, when exposed to the same pressures of military training. One result of this study was that high pepsinogen secretion wasn't enough to cause ulcer formation: there had to be a number of psychological factors present as well. These included the unconscious wish to be fed and looked after, and the wish for bodily closeness with others.

While ulcer formation was a favourite topic of study in the 1950s, there was much less interest in the timing of ulcer perforation. One report from the Boston City Hospital on twenty cases of perforated ulcer noted how factors like alcoholism and diet were certainly important, but the exact moment when the ulcer perforated would be in response to a situation in which the patient felt unable to cope and no defences were available. The importance of studying the individual case is shown by the story of one patient who led a rather dissolute city life, consuming large amounts of alcohol and subsisting on a diet of fried food, yet experiencing no gastrointestinal problems until his visits to the family home where he was fed properly and would follow an ostensibly healthy lifestyle. Each visit home would trigger ulcer activity, due, apparently, to his intense envy of his preferentially treated brother and his anxiety at the proximity with his dominating mother.

More recent work has confirmed the significance of timing, but from a slightly different angle. If you lead your life at a frenetic pace, hydrochloric acid secretion in the stomach decreases. Over a period of weeks, with less acid around to attack its lining, the stomach secretes less of the mucus it uses to protect itself, and also cuts down on the production of the neutralizing alkaline bicarbonate. When it's time to take a break and actually relax, acid production increases again but now it encounters walls which are not so well defended. If this process is repeated several times, an ulcer may develop. In this case, the calmer you are after a tense and busy period, the more you will be at risk.

Other studies found psychologically disturbing situations to be the principal factor in the timing of perforations, yet the psychiatrist Pietro Castelnuovo-Tedesco noted that, in the cases he worked with, the patient did not automatically link the onset situation with the actual occurrence of the perforation. In about half his cases, the patient would not recognize that it had been preceded by difficult events, and in the other half they would be acknowledged but explained as a coincidence. Isn't this relevant to the idea we put forward at the end of the last chapter? It is possible that the very mechanisms which allow patients not to recognize these factors may be relevant to their falling ill. The absence of connection between the precipitating psychological situation and the illness may itself be the connection. Could there be a link between this refusal to recognize the role of emotional factors in one's life and what happens to our bodies?

There is a long tradition in psychosomatic research of exploring the factors involved in the timing of illness and recovery. Young polio patients living in iron lungs in the 1950s would be able to benefit from greater air flow after a phone call or visit from a parent. Parents, indeed, are familiar with the fact that mood changes in their children often precede rather than follow the onset of an illness, even one as slight as a common cold. US Army studies conducted between 1963 and 1966 showed how a person's psychological state before an infection could affect the severity of the illness to follow. Being depressed and unhappy could impact on one's vulnerability to streptococcal infections, for instance, and to a range of respiratory conditions and other illnesses. Hundreds of animal experiments were deemed necessary to prove that after inoculation with bacteria or viruses, tense, unhappy situations hasten the development and increase the severity of physical symptoms – something which many parents will have learned from their children without a government grant.

Likewise, the famously enigmatic cycles of exacerbation and remission in autoimmune disorders have been linked to psychological factors in countless studies. They have been found to play a role in the onset of rheumatoid arthritis, systemic lupus erythematosus, ulcerative colitis, iritis, thyroiditis and many other of these diseases in which the immune system reacts against the body's own tissues. Curiously, textbooks on autoimmune disorders usually contain no reference to such research, even to dismiss it. Yet for years, studies have been appearing on the links between the onset of diseases like juvenile (or type 1) diabetes and traumatic situations, such as separation from the mother or the birth of a sibling. Research shows that even the mildest form of type 1 diabetes – in which the body lacks insulin-producing beta cells – fluctuates in severity, and the symptomatic increases in glucose, water and chloride secretion may all be precipitated by emotional factors.

In the case of the eighteen-year-old diabetic girl we discussed in Chapter 1, it was not only her relation to the medication that was profoundly influenced by her unconscious ideas, but also the timing of the onset of the disease. After the separation of the parents while she was still in her mother's womb, she was left with her grandmother at eighteen months and only returned to live with her mother when she was four. The mother later remarried and became pregnant again. It was at the moment of the birth of her half-sister – when she was twelve – that she developed diabetes. 'I felt completely deserted,' she said when describing this period, as if it revived memories of the abandonment at eighteen months.

If an association between the development of the illness and the birth of the sibling seems likely, what of her actual experience of being diabetic? As we saw earlier, her descriptions of this matched word for word her descriptions of her father, and she had constructed an unshakeable association between them: she had diabetes, she thought, because she didn't have a father. One day, after speaking about him, her attention was suddenly attracted to a Kandinsky picture hanging on the wall. Why, she asked, was there a small wheel painted as if floating in a void? 'What's that wheel doing all alone?' she said. 'No thread is holding it!' This thread, she continued, was what would link her to her father, and the wheel was like herself. Unstable, isolated and insecure in her relationship with her mother, she regarded the thread joining father and daughter as the only point of consistency in her world. As she went on to speak more and more about her father, her diabetic condition improved significantly and she began to take her medication more responsibly. And not long after breaking this taboo of silence about her father, she made the decision to go to meet him.

This case, like many others, shows the advantages of combining medical treatment with an exploration of the patient's emotional life. It sheds light not only on the course of the illness but also on the timing of its emergence. Clear correlations have been found in many other studies between the metabolic process and the vicissitudes of emotional life. While the amazingly detailed medical knowledge of the biochemical mechanisms involved in diabetes may have drawn attention away from this, hundreds of case reports indicate relations between sugar output and factors such as disappointment, loss and frustration. Three centuries ago, the physician Thomas Willis remarked that the disease seemed caused by 'prolonged sorrow'. And from the 1930s onwards, numerous studies have demonstrated a correlation between anxieties and insulin requirement. In one experiment, the level of sugar present in their urine was even measured at regular intervals during the psychoanalysis of two patients.

As for type 2 diabetes, in which the insulin-producing cells are present but the body has become more or less resistant to insulin, a recent British research project found that Whitehall civil servants who spend their working lives being told what to do are nearly three times as likely to develop this disease as those who tell them. Ten thousand civil servants were monitored from 1985, and after having controlled for factors like diet and exercise, it was claimed that a low 'effort–reward' ratio was the critical variable. The frustration generated by the feeling that one was receiving far less back from work than one was putting in was creating a level of tension that seemed to favour the health problem.

Personal setbacks and grief have been found to precede the onset of both varieties of diabetes, as well as of auto-immune disorders like rheumatoid arthritis. This is a disease often associated with rigid self-control, one of the most common observations being that sufferers are locked in a masochistic relationship they feel unable to leave. Love and hate towards the partner are combined, and, unable to separate, the person endures their hatred over many years. Estimates for the percentage of patients with psychological factors playing a role in the onset of rheumatoid arthritis range from 20 to 100 per cent. Similarly, with the still poorly understood juvenile rheumatoid arthritis, emotional factors have been linked to its onset in a significant number of cases. Several studies have found that important separations or changes in the child's life have taken place prior to the onset of symptoms.

Multiple sclerosis is another good example here. Many studies concur that difficult psychological situations correlate with the emergence and exacerbation of symptoms. One study found that nearly 90 per cent of patients experienced heightening of symptoms following difficult situations, which often involved the feeling of helplessness, while another focused on the arousal of anxiety as an antecedent. In one case, a 34-year-old woman saw her three-year-old son being hit by a car. She assumed (wrongly) that he was dead, and experienced a sudden sensation of bodily weakness, particularly in her legs. She was unable to move, and her body, she said, was not 'itself' from then on. Progressive symptoms began to affect her legs and gait, and eight months later MS was diagnosed.

In another case, a woman was unable to get out of her chair to accompany her husband on a doom-laden visit to hospital. He died a week later, and the weakness she had felt in her legs continued, with MS diagnosed a year later. In another report, a 28-year-old man developed MS shortly after his brother was married. Both had lived with their mother, and when the brother got married he thought that now he would have to start to 'look for a girl' himself. Before he could do this, however, the illness appeared.

The reader might feel exasperated here at so much anecdotal evidence, colourful stories thrown in from the great melting pot of medical literature. But we believe strongly that statistics on their own will rarely tell us much, and that individual narratives are of the utmost importance. A more interesting criticism would be to argue that people tend to try to give meaning to their symptoms, and so construct false narratives to explain their medical situation. In the example of the woman who saw her son hit by a car, it is quite possible that the symptoms emerged either much earlier or much later than the moment of the accident. Perhaps unconsciously, she telescoped them together so as to build up a story with a coherent narrative.

Such processes have been called 'infantile medical theories', to evoke the 'infantile sexual theories' described by Freud. Freud's idea was that, at the points where children can make no sense of a mystery such as sex or childbirth, they will invent their own personal explanation, which may then persist unconsciously for the rest of their lives: for example, the theory that babies are made from food, or that birth is an anal process. On the same lines, infantile medical theories would aim to give a meaning to the hard-to-grasp realities of illness, pain and mortality, even if this means rewriting the apparent facts involved.

Take the case of an eight-year-old girl, forced to choose between living with her parents or her paternal grandmother. Choosing the parents meant, for her, being torn away from her beloved grandmother who had brought her up until that time. She would later equate this moment of separation with the emergence of her diabetes, which she saw as quite literally a consequence of her choice. She also believed that her illness had been inaugurated by an episode of coma that took place not long after this, a link which ran counter to the medical evidence. Her diabetes had in fact appeared when she was six.

Such reformulations of history are ubiquitous in human life, so reconstructing a patient's medical biography is never straightforward. In psychoanalytic practice we often come across people who believe that their physical symptoms are linked to a particular event in their past. Sometimes, they display a delusional certainty. In other cases, the patient suspects a link but has doubts about it. This spectrum alerts us to the significance of the position people take up regarding the very idea of a connection between somatic illness and any kind of cause, be it an external trauma or an inner tension. In the example above of the woman with MS, there is no evidence that the patient herself actually insisted on the link between her son's accident and the illness. For her, perhaps, it was purely coincidental.

We should also be careful when speaking about 'onset'. The psychoanalyst Françoise Dolto discusses the case of a woman, apparently free of somatic symptoms, who suddenly experienced a knife-like pain in her stomach at the moment the coffin containing her dead son was being lowered into the ground. Examination revealed a cancer and she died one month later, on the same day of the month that her son had died. Since a cancer could not possibly have sprung into existence there and then, we should separate the time of onset from the moment of becoming aware of the bodily sensations in her stomach. Some cancers will take decades to become established, the initial damage to a cell occurring even thirty years before proliferation begins. After the atomic bomb was dropped on Hiroshima, cases of leukaemia took around 6–7 years to be detected, and the average growth time to detection for breast cancer is 7–11 years.

Some illnesses have clearly visible start dates, but others do not. Autopsies on young soldiers killed in the Vietnam War found atherosclerotic plaques in their arteries of the kind that would be indicative of future heart disease. Had these young men lived, how long would it have been before they developed any symptoms? And, as we have seen, diseases like cancer may have their inception many years before any symptoms become noticeable. Pathologists have noted that autopsy may reveal pathological conditions which were not the actual cause of death. For instance, 25–30 per cent of deceased women are found at autopsy to have microscopic breast malignancies which have never become symptomatic. It is also well known that small and previously undetected prostate cancers are quite commonly found in men who die from entirely unrelated causes. Similarly, diseases like congestive heart failure and hyperthyroidism begin with vague symptoms like weakness and malaise, so an exact onset date is difficult to pin down. To complicate matters further, these signs may often be predisease reactions that will not necessarily result in the symptoms of somatic disease as such. It is thus often difficult to equate onset with a discrete, specific moment.

Individual cases must be studied here in detail, and we could see the large-scale statistical projects as a form of complementary medicine, in the sense that they can be used as complements to the individual case. Both of these forms of research suggest that the timing of illness is significant, and this has perhaps been most clear in the field of bereavement research. One study has even claimed that the death of a loved one has a stronger correlation with mortality than any other known variable. The media often report cases of death following the loss of a partner or sibling, and it has been a subject of continual fascination for writers and filmmakers. The former British prime minister James Callaghan died just eleven days after losing his beloved wife Audrey, the singer Johnny Cash a few months after the death of his wife June Carter, while the Puritan general Oliver Cromwell died of what many took to be a broken heart soon after the loss of his cherished daughter.

In one of the earliest research projects, Eric Lindemann

found in 1945 that 75 of 87 patients had suffered a bereavement prior to the onset of the disease they were suffering from. In a later, large-scale study of 95,647 people, the highest relative mortality occurred directly after bereavement, with greatest risk of death via ischaemic heart disease. After the first month, female mortality rates returned to normal, though men continued to be at greater risk. In fact, for every major cause of death, the rates for divorced, single or widowed males are higher than for those who are married. Almost every type of cancer is influenced by marital status, with the widowed, divorced and single having consistently higher death rates. Risks have also been shown to increase after bereavement for a wide range of specific diseases from diabetes to ulcerative colitis, tuberculosis, glaucoma, skin rashes, gum abcesses and the pituitary disorder Cushing's disease.

The British psychiatrist Colin Parkes found, in a famous series of studies, that mortality was highest in the six months following a bereavement. He was interested in the role of loss and grief in different types of 'life change', and felt that grief was a key factor in understanding trends in illness and mortality. In most of the cases he studied, the cause of death was defined as atherosclerosis or coronary thrombosis, and he tried to focus attention on the social situation of the bereaved. It wasn't just about who had died, but about whether that person had been in a relationship and whether there had been any other deaths in their immediate circle.

Another study showed that women under sixty-five who had experienced the death of a significant other in the previous six months were six times as likely to die of sudden cardiac arrest than those who had not been bereaved. Dewi Rees and Sylvia Lutkins, a GP and statistician, found that relatives of a person who died had a much higher mortality rate during the first year following bereavement than a control group. They followed 903 close relatives of 371 people who had died following a disaster in a small village in Wales, with a non-bereaved control group of 878 from the same community. In this time, 12.2 per cent of widowed people died, compared to 1.2 per cent of the control group.

Bereavement has also been found to correlate with a lowering of the immune system's efficacy. One study found a tenfold reduction in lymphocyte function, a basic immune defence cell, and specifically in T-cell response to reaction-producing chemicals known as mitogens. This was notable at five weeks after the bereavement, but not at two weeks. Women's immune systems seem to recover faster here, while men's are still compromised even a year later. The effectiveness of natural killer (NK) cells – another type of immune defence cell – is also lowered, and may be notably reduced during a loved one's illness as well as after their death. Again, this is significant given that NK cells play a role in helping us in our response to viral infections, autoimmune disorders and some forms of cancer.

Although bereavement studies tend to put the emphasis on the 6–12 month period following the actual loss, this may be missing the point in a high percentage of cases. Computer records can be used to show that many patients pay their GP a visit in the same month of every year, and even when their visits are spaced out by intervals of several years, they still come back on the same date. Such phenomena have been noted in fields of medicine as diverse as ophthalmology and cardiology. The patient is hardly ever conscious of the significance of the date, but with detailed questioning, it turns out to be the anniversary of a loss or a traumatic event, *as if physical symptoms were commemorating that event in the place of conscious memories*.

Exploring the psychological context of acute glaucoma, the ophthalmic surgeon William Inman was struck by how often his patients had become ill on the anniversaries of significant dates. In many cases, the loss or trauma had occurred decades previously, yet still even forty or fifty years later the patient would develop symptoms on the relevant date. Although the obvious explanation was that they had been unusually stressed due to the painful memories evoked by the date, Inman was surprised to find that in most cases the patient was completely unaware of the connection. It was only after detailed questioning that the significance of the date was discovered. No conscious stress would be reported. Perhaps it was this very absence of acute emotions that played some role in the emergence of the illness. The symptoms marked the anniversary where conscious thought processes could not.

Varda Mei-Tal from the University of Rochester discusses the case of a man whose family had been murdered in the concentration camps during the Second World War. The only known anniversary for any of the deaths he could be sure about was that of his brother, and it was always at this date in the year that his multiple sclerosis would worsen. These so-called 'anniversary reactions' involve the emergence or exacerbation of physical symptoms on the anniversary of an important date, often that of a bereavement. The Hungarian psychoanalyst Sandor Ferenczi introduced the term, developing the idea from Freud, and many studies from the 1950s to the '70s studied anniversary reactions in the context of mortality and illness. Psychoanalytic exploration would reveal how the first symptoms or premonition of illness in some cases began at a particular date of the week or month, or when a particular age had been reached. And these dates, it would turn out, had frequently been those associated with

the death of a parent or someone who mattered to the
patient.

The American psychoanalyst George Pollock noted how
if men often fell ill on the anniversary of the death of their
father, women would sometimes become sick when they
reached the age at which their mother had been when their
father died. Deaths, anniversaries and illnesses were bound
up in a complicated logic that involved several variables all
at once. Everyone is familiar with the so-called 'nemesis' idea,
the conviction that, despite all rational belief, one will die
before a certain specific birthday or date. Freud was sure he'd
die between the ages of forty and fifty, and then settled, for
a time, on the idea that he would not live to reach the age
of fifty-one. He was even known to say to his friends, on
parting, 'Good-bye, you may never see me again,' despite
living till the age of eighty-three. This is a very common
belief: people have a feeling that they won't live longer than
a set number of years, which often turns out to be the life-
span of one of their parents or relatives.

Another early study showed how coronary occlusions may
occur on significant anniversaries, and the psychoanalyst and
medical researcher George Engel observed changes in his
own health over a decade, noting how significant symptoms
emerged on the anniversaries of the death of his father and
twin brother. After his twin died of a heart attack at the age
of forty-nine, Engel became convinced that if he did not die
of a heart attack within one year of the date of this death,
he would never suffer a heart attack in the future. Eleven
months later, he gave a lecture which included projecting
slides of himself and his brother to medical students. He
knew that his brother had lectured to the same class, and
that his appearance there would be greeted with nervous
laughter, a common reaction to the uncanny resemblance

between them. A few days later, after having kept himself unusually busy and with the prospect of an unpleasant meeting with someone whom he identified closely with his brother, the heart attack came, just one day before the day of the month his brother had died on.

Graeme Taylor records another case of a 45-year-old female patient with no prior history of angina who was admitted to hospital after suffering severe chest pain at five o'clock one morning, where it was confirmed that she had suffered a heart attack. He discovered that it was six years to the day that her husband had woken up at 5 a.m., fallen into her arms and died from a massive heart attack. The timing in this case seemed to be determined also by the imminent death of the patient's father from leukaemia, and the recent departure of her only child to attend a university in another city. Since her husband's death, she would frequently wake at 5 a.m. and relive in her imagination the terrible events of that morning.

A recent article on the weakening of heart muscle subsequent to emotional shock mentions the case of an elderly woman admitted to hospital with what appeared to be a flaring up of her chronic emphysema. The doctors were worried she was experiencing heart failure, and as her records were reviewed it turned out she had been admitted to hospitals three times in three years with similar symptoms. These admissions, indeed, had been on the same date of each year, which her daughter confirmed had been the anniversary of her husband's death.

As we multiply these examples, we should be careful to note that there is no simple correspondence between the experience of a loss and an illness. In some cases, other losses will be necessary to revive memories and affects linked to earlier ones. One of the most consistent findings of early mind–body medicine was that if a loss or separation seemed to impact powerfully on a patient, it was often due to the fact that it stirred up issues surrounding an earlier loss. This would be especially relevant in those cases where the second relation had been built up as a compensation or replacement for the earlier, broken one. When this is lost or threatened, the person is thrown back on to the earlier, traumatic loss.

The context of each loss needs to be carefully considered. If someone becomes ill at the age not of a parent's death but at the age the surviving parent was when their spouse died, then it is important to explore how that person's mourning was perceived by the patient. There is undoubtedly a difference between a case where the surviving parent shows no grief and one where their mourning is articulated. If no grief is registered, then it may be left to the child to shoulder the burden of mourning in the family. And this, as we've seen, may be embodied in physical symptoms which act as commemorative markers. As with the life changes we discussed in the previous chapter, it isn't just what happens that matters, but how what happens is registered by other people.

Let's take another example here, which involves the anniversary reactions we have discussed and the question of unarticulated loss. A 25-year-old woman starts to experience blurred vision in one eye while teaching a class at school. Since she is five months pregnant, she assumes it is simply yet another effect of the physical changes occurring in her body. She doesn't worry and the symptom doesn't particularly bother her. A few weeks later, she develops similar problems in her other eye, and her GP tells her that it is most likely to be a mild case of optic neuritis, an inflammation of the optic nerve behind the eye. She has no anxiety and the symptoms don't get any worse.

After the birth of her son, she becomes pregnant again, and one evening is playing a game with him on the stairs when she suddenly loses all vision in one eye. Again there is no anxiety, but a visit to an ophthalmologist changes this. He suggests a brain scan, worried that the loss of vision may be the effect of a brain tumour. Terrified, she walks home thinking that she might drop dead any minute. The scan reveals nothing, yet not long after this another symptom appears. Getting dressed one morning, she loses sensation in the left part of her body, starting most noticeably with her toes. A scan and lumbar puncture reveal MS. She consults one of the country's top specialists, who tells her that her condition will certainly worsen and advises that she sell her house and move to a bungalow.

Despite this grim prognosis, she is convinced that there is something more to her symptoms, and after a visit from her parents a decisive change takes place. They had arrived in the afternoon just before the diagnosis of MS was about to be confirmed by the latest round of tests, and as they are sitting in the kitchen talking, the mother picks up a photograph of the patient as a young girl. Holding it up she says, 'She was such a lovely daughter.' Amazed, the young woman retorts, 'I'm not dead yet!' Almost immediately, the mother starts to have a pain in her stomach, and screams that she's got cancer. The father hurries into the room and insists that they leave to take care of the mother. The patient is left feeling unrecognized and alone, unsupported by her parents. She sees them, perhaps for the first time consciously, as deeply alien and absent figures.

This episode marks a moment of change. 'I woke up to something,' she says. She begins an active study of literature, starting a master's degree which involves the study of psychological texts and, in particular, a novel about a man's quest for his father. Later, she will start psychotherapy. Thrown into this pursuit of individual, subjective truth, and redefining her world as a result of this, her MS symptoms completely disappear. Today, more than twenty years later, there has been no relapse. She had created a cure for herself, which involved the exploration of her own history and of the power of words to create destinies. So what exactly had precipitated her illness?

The patient had been raised by a rather cruel, sadistic mother and a kinder, more loving father. The mother would often tell her, 'I hope you die in agony' or 'I wish I'd never seen the sight of you', voicing through this battery of insults her death wish against the one daughter she felt to be plainer than the others. The father was a draughtsman, who gave a special value to the sense of sight, which he depended on for his livelihood. Once, when she was nine, the patient accidentally flicked a button, which hit her father in the eye. She imagined that this was the cause of an eye problem which he developed some time after this. The problem vanished soon enough, however, and her father regained his vision.

The father's own life had been deeply affected by the death of two of his sisters. One, born with a heart problem, had died at the age of four from what was described as heart failure when she witnessed some boys killing a dog. The other had died suddenly of meningitis at nineteen, and it was after this aunt that the patient herself had been named. The mother had insisted on this name, against the father's wishes. Despite this, the patient had been told by her mother never to mention these two dead sisters to the father, as if their memory had to be obliterated lest a wound be opened. She also had a special bond with two of her own sisters, and her first child was born on the birthday of one of these sister's own sons. It was this same sister who had been taken in her teens to hospital by the father for some tests. Climbing the steps to the hospital, the father had collapsed with a heart attack.

What effect did these family myths and events have? The patient had been named after a dead woman, the aunt whose story had to be kept silent, and she had always been convinced that she would be dead by the same age: nineteen. Yet when had she in fact fallen ill? Not on the anniversary of the aunt's death, but at twenty-five, the age at which the father had lost his nineteen-year-old sister. This was the moment when the patient had developed her first symptoms of MS. Like her father and, indeed, like the first of the aunts, she had experienced what she called 'a disturbance of vision'. And like the second aunt – her namesake – her next symptoms involved the one region of the body she believed had been implicated in the meningitis: the toes. She had been acutely aware of a strange change in her sensation of her toes at the time those symptoms had occurred. Although these can of course be explained in purely biological terms, with optical neuritis a common first symptom of MS, the series of coincidences is too striking to be dismissed. There is a sense in which anniversary reactions are being played out. But to what end?

The MS embodied the convergence of different currents of her psychical life. At one level, there was an identification with the dead aunt, specially valued as the one whom the father had so cherished. At another, the timing and location of the symptoms suggested an identification with the father himself. Like him, she had experienced a loss of vision. Like him, she had been afflicted with a black-out on some steps, and it is hard to ignore her choice of game to play with her son: going up the stairs repetitively, as if to mimic the scene of the heart attack. And like him, she had been twenty-five when tragedy struck. The scenes in question here involve the father's relation with a beloved girl: he is twenty-five when the sister dies, and has his heart attack on the steps when he is caring for the patient's sister. What is perhaps being evoked is the unconscious idea 'a father cares for a sister'.

But the symptoms also suggest another strand of her life. Her mother had named her after a dead girl against the father's wishes, and had made no secret of her own rather murderous propensities. Couldn't the MS symptoms also embody this maternal death wish? They had emerged, we should remember, during each of her two pregnancies. Each time she was about to become a mother, it was as if the mother's death wish had become actualized. Each time, she was struck down. But this hypothesis still leaves one question unanswered. Why did she experience so little anxiety?

Could it be that the symptoms revived the unconscious formula according to which a father cares for a girl? This idea may have been precisely what guarded her from the malevolence of the mother, acting as a kind of barrier. This would explain why none of the symptoms produced anxiety: as a defence, it was precisely anxiety that they protected her against. When, on the other hand, she was terrified lest she drop dead on the way home from the ophthalmologist, she remembered that this fear was exactly what she had experienced as a child, imagining herself in the place of the dead aunt. The key, however, may lie in the details: perhaps it was not the symptom itself that caused the anxiety here, but the malediction, the warning uttered by the opthalmologist which evoked the maledictions of the mother. In her mental universe, after all, on the side of the mother were death wishes and curses, while on the side of the father was care and concern.

Both of these currents, perhaps, played a part in the onset of her MS.

We could ask one further question here. Why didn't her parents' visit that had ended so badly cause her symptoms to worsen? She had been confronted, after all, with her mother's death wish – when her mother had referred to her as if she were already dead – and also with a profound disappointment in her father. Rather than caring for her, and hence illustrating the unconscious idea of a father caring for a girl, he had chosen the mother instead, taking her theatrical panic seriously and leaving with her. If psychological factors were indeed playing their part here, surely this would have been enough to send her symptoms spiralling?

There is of course no way of answering this question with any certainty, although a clue may lie in another of her childhood memories. When she was a young girl, she had been impressed at catechism when listening to the curate's sermon against untruth. Later that day, after her mother had once again done her best to undermine her, she had returned to attend mass at the church. Seeing her father standing outside, she had run to him, to be knocked over by a car, fracturing her pelvis. Her father picked her up and carried her into the church, expecting the worst. She cried out, 'It hasn't happened. Tell me it hasn't happened,' and was surprised when the curate agreed with her. 'No, it hasn't,' he said, undoing his sermon of that very morning against lying. Her father, on the other hand, told the truth. 'Yes, it has happened,' he said, 'but it's going to be OK.' These paternal words echoed in her mind many years later, and she thought of them when the MS was diagnosed. Once again, it was in the father that she found her support. This incident, she later observed, happened when she had reached the age she imagined the father's first sister had been when she died.

Perhaps encouraged unconsciously by her father's words, rather than succumb to illness after her diagnosis and the disastrous parental visit, she managed to find her own form of solution. The search to find words to explore and articulate her family history began at this moment. Rather than submitting to the imperatives of the mother and the lethal images of the dead aunts, she began actively to explore her past and that of her parents. And in her studies, the book she chose to focus on was about a man's quest for his father. Perhaps it was this that allowed her to elaborate her unconscious expectations and ideas about her father beyond the setback of that dreadful afternoon.

If illness and death can be determined, even in a few cases, by psychological factors, we need to take the consequences seriously. Bereavement studies show us that a loss can have significant effects on one's cardiac health and immune system. And anniversary reactions, which can range from the flaring up of an autoimmune disease to a heart attack, imply that the body contains memory systems which bypass conscious thought. A watch is ticking and it isn't the one on our wrist. The forms of time-keeping here are for the most part unconscious. When an event can't be processed or made sense of, it may leave its traces in the body. This might exploit a vulnerable point in the patient's body or, in some cases, create a replica or copy of someone else's symptoms.

This suggests that systems for storing, recording and registering must be highly active throughout our lives. But why will they be associated with the timing of illness in some cases but not in others? Is it possible that some of these systems can never be fully translated, so that traces of feelings, events or thoughts from one system will never be able to be inscribed or represented in others? Was there something so unthinkable for the man who lost his family in the concentration camps that the worsening of his physical symptoms was the only way for him to mark the traumatic losses? These are some of the questions that the timing of illness raises. They all converge on the issue of how we are able – or unable – to process our mental life. Perhaps the less something can be thought, the more likely it is to return in the body.

But what guides this return? Would the physical illness be a 'downstream' effect of a general weakening of the body, or, on the contrary, a highly specific response? We have seen examples of symptoms mirroring those of lost loved ones, as if they have been formed using the information received about their death. If this can happen, language must play a role in the development of at least some symptoms. Words and ideas must be shaping – in some cases – the particularity of physical ailments. But how can mere words affect our bodies?

5. Words and Beliefs

Can words make us ill? We may all be familiar with experiencing a headache, nausea or even a feeling of faintness on hearing some bad news. At other moments, we might blush if we've said the wrong thing. But can words generate permanent changes in the very tissue of our bodies? A good place to start here is with hypnosis. Hypnosis, after all, is about the effect of words: a person listens to someone else's voice and then 'suffers' the consequences. Shiny swinging objects and piercing eyes are just the icing on the cake. The active ingredient is always speech.

In *Emotions and Bodily Changes*, her vast review and bibliography of psychosomatic literature published in 1935 and updated until 1946, Helen Flanders Dunbar listed several thousand studies that today have for the most part been forgotten. Many of them involved hypnotism, and if we believe what we read, almost every disease known to man will respond in some way to hypnotic influence. What's so fascinating about juxtaposing these with later work is that the old studies are primarily concerned with *words* and *beliefs*, the hypnotizer transmitting a verbal instruction to the subject, whereas many of the more recent studies claim to be about *emotions* and *feelings*.

Yet thinking and feeling cannot be so neatly separated. As Freud pointed out in 1905, 'all mental states, including those that we usually regard as "processes of thought", are to some degree "affective", and not one of them is without its physical manifestations or is incapable of modifying somatic process.' Even quiet, contemplative thinking will be accompanied by minute muscular changes and a string of observable effects in the body. Thinking is a process that is saturated with feelings. We will follow certain trains of thought and not others in order to avoid the experience of pain, for example. Thoughts themselves can be felt as intrusive, unwanted, persecutory, comforting or pleasant.

When thoughts are suggested by hypnosis, they can have an effect upon blood pressure, on the widening or constriction of our bronchial tubes, upon heart rate and even on blood-sugar levels. A number of famous experiments have shown how a blister can be raised on the skin, and then removed, by hypnotic suggestion. Experiments with skin response were particularly popular at one time, as they showed how blood flow to a part of the body could be influenced by both conscious and unconscious beliefs. Today's mainstream experiments mostly dispense with hypnosis, yet use other techniques involving suggestion. In a study of contact dermatitis, the Japanese researchers Ikemi and Nakagawa took thirteen hypersensitive subjects and touched them on one arm with leaves from a harmless tree, telling them they were from a lacquer tree, which produces effects similar to poison ivy. They then touched the subjects on the other arm with real lacquer leaves, telling them they were from the harmless tree. All thirteen subjects had a skin reaction to the harmless leaves, while only two reacted to the 'real' irritant leaves.

Technology is useful here, as a machine can often embody the authority and power we might formerly have ascribed to a hypnotizer. In a study at Eastman Dental Hospital, patients who had undergone painful tooth extraction were divided into several groups, each comprising around 25 people. One group was given no form of therapy, another ultrasound, a third mock ultrasound with massage, a fourth

mock ultrasound without massage and a fifth were invited
to massage themselves. The researchers found that the
greatest post-operative benefits were in the group who had
experienced mock ultrasound with no massage. They had
the greatest reductions in swelling, as well as less pain.

Relief from pain may not be such a surprising result, but
the reduction in swelling shows real physical change. In
another well-known experiment, asthmatic subjects were
exposed to a harmless saline solution, but told they were
inhaling irritants. Almost 50 per cent experienced increased
airway resistance, and those of them who had the most severe
attacks found relief after they were given the same saline
solution when it was offered to them as an antidote. In a
further study, asthmatic subjects were divided into four
groups. Two groups were given a bronchodilator and two a
bronchoconstrictor, but half of each group was told that they
were in fact receiving the opposite medication. For each of
these falsely labelled items, the experimenters found that its
efficacy was only reduced by between 40 and 50 per cent.
They were still working. Suggestion was once again having
real effects in the body.

Such studies are becoming rarer in the pages of mainstream medical journals. The use and study of suggestion is
increasingly the domain of psychologists, and there is often
less of a dialogue with those exploring somatic disease.
Hypnosis is supposed to be a dubious business, with wild
variables such as the degree of suggestibility of the hypnotized subject or the extent to which the hypnotizer believes
in what they are doing. It is worth noting that the lacquer-
tree study we just mentioned was conducted in Japan, where
one might guess that the relation to authority figures – and
hence the ease of suggestion – may be somewhat different
to that found in other parts of the world. In addition, for

someone to become a volunteer in a medical trial suggests that they have a certain belief system. Although the motive may be financial, there is often the idea that one is helping to further science. It is thus difficult to accept the idea of a neutral volunteer who isn't searching for a master to believe in, or some form of knowledge in which to put their faith. The problems in replicating many of the older studies of suggestion may be due to precisely this kind of factor: as our trust and acceptance of symbolic forms of authority has been undermined in the modern Western world, so the practices which relied on them no longer work so smoothly.

When the Baltimore City Hospital recorded the case of a woman who died after hyperventilation on the day before she turned twenty-three, it was noted that at her birth, on a Friday the 13th in the O'Kefonokee Swamp region of Florida, the midwife had told the family she was hexed to die before she reached the age of twenty-three. She had made the same prediction for two other girls delivered on that day, and these two, it transpired, had died within one day of the predicted date. Now, the only hypnotic suggestion here is that of speech and the belief systems at play in the families and the culture concerned presumably made the hexes real, together with the authority conferred on the midwife in these systems.

In another case, a man died as a result of what could be seen as a more personal kind of hex. The patient was caught up in a very close relationship with his mother, a woman he described as a wonderful lady who always made the correct decisions for the family and who had never encountered a situation she couldn't deal with. He lived with her till he was thirty-one and his two marriages during this period both ended in divorce, predicted each time by the mother. With

her help, he now bought a nightclub which proved successful and profitable. She kept the accounts and ran it for a year
while he was doing his military service.

At the age of thirty-eight, he married once again, but his
wife resented what she saw as his dependency on his mother.
A son was born, the business prospered and life went on in
an apparently uneventful way for the next fifteen years or
so. At this point, he received a very attractive offer to sell
the nightclub. His mother became distraught and opposed
the sale, yet, with the support of his wife, he went through
with the transaction. Learning of the imminent sale, his
mother admonished him: 'Do this and something dire will
happen to you.' Two days later he had his first attack of
wheezing and an asthmatic condition was diagnosed. He had
no previous history of respiratory problems and had seemed
to be in excellent health until then.

Not long after this, the sale of the club was completed.
During the next few days the man's asthma worsened, and
he was hospitalized. The mother had been furious about the
sale, and repeatedly reminded him of her predictions, adding,
'Something will strike you.' Medical help proved less and less
effective, and the man dwelt on his mother's grim prophecy,
telling his doctors that she was always right. Further spells
in hospital followed, and during his last interview he told
his doctor about plans to invest the money from the nightclub sale in a new business in which he would not include
the mother. He discussed the problems this might cause, and
ended the interview with a renewed expression of terror at
his mother's predictions.

The interview took place at 5 p.m. and his physical condition was checked. Nothing seemed untoward and he was
deemed to be in excellent health. At 5.30 he telephoned his
mother and told her of his new business plans. The mother

made no attempt to dissuade him, but at the end of the conversation stated that, whatever his doctors had said, he should remember her prediction and be prepared for 'something dire'. Within the hour following the phone call, he was dead. An autopsy reported the cause of death as acute ventricular dilatation and bronchial asthma.

Words and beliefs here clearly contributed to this unfortunate man's death. His belief in the power of his mother's speech was so strong that her prophecies triggered bodily processes that killed him. Suggestion was functioning at its purest, and this is something that orthodox medicine doesn't like to get too close to. There are huge prejudices when it comes to thinking about how pervasive suggestion is, and especially how it is present in all medical encounters. In an extreme but perhaps exemplary exchange, an American doctor tried to treat a case of the autoimmune disorder systemic lupus erythematosus in an Asian woman using conventional medicine but without success. However, when she visited a native healer in her village she made a significant recovery, without the usual corticosteroid drugs used in the West. Rather than explore the mechanisms of what the American doctor took to be a cure by suggestion, one medical commentator argued that the doctor might have confused his patient with someone else, given the fact that Westerners find it difficult to tell Asian faces apart!

This distrust of studies involving suggestion is perhaps clearest in the case of warts. The history of wart treatment would make a marvellous volume in itself as it illuminates so many of the prejudices and belief systems that we find in medical research. Caused by a virus, warts have been treated historically by practically every remedy under the sun, from pork fat to lemon juice to incantations to excision to castor oil, silver nitrate and radiation. Reviewing this wide range of treatments, it is clear that the same methods could be successful in the hands of one person but not another. There is little doubt that suggestion is the key factor.

A British study published in the *Lancet* in 1959 provided further confirmation that hypnotic suggestion not only worked, but was ten times faster than spontaneous cures and, even better, could get rid of warts without leaving a scar. Once the patients were hypnotized, two suggestions were given: that the warts on one side of the body would disappear and that, on waking, the patient would open the door when the hypnotist blew his nose. Of the nine patients who indeed opened the door, all of them were cured of their warts on the side of the body in question, with the warts remaining on the other side.

If suggestion works so well, why not use it to treat warts? Although it won't work on the under-threes, it's faster, cheaper and generally more effective than anything else on offer: so why not? The answer is that suggestion is not deemed to be a genuine cure, and its efficacy unscientific. As the authors of the *Lancet* study noted, 'there is still considerable public and professional prejudice against hypnosis, and the practitioner may suffer in reputation.'

Today, a National Health Service website dispenses information to the public on, among other things, warts. It mentions hypnotic treatment, but says that this is to be discouraged since it has been explored only in small-scale studies. This is surely symptomatic of this very prejudice. Since these small-scale studies have been so positive, why not suggest on the website that *large-scale studies should be encouraged*? Despite the odd contrary or equivocal result, the balance in medical literature is firmly in favour of hypnosis. Aversion to its use is not only irrational here, but signifies an avoidance of thinking about some of the very processes that conventional medicine relies upon.

It could be argued that every single medical transaction involves a form of hypnotic suggestion. Since it requires the meeting of at least two human beings, both conscious and unconscious beliefs and thoughts will come into play and have an effect on the outcome. A person's attitude to doctors, nurses and other medical staff is unique, determined by their own history and by what they have heard from others. Visits to see a doctor or to hospital in one's childhood will colour later experiences, as will stories of the medical treatment of parents or relatives from previous generations. A study in the *British Medical Journal* found that patients re-covering from heart attacks would be more likely to die during ward rounds conducted by the chief surgeon than at any other time during their hospital stay. The less feared the surgeon, perhaps the less chance of this, but wouldn't that in itself detract from the beneficial effects of believing in a surgeon's power?

This can be seen also in the way that physicians are often recommended as the physicians of some celebrity or aristo-cratic figure. We might learn next to nothing of the actual success or failure of their treatments, but there is a certain magical effect created by the association itself. Newspapers and glossy magazines continually tell us that a particular doctor or healer is frequented by the stars, and it is hard not to think here of the ancient belief in a king's ability to cure scrofula by touch. Just as contact with the royal figure removed disease, so contact with someone who has touched the celebrity will restore one to health.

It is no accident that the ancient tradition of the laying on of hands can still have a powerful effect. Touch is assumed to possess a magical quality, and it has been observed that nearly all of the world's medical systems, apart from that in the West, include extensive forms of bodily contact. This is especially significant given that the ailments being treated are not exclusively musculoskeletal. Indeed, patients here in the West often admit their disappointment if their doctor *hasn't* examined their body during the consultation.

The background system of beliefs can work through touch, but also through many other channels. At the most basic level, since any medical encounter will involve speaking, suggestion will be at work, since its prime vehicle is speech. It is words, after all, which have an effect on us in hypnotic states. A recent experiment at the University of Hertfordshire set out to explore the suggestion at play in spectacles of metal bending. Two groups of students watched a video of a psychic bending a key, which ended with a sixty-second close-up of the key on a table. One group was told that the key was still bending, while the other received no spoken commentary. Forty per cent of those who had been told the key was bending believed it to be so, compared with only 5 per cent in the other group.

The 'psychic' was in fact a magician, and the key was certainly not bending. The experiment was then repeated with two further groups, but this time they were not asked afterwards if they believed the key was bending. Instead, they were asked to write down in detail exactly what they had seen. Of those who had reported seeing the key continue to bend when it was left on the table, only one in ten mentioned that this had been suggested to them by the voice-over. Nearly all of them, it turned out, had forgotten what the magician had told them. Their reality was being shaped by the words they had heard, yet these words remained outside conscious thought.

Although shiny objects may be used in the more showy instances of hypnosis, the above results show how it is really speech that 'drugs' us. Words get into our heads and continue to influence us even years after we have heard them. They mould our very experience of reality, of what we believe we see, hear and even touch. Those who had been told that the earth is the stationary centre of the universe would see a sunset rather differently than those brought up to believe that the earth rotates around its own axis and revolves around the sun rather than vice versa. Even at the level of bodily sensation, what we hear shapes us. In one particularly intriguing study, it was shown how women in eighteenth-century Saxony would complain of a wide range of symptoms which involved the experience of the body's interior as a fluid. Physiological processes could transform into each other, and shift from one part of the body to another with astonishing agility. Pains would move around the body just like the somatic symptoms, in a flowing process that echoed the language of seasonal change and movement prevalent in that agrarian society.

Medical anthropology also shows us how the language used in a culture will determine people's experience of the body. Feelings of a blowing sensation in the ears, a dryness in the chest or the painful retraction of the genitals into the body might be uncommon in the West, yet they form part of the common currency of illness in other parts of the world. The words that shape us as we grow up are playing an active role here in influencing what we think we are feeling in the body. To take another example, a man suffering from sharp pains in his appendix and terrible fear of appendicitis was surprised to learn one day that his appendix was actually on the other side of his body. Suggestion is not limited to the slogans of advertising, and during our formative years what we hear from those around us will serve to shape the way we perceive the world.

Words tell us how to react and respond to those around us, sculpting our relations to others, and forging our ideals, our aspirations and our goals. Often, it is only through the detailed exploration of mental life allowed by psychoanalysis that such words can be remembered or their importance grasped. The words that have mattered may be forgotten yet acted out repetitively throughout one's life. During therapy, a drug addict was stunned one day when a childhood memory came back to him with all its force. He had been playing with his sister while his mother chatted with a friend, and some friction had erupted between them over a packet of sweets. Separating the feuding children, the mother had remarked, 'A boy always needs something inside him.' This comment had perplexed him: What did it mean? What was the 'something'? Why had the mother said it? Yet it informed every moment that he was called on to assume his place as a male – his school graduation, his first sexual encounter; on such occasions he turned compulsively to the ingestion of drugs.

There is an enormous literature on how words affect us unconsciously and the hidden suggestive processes that are set in motion by words in even the most casual medical encounter. Take this vignette reported by the French paediatrician Leon Kreisler. A five-year-old girl developed recurrent laryngitis and an inflammation of the windpipe, with a residual cough present between episodes. Her father had left the family to work overseas, and one day had the idea of sending her a special packet containing a sweet which, he assured her, had been made by locals as a cough remedy. After eating it, her symptoms completely disappeared.

This kind of miraculous story always arouses suspicion. But it serves as a useful example of how objects – like forms of medication – are involved in relations between people, relations which involve not only belief systems but expectations and questions of love, desire and disappointment. If a sweet sent by the right person at the right time can help cure an illness, couldn't it – or its absence – also help to create one? And isn't the same kind of process involved in even the most mundane medical prescription?

The physician and psychoanalyst Michael Balint pointed out in the 1950s that the most frequently used 'drug' in general practice medicine was actually *the doctor themself*. What mattered wasn't just the pills in the bottle but the way the doctor prescribed them, and the whole atmosphere in which they were given to the patient. Even the simplest psychological perspective on human transactions will show how material objects like pills become signs of many other things, just like the presence and manner of the doctor and the other props and procedures of medical practice. We asked one doctor why he chose to wear his stethoscope at all times, and he replied that it helped his patients to see him as a doctor, even though he hardly used it during the course of a normal working day.

One well-known study showed how a few words from the anaesthetist prior to surgery had tangible effects on post-operative pain and the length of time spent in hospital. Ninety-seven patients due to undergo abdominal operations were divided into two groups. They were all visited by the anaesthetist before surgery and told about the preparation for anaesthesia, the duration of surgery and other details. But only one group was told about post-operative pain – where they would feel it, how severe it would be and how long it was likely to last. None of the patients knew that a study was being conducted, and the surgeons didn't know which patients belonged to which group.

After the operations, the results were significant. The patients who had received instruction from the anaesthetist requested less painkilling medication, and were discharged nearly three days earlier than the other patients, despite the fact that the staff responsible for sending them home were unaware of which group they belonged to. The simple explanation given to the patients in the experimental group was enough to have a real effect on their experience of pain and their post-operative health. Words formed a crucial part of their medical experience.

Research in this area is often grouped under the heading 'placebo effects'. Yet surprisingly, much of it supposes that suggestion can be removed experimentally from human transactions. There have even been proposals to study 'placebo psychotherapies', where the therapist would be untrained and not administer any 'therapy' to the patient. This is especially confused, since therapy involves a relation between two people. If one person attributes knowledge to the other, this may facilitate the speaking process and turn anything the therapist says into a meaningful intervention, regardless of what the therapist intended. We could think here of the *New Yorker* cartoon in which two shrinks pass each other by in the street. After they exchange a 'Good morning', each walks off with the thought bubble 'What did he mean by that?'

Suggestion is present in *every* human transaction and cannot be removed at will. Since most of our beliefs are not conscious, they cannot be added or subtracted in an experiment. Even if subjects are told that someone knows absolutely nothing and has no training or is a fraudster, there may still be powerful beliefs in that person as a result of the unconscious processes mobilized by human interactions. They may remind us of a childhood figure or simply give us a means of posing a question about ourselves. For this very reason the heartless Don Juan may remain popular despite repeated warnings about his unscrupulousness. As he is some-one who is believed to know a great deal about women, others may be drawn towards him as a way of asking a question about their sexual identity: What is a woman? What does a man see in a woman? And so on.

This means that suggestion is everywhere and that there is no such thing as an inactive pill or process. As infants, we are given things or have things taken away which matter not for what they are as material objects but as signs of love or the withdrawal of love. The child who nags for sweets at the supermarket checkout is not necessarily interested in the sweets themselves, but in whether the parent will comply with their demand. And we can all remember gifts received in childhood which took on their value due to who it was that had given them rather than what they actually were. The loss of such a trivial object can be devastating for us even decades later.

Objects become signs of relations between human beings, and it is impossible to subtract this dimension from human interactions. To give or receive anything will have a *meaning* for us. Placebo effects can therefore be operating in the presence of a doctor or when one is alone. They depend not on some objective reality about what is pharmacologically effective and what isn't, but on complicated systems of unconscious beliefs and expectations. It is very difficult for a human being not to suppose that, somewhere, someone knows more than them. This belief will then shape to some degree their relations with other people.

There is a myth that one-third of patients are placebo responders, as if such a category could be distinguished. Actual effectiveness rates have been reckoned at between 1 to 100

per cent depending on the particular conditions of an experimental trial, but there is no human being who does not
operate on an everyday basis using placebo mechanisms.
Thought itself, we could argue, is a placebo, since it invites
us to follow false paths in order to avoid pain and supplies
false rationalizations of these detours. On a daily basis, we
construct mistaken explanations of reality in order to protect
ourselves from what we don't want to know. We interpret
events and ascribe mental states to other people – and to
ourselves – to ward off any engagement with the realities of
unconscious desires and feelings of hostility.

Take the example of the teenager's fits we discussed in
Chapter 3, which always took place only when he was alone
in a room with his younger sibling. If we agree that these
were manifestations of his unconscious hostility, surely the
common-sense, medical diagnosis of an epileptic-type attack
would count as a placebo? It would be an empty explanation that might have beneficial effects for the patient, giving
him some short-term relief from his anxiety and perplexity.
Believing this could have a protective function, but it
wouldn't address the source of the problem.

Let's take another example. A government official went to
consult Freud, who noted that the banknotes he paid with
were always perfectly clean and smooth. One day Freud
remarked that one could always tell a government official by
the brand-new currency withdrawn from the state treasury.
The man replied that actually he ironed the notes at home,
as it was a matter of conscience not to hand over any dirty
paper money. Banknotes might harbour dangerous bacteria
and hence harm their recipient. When Freud later quizzed
him about his sexual life, it turned out that he would regularly take the daughters of respectable families he knew for
trips to the country, arrange to miss the train home and then

creep into their hotel room at night to masturbate them. His unscrupulousness with these young girls was thus displaced into his fastidiousness with money: what they had in common was the idea of the dangers of a 'dirty' hand. Yet the patient's explanation for his passion for clean money presented no problem for him. It was a false belief that protected him from acknowledging his sexual impropriety.

Placebo studies turn up some curious details. Injections have higher placebo effects than pills, and large pills do better than smaller pills, although very small pills score higher than average-sized ones. All of this will depend on the *representation* of injections and pills in a particular family and in a particular culture, since we will associate the different sizes and forms of medication with what we know about them already from our experience of the world and our relations with other people. The current overprescription of antidepressant medication would be worth studying here, as it highlights what society pressures people to accept as a valid means of confronting sadness and pain. Prozac is consumed so widely in Britain that traces of it can now be found in tap water. The fact that so many take these drugs endows them quite naturally with a large dose of placebo effect, which has been reckoned at between 60 and 70 per cent.

Although we often hear the phrase 'It's just placebo', there is never any 'just' about placebos. Suggestion is a powerful phenomenon, and so medical encounters become highly potent meetings. As the neurologist and analyst Roy Grinker pointed out, an ill-advised sentence, a mistimed jocular remark, or a serious statement wrongly emphasized can damage the patient's recovery processes and result in a tragic outcome. The same may be true for the very act of communicating a diagnosis. Being told one has heart disease by a respected authority figure will certainly have effects on a person's life. Even if a second authority figure disagrees, the seeds of doubt are still planted, and this pressure may well contribute to the person's ill-health.

Medical anthropologists have compared the act of communicating a diagnosis to the hex or spell familiar from witchcraft, and the 'second opinion' to the effort to find a more powerful witchdoctor to undo the hex. This is shown clearly by the fact that, as recently as 1961, 90 per cent of physicians interviewed in a US study would not usually reveal a cancer diagnosis to a patient. The medical journals of the time include articles with titles like 'Do cancer patients want to be told?', 'Should cancer patients be told the truth?' and 'What Philadelphia physicians tell patients with cancer'. By 1978, however, 97 per cent of doctors *would* give their diagnosis to the patient.

One might think that this startling change is due to improvements in cancer therapy itself, so that diagnosing the disease is no longer equivalent to delivering a death sentence. But this is certainly not the case for all forms of cancer, and, indeed, it has often been argued that a diagnosis with negative connotations for the patient will have detrimental effects on their physical health. If the patient thinks the disease is serious, and if this belief is supported by those around the patient, the medical diagnosis may well only reinforce a downward spiral. We can see this illustrated in extreme form in the story we discussed earlier of the woman who died on the eve of her twenty-third birthday.

Even in the case of some patients with malignant disease, the realization of impending death may result in death before the malignancy has actually got far enough. The diagnosis *becomes* a 'cause' of death. Words are impacting here powerfully on the body. If we agree that suggestion is so important, then in the interests of the patient's health, why not tell them that they have one condition and not another, or that their prognosis is much better than the physician thinks? Doesn't this raise the very basic issue of truth versus the best interests of the patient?

It seems as if truth wins out here over best interests in many cases. The main explanation for this is legal. Doctors and hospitals don't want lawsuits, so transparency is maintained at all costs. Patients and their families are told frankly of worst-case scenarios and poor prognoses. But is this really 'truth'? Why shouldn't the doctor also mention the other end of the statistical spectrum, and even the rare cases of a miraculous remission? Beyond the legal issues, there is still the fundamental philosophical question of truth versus well-being. To choose truth over well-being is an ethical decision. With some cancer cases, it appears that what the doctor considers truth triumphs. But the reverse seems to hold for conditions such as depression, and the scenario is complicated with something like warts where less efficacious remedies are privileged over other proven treatments. Is it the gravity of the condition that determines the choice?

The act of diagnosing is thus never simply an external label applied to an existing and stable situation, but *an active ingredient that can change the situation itself*. According to a well-known slogan, 'Diagnosis is treatment'. Heart disease is a good example. It has been observed that if someone were to have monthly check-ups after certain kinds of heart problem, one day a false positive would show up. The act of communicating this result could not be reversed, and the patient would be placed under huge pressure to make a decision about medical intervention, not only from themselves but from their family and those close to them. The diagnostic act in itself can have massive, practical consequences.

Indeed, studies have shown that even the simple act of taking someone's blood pressure will often precipitate an increase in blood pressure.

This raises a number of clinical questions. If we remember from the last chapter the atherosclerotic plaques found during the autopsy of young soldiers, we could speculate on the kind of prognosis given to the patient were they still alive. Given this wide cross-section of reasonably healthy young men, if they had not died in battle, many of them would presumably have lived to an advanced age despite the presence of the plaques. Likewise, we often find debates today about whether all tumours should be treated indiscriminately, with the suggestion that there are some cases where it would be more beneficial for the patient to keep an eye on – or even try to ignore – their symptoms, instead of immediately undergoing an operation or course of medication. Sometimes, doctors give conflicting opinions, leaving the patient in the difficult state of not knowing what to do or whom to trust. Given the brevity of most medical encounters, it is almost impossible to predict exactly what the effects of a diagnosis are going to be.

Robert Aronowitz reports the case of an engineer in his seventies who thought it would be wise to screen for prostate cancer. The blood test was positive, but no cancer could be found on the ultrasound. Six 'blind' biopsies were carried out, and the last one contained a small cancer. The patient, after much family pressure, decided to undergo radiotherapy, and it is a question of whether he would have taken the decision to endure the side-effects of this therapy if the dreaded word 'cancer' had not been mentioned. Far more men die with prostate cancer than because of it. Specialists will sometimes give differing views here, and disagreement over a range of illnesses is not uncommon. Different and contradictory views will be more likely if each specialist is unaware of the diagnosis made by the other.

Diagnosis also poses the question of what it means to have an illness. Labels in the media allow and actively encourage the identification of medical conditions, and these have certainly become more diverse as health pages burgeon. Many syndromes which were never traditionally counted as illnesses have become so. During the latter part of the twentieth century, risk factors for several well-known diseases came to be seen as diseases in their own right. High blood pressure, for example, was no longer just a latent variable which might increase one's chances of becoming ill later in life, but a fully fledged illness in itself. What was once a risk is now an illness. High cholesterol and clinical obesity were both once seen as factors increasing the risk of other illnesses, yet they are now illnesses in their own right. Acid reflux is another recent addition: a common ailment not considered too serious in itself, it has now been upgraded into acid reflux disease. The new epithet confers new gravity on to this unpleasant problem, and so makes requests for medication more likely.

Mental-health labels have also been burgeoning. A new entity like 'social phobia' that has been recognized by the World Health Organization is largely the result of marketing by pharmaceutical companies. If a drug needs a market niche, the more illnesses there are, the more chances it will have to succeed. The expansion of 'addictions' is another case in point. Problems of human behaviour become medicalized, so that tastes in love and sex become addictions rather than subjective choices. It won't be long before smoking becomes an illness rather than a risk factor for an illness. First, smoking is seen to increase the chances of contracting a cancer. Then, it is deemed an addiction. And soon enough addiction becomes illness.

Labelling illness generates a host of problems. Psychiatrists and anthropologists have studied so-called 'illness behaviour', where the patient's relation to their role as a 'sick person' is explored. Some people seem to resist this role, others to embrace it. But what if the sickness itself is not so clear-cut? Illnesses are often far less homogeneous than we expect them to be, and disease recognition, naming and classification depend more than we might like to think on social factors. There is a constant pressure today to turn a variety of quite vague illness pictures into discrete disease entities, as if this would somehow make things more real and manageable.

When the physician Francis Crookshank wrote in the *British Journal of Medical Psychology* in 1931 that emotional weeping would one day be reclassified as 'paroxysmal lacrimation', with treatment by local application (a handkerchief), a salt-free diet and restriction of fluid intake – and failing that, early removal of the tear glands – his jest was in fact an accurate prediction. There has even been a reported case of a man who consulted an ophthalmologist for precisely the above reasons, only to be told that he was, in fact, crying! Although this is an isolated case, new diagnostic labels are flourishing. 'Addictions' now flood the marketplace, and there is a steady march of new diagnoses that demonstrate the difficulty medicine has in accommodating suffering which is not framed in its own terms.

Patients might want to upgrade their set of symptoms into a disease for many reasons: to gain understanding and recognition of their suffering, as if the label renders it legitimate; or because treatment, insurance payments and compensation may be more readily available if the right diagnostic label is introduced. At a psychological level, there is a powerful tendency, much studied by analysts, for people to move in the direction of labels. This may be to demonstrate that one cannot be reduced to that label, in which case one's symptoms are experienced as not quite fitting it, or, on the contrary, to show that one can be. Naturally enough, these different relations to diagnostic labels encourage people to form groups: people congregate together if they think they share an ailment or an addiction, or if they think they have been wrongly diagnosed. Pharmaceutical companies keep their eye on these trends and actively try to shape them. A new product, after all, needs a place in the market, which means, at times, a new diagnostic category.

Like their patients, doctors often disagree about labels. Certain doctors are well known in the trade to be believers in chronic fatigue syndrome, while others are sceptical. The same goes for some neurological conditions, where certain doctors will recommend life-long pharmaceutical regimes, while others will make alternative diagnoses and prescribe short-term medication. This is also often the case with decisions about the benefits of surgery. Advice on the pros and cons of even major surgery can vary dramatically from one physician to another, as we found when we accompanied patients on visits to different consultants. The same holds for some blood-sugar conditions, in which a patient may be urged to start a lifelong medication regime before sufficient time has passed between tests to monitor it. Spontaneous remissions from such illnesses are little studied by medicine.

To take another example, in cases where the sex of an infant is ambiguous, it has been shown that surgeons and paediatric endocrinologists will make radically different decisions as to which procedure to follow. The endocrinologists tend to be swayed more by the chromosomatic sexuality of the infant, the surgeons by the possibility of building a sex organ. Parents may be given advice to turn the infant into either a boy or a girl, depending on whom they choose to believe.

There are cultural differences here too. Some countries are well known for overprescribing drugs, others for underprescribing. France, for example, has a very high rate of prescription per GP visit compared to the UK. Surgical procedures are also carried out more in some places than in others, and one study even claimed that only 2–3 per cent of the surgical interventions of tonsillectomy and adenoidectomy were medically necessary. In 1976, a House of Representatives enquiry found that there were 2.3 million cases of unnecessary surgery each year in the US, and the current figure stands at more than three times that. This is an intriguing aspect of medical history, especially so given that surgery and medicine are relatively late companions, the two disciplines having been separate for centuries. While drugs today have to undergo scrupulous controls, with double-blind trials and a whole battery of tests, this is not the case for surgical procedures. If a drug is tested with trials involving thousands of people, could there be any comparable procedure in surgery? And what place would there be for placebo surgeries?

Surgery is interesting here, since it often has quite disparate effects depending on the psychological situation of the patient. Some psychotic people find that the symptoms of their psychosis are much improved after a surgical operation unrelated to the psychosis, while many neurotics will fare worse. It is worth remembering here that shamanistic treatments in many cultures involve ceremonies where an object is symbolically removed from the body, as if malign influence had been condensed into it. Once this object is removed, the evil force is subtracted, and the patient can recover. We might wonder to what extent these clearly psychological factors play a part in some of the results that surgical procedures produce. If, for example, surgery is seen unconsciously as a punishment, it may bring a certain feeling of relief from guilt. And this may help to explain some of the early opposition to the use of anaesthetics. Pain, it was argued, formed a necessary part of the procedure: without it, surgery would be less effective.

What about the cases where something is not subtracted but added to the body? Isn't it curious that myths and folklore in so many different cultures tell stories of heroes and heroines being helped on some quest or journey by a kindly donor who gives them a magical object to help them in their task? We could think of the winged sandals and cloak of invisibility given to Perseus by the Nymphs; or their modern equivalent, the high-tech gadgets given to 007 by Q in the James Bond films. Here again we find a kindly donor of magical objects, and who tends to remain in the same place, in contrast to the hero who is forever moving around. Is there something of this in the everyday medical encounter? And could this be one of the reasons why people so often feel disappointed if they leave the doctor's surgery without a prescription?

6. Can Illness have a Meaning?

Doctors and patients often disagree about anatomy. A patient may insist that pain is localized to a part of their body where the doctor can find no medical ailment or injury. If this part is supposedly an internal organ, it may turn out that there is no real organ in that area of the body. Doctors in the late nineteenth century studied these problems in great detail. It seemed to them that in many cases the body experienced by the patient was not the body described by anatomy. Yet for the patient this body was absolutely real. The pain it felt was not invented.

Freud showed in the 1890s that many physical symptoms that seemed to have no organic basis were the coded expressions of unconscious fantasies. A patient might complain of a paralysed arm, but even if there was a complete anaesthesia in some part of the arm, its anatomical location would not tally with medical knowledge about the distribution of nerves. An organic paralysis might mean that a certain part of the nerve a bit further away from the site of the main paralysis should also be unresponsive. Using such tests, Freud argued that patients did indeed have symptoms in their bodies, but that these bodies were imaginary ones and quite different from the bodies that medicine described.

These imaginary bodies were made from words. Expressions like 'I'm sick to the stomach', 'I've got a broken heart', or 'You're a real pain in the neck' could actually generate symptoms in what were imagined to be those same parts of the body. Such coded messages would depend on what each particular person had learned or surmised about particular parts of the body and their functions. Parents often find their children have an ache where they imagine the heart to be, and see their own words echoed back in their child's body. Medical students are certainly not immune to this kind of process, and with the huge amount they have to learn about the body, it's not surprising that they experience a wide range of novel symptoms. Since they meet with over 10,000 new technical words in an average medical training, how could some of these fail to generate an exotic variety of symptoms?

Strange as it may seem, this process may actually be taken as a sign of 'normal' development. It suggests, after all, that words and thoughts are being incorporated into our bodies. Our bodies are being constituted by words and the representations transmitted to us by our family and environment. We are developing a sense of the body. Listening to the early history of adult patients, it is often a positive sign to come upon memories of localized and time-specific symptoms in childhood that appear to be the effect of words. But as well as testifying to the way our bodies are constructed, the hidden messages we find in these symptoms are also indicating that other means of expression are unavailable. Sometimes we speak through the body when other routes are blocked.

Let's say we have a disturbing thought, perhaps concerning sexuality or violent wishes. Freud studied the ways in which such thoughts could be split off from consciousness. When the thought was deemed incompatible with other currents of our mental life, two things could happen. It could be maintained in consciousness, but have all the feelings connected to it split off and displaced to some neighbouring idea. We see this in obsessive states, where the person is aware of the odd sexual or violent thought but regards it as trivial and innocuous. By contrast, an adjacent trivial thought suddenly becomes magnified to incomprehensible proportions: the cupboard door always needs to be kept closed or the salt separated from the pepper. The anxiety linked to one idea has been shifted to another.

The disturbing thought may be otherwise transformed in a process Freud called *conversion*. Here the idea is repressed and pushed out of consciousness completely. But the strong feelings linked to it, prevented from obtaining a voice in our conscious mental life, will be diverted into the body. The strength of the thought is rendered less threatening by its transformation into something somatic. The choice of body part or process to be affected will depend on the details of what was happening at the time of the disturbing thought or on our knowledge of the body. This may be complicated by the fact that a thought that appears innocent at one moment may seem conflictual at another. Think, for example, of the way that children learn about sexuality over time. Childhood sexual games may generate guilt and self-punishment long after they have actually ceased, when the child learns more about adult perceptions of sexual practices.

Freud believed that these symptoms are like memory traces or commemorative 'monuments' within the body. The body bears witness to the original perturbing thought or experience, even if consciously we know nothing about it. Something too disturbing to think about, like a sexual or hostile wish directed to a loved one, is articulated in the body rather than voiced consciously, and it is the psychoanalyst's task to deliver the hidden message from the physical symptom. Crucially, since the conversion symptom can copy what one knows about the body and its ailments, it has to be carefully distinguished from other physical symptoms. The most common conversion symptoms include back pain, headache, intestinal problems, skin disorders and, in innumerable forms, pseudocyesis or imaginary pregnancy. Pseudocyesis is incredibly common, and can take the form of morning sickness, the build-up of intestinal gas and adipose tissue and abdominal swelling. In fact, *anything* that the person associates – rightly or wrongly – with pregnancy can be used to generate symptoms, even, for example, the sudden desire for some unusual food. The person will be aware of these often painful symptoms, but much less aware of their unconscious interest in pregnancy.

Conversion symptoms are full of meaning. A blurring of vision might in one case express the desire not to see something, just as a freezing of one's hands might express the idea of being 'left out in the cold'. Paralysis of the arm might express the wish to touch someone else, or oneself, in a sexual or hostile way. These everyday symptoms express wishes, fantasies, feelings and prohibitions that could ultimately be put into verbal form. What they have in common is this basic fact of *expressing*. Conversion symptoms, according to Freud, are a form of language and hence need to be listened to and deciphered. It is just a question of learning the individual code.

This code can be direct or indirect. In one case, a woman's facial neuralgia was traced back to a remark made by her husband which was felt as a bitter insult: 'It was like a slap in the face.' But how, asked Freud, could such a specific and apparently direct translation take place? Why was it a trigeminal neuralgia restricted to the second and third branches that was aggravated by chewing but not by talking? It turned out that what seemed to be a direct symbolization of the hurtful remark was in fact a more complex conversion. Freud linked it to a much earlier episode in which she had been experiencing both facial pains and toothache when she happened to witness a painful sight followed by feelings of self-reproach. This, he thought, had set the ground for the particularity of her symptom. The original neuralgia had merely been associated *in time* with disturbing thoughts, yet was used later on as a conduit to symbolize other, perhaps unrelated, problems.

In another example, a patient was afflicted with violent pains in her right heel that made walking impossible. Analysis linked this to the time when she had been staying in a sanatorium and was being taken by the house physician to the dining room. The pain had started when she took his arm to leave her room with him, and she had been terrified that she would not be 'on a right footing' with the other people present. Freud did not think that the symptom resulted directly from the thought, but that she had simply chosen from among her many physical symptoms at the time the one that was most symbolically appropriate to express the thought. This was what gave it a special persistence. In fact, Freud believed that direct, fresh conversions were very rare. More often, they would use associations, old illnesses and previously vulnerable parts of the body.

Freud noticed that conversion symptoms tended to require an addressee. They called out to be deciphered, which was why they often emerged only when particular people were present. Someone had to be there, although not necessarily physically present: they could be nearby, or simply somewhere in the patient's thoughts. What mattered was the unconscious idea of there being an addressee, some-one who could potentially listen. And this someone was often associated with a source of knowledge, be it medical knowledge or knowledge about some aspect of sexuality. It was as if the symptoms were appealing for a response, some answer to an intimate question about the body, sexuality and love.

Although conversion symptoms had symbolic meaning, they were believed – wrongly – by many analysts not to involve changes to the actual tissue of the body. An example can clarify the conversion process here, and illuminate its logic. It's the case of a 24-year-old woman seen at the Strong Memorial Hospital in New York for a variety of symptoms, including anxiety, vomiting and unexplained crying, which her physician worried might risk exacerbating a previously diagnosed gastric ulcer. During the physical examination, when questioned about a small patch of eczema on her left wrist, she explained that it was much better than it had been, and she wore a band of cloth to protect her skin from the wrist watch which she saw as the cause of the skin reaction. She also wore bands of cloth on her fingers to protect them from contact with her rings.

After some time in psychotherapy, more details of her symptoms emerged. The cloth protected her from contact with nickel, and whenever she touched it her skin would become red, swollen and itch at the point of contact. The eczema would always last between two and four months, regardless of the treatment she used. Asked when exactly her allergy had started, she said without hesitation that it had been when her father had given her a gold watch a few days before her graduation from high school. Symptoms immediately appeared, and these recurred sometime later when, working in a Children's Court, she had rested her arms on the judge's bench and come into contact with a strip of metal.

Her doctor had told her it was a nickel allergy, after testing her skin for reactions to various metals and finding that a swelling and irritation appeared when he pressed a five-cent piece to her back. These symptoms seemed marginal to her therapy, which focused on problems in her relationship with her boyfriend and family, until a particular moment. She had finally lost her virginity to the boyfriend, and was seeing her family for the first time since this important event. As they were doing the dishes after dinner, her mother exclaimed, 'What are you doing with your watch on?' The mother had not known that the allergy had more or less cleared up, and that she had been able to wear jewellery and metal against her skin without getting eczema. On hearing the mother's question, the young woman felt as if the world had come to an end: she suddenly felt a pain in her wrist where the watch was and began to scratch. Her arm was soon red and swollen, hives appeared and she had to go to lie down.

Now, why didn't she just tell her mother that her allergy had cleared up? As she explained to the therapist, on hearing the question she instantly thought about what had happened with her boyfriend, and took it as an accusation. Her first thought had been 'Shame on me', and, when asked if anything similar had occurred previously, she revealed emotionally a number of details. At the age of ten, she was going to be confirmed and had to attend confession. She was very uneasy about this, knowing she would have to confess all her sins and that she had to be pure to be 'wedded to Jesus Christ'. She felt that, however much she confessed, she would still be impure on account of all 'the filth' she had heard, of which she didn't know the meaning. She was tortured by the thought of whether having heard filthy things was a sin in itself or not, and how she could confess something she didn't know how to name or put into words.

Convinced that she was unclean, she took Communion,

and after the ceremony her aunt hung a metal necklace with a crucifix around her neck, telling her she was a grown-up now. Almost immediately, she broke out with a skin eruption over her neck and shoulders. When, years later, she had worked in the Children's Court, she complained that she had also then 'heard filth', especially the idea that people could have children without getting married, and it was at this exact time that her symptoms had emerged once again. The physician discussing the case noted that, given her sensitivity to the theme of marriage, she had understood Communion to be about a marriage to Christ, when strictly speaking, this would apply only to a nun taking her vows.

The conversion here presumably concerns the sexual thoughts she had and the defence against them. In the first scene, the religious ritual introduces the idea 'I cannot wear the crucifix as I am unclean', which is literally made flesh by her skin reaction. The symptom expresses both the sexual wishes and perhaps the punishment for them. The father's graduation gift, also at an important symbolic time, revives this earlier scene, when she is told that she is a grown-up woman. Later, when working at the Children's Court, she hears 'filth', and this confronts her again with the question of marriage. Finally, her mother's question is heard as an accusation of being unclean, following this same logic. The symptom thus inscribes in her flesh both an admission of and a punishment for her sexuality.

This is a classic example of a conversion symptom, and although Freud's idea was limited to very specific instances, many of the early analysts expanded the concept to find conversion symptoms just about everywhere. Even diseases like cancer were at times understood to be symbolic expressions akin to the coded message of a hysterical paralysis or skin eruption. Such interpretations seem far-fetched today, but they bore witness to what was a real clinical problem. Someone suffering from an organic disease will always associate old fantasies with it. They will be overlaid on the symptom, yet without necessarily being its cause. In one case, someone with a stomach ulcer had dreams and waking thoughts indicative of a fantasy of being stabbed in the stomach. In another, a woman saw the tubercle bacillus she harboured as the image of her invasive mother. There is a difference here between causes and overlays.

Some forms of today's behavioural therapies work in exactly the same way. Patients suffering from somatic illnesses are asked to visualize their body surface, cells or immune system in a positive way, as if this secondary overlay can affect the course and experience of the illness. Results seem to suggest that, in many cases, it can, and we will look at some possible mechanisms in Chapter 14. It is curious that often the very people who deny that thoughts and fantasies can contribute to somatic symptoms use what is presumably a parallel process in their attempts at improving the patient's condition once they are already ill. One behavioural technique for those suffering from heart problems is to encourage them to imagine that there is an unstressed, relaxed fellow sitting on their shoulders, directing their actions. Isn't this quite similar to the ulcer patient's idea that there is someone trying to stab him? In both cases, a thought or image is grafted on to what is a pre-existing problem. Yet why should one have physical effects and not the other? If an overlay – like visualization – can have effects on, say, the immune system or blood pressure, why couldn't the same mental process have contributed to the symptoms in the first place?

Freud did not believe that all symptoms were conversions. As well as somatic symptoms with no psychological roots, there were the symptoms of what he called the 'actual neuroses', where frustrations and dissatisfactions would produce physical symptoms, even if these symptoms *didn't hold any disguised message*. It was rather a question of economic balance: what was dammed up in one part of a person emerged in another part. Similarly, Freud described how feelings may bring about diseases of the nervous system accompanied by anatomical changes and also diseases of other organs, given some predisposing factor to the disease in question. Freud's students elaborated on this idea, proposing the category of 'vegetative' – in the sense of not consciously directed – symptoms, which had no symbolic meaning and were not necessarily the consequence of an economic factor either. As one analyst put it, in these cases 'there is no symbolism in the symptom'.

Franz Alexander spent decades researching this kind of problem, and he was responsible for inspiring much of the American work in the 1940s and '50s. After training in Vienna and Berlin, Alexander moved to the States and founded the Chicago Institute for Psychoanalysis. He was interested in what he called the physical 'concomitants' or accompaniments of mental states. Psychological reactions like rage, panic and relaxation would have specific accompanying physical states, different for each of the core reactions. Alexander's guiding hypothesis here was that, if mental states had specific physiological correlates, when ideas and feelings were blocked and unable to gain expression, the accompanying action of the autonomic nervous system would be blocked as well. The energy would then be maintained chronically, causing tissue damage.

For example, the wish to receive and give will have as its accompaniment the activity of the upper intestinal tract, since this deals with the first intake of food. Given that the infant's first experience of love is bound up with its first experience of feeding, food and love become inseparable at an unconscious level. If the person then feels rejected and craves love, yet cannot express this, the stomach will respond. Acting as if preparing for food, the continuing secretions in the stomach, with their high acidity, will prepare the ground for an ulcer. Alexander elaborated similar models for asthma, hypertension, ulcerative colitis and a number of other diseases.

Despite their differences, Alexander thought that all of these diseases had something in common. They all revolved around conflict. This could be the conflict between the feeling of dependency and its denial, or between the feeling of aggression and the measures taken against it. We start life in a dependent state, but still wish to assert our autonomy. We feel hostility towards those closest to us, yet must inhibit this so as not to risk losing their love. According to Alexander, these conflicts will introduce tensions that may later have real effects on our health. His ideas were once tremendously influential, and they raised a number of new questions.

Since psychoanalysis was all about speaking, undoing symbolism and accessing coded fantasies, symptoms which had no meaning were tricky. How could one work with them? What could one do if interpreting them in the traditional way was ruled out? On Alexander's model, the ulcer didn't *mean* anything. It wasn't sending a coded message, and it wasn't symbolizing any fantasy about being stabbed. It was merely the bodily accompaniment of a psychological conflict or state of tension. Alexander was also careful to emphasize that these factors were only one part of a bigger picture. For somatic symptoms to develop, there had to be the right kind of precipitating event and also a mysterious 'X factor' which involved the body's propensity to fall ill. This could be seen as a constitutional or genetic or otherwise 'pre-wired' component.

This idea seemed to fit with a lot of the exciting work in physiology at the time. Remember how Walter Cannon had been interested in the way an organism reacts to acute situations with bodily change: increases in heart and respiratory rate, muscular tension, sweatiness and lower intestinal activity. Cannon wanted to investigate the human somatic reactions to states like rage, hunger and panic. Might it be possible to find specific physical manifestations for each of them? He found a common pattern in both human and animal research that is known as the 'fight-or-flight' reaction.

Despite the fact that the end results of fighting or fleeing will be very different, both involve the rapid mobilization of resources to enhance physical and mental functioning. Fight occurs if rage is prevalent, and flight if fear is prevalent. And this is where the model was useful in terms of understanding the formation of symptoms. If the body mobilized itself for an action that never came, there would be a prolonged overstimulation of the heart, adrenal glands and other organs. In the case of sudden death, for example, if the emotional state had persisted for a long time, without the possibility of action, the overactivation of the sympathetic nervous system (the branch of the autonomic nervous system that prepares the body for action) could have caused a fatal fall in blood pressure. Unlike a conversion symptom, the fall in blood pressure wouldn't be a symbol or need any deciphering.

Cannon and Alexander thus shared the idea that a state of tension could produce bodily symptoms. These would be different from the specific coded messages of conversion symptoms: if conversion symptoms had a meaning, vegetative symptoms didn't. It had also been argued by other analysts that where conversion symptoms didn't involve any actual damage to body tissue, affecting mostly the neuromuscular and sensory systems, vegetative symptoms could involve lesions and significant tissue change. The implication was that conversion symptoms were less serious in terms of potential risks to one's health than vegetative ones, and that different modes of treatment would be called for.

But could they really be separated so neatly? What would happen, for example, if a conversion symptom persisted for years? Wasn't there the possibility that this might generate local tissue damage? If someone had the wish to reject someone close to them, and this wish could not be articulated, it might produce the conversion symptom of nausea and vomiting, for instance, as if the other person were being vomited out. When Madonna famously mimed the gesture of vomiting after receiving a patronizing comment about her show from Kevin Costner, this could be read as a parody of this kind of conversion: she was vomiting up both Costner and his remark. And refusing to incorporate it.

Now, what would happen if this symptom of nausea and vomiting, combined with acidic hypersecretion in the stomach, continued over a long time? Could it result, for example, in the formation of a peptic ulcer? Skin disorders are another good example here, as they are so often symbolic, yet involve tissue change. In one case, a twenty-year-old soldier developed a nettle-like rash on the back of his legs, thighs and buttocks. The rash had an odd transverse linear pattern to it, resembling the welts one might receive from a whipping. It turned out that, as a nine- or ten-year-old boy, he had been whipped for the offence of peeking through the window of a girls' dormitory. The recurrence of these lesions ten years later took place immediately after he had been apprehended loitering on the grounds of the nurses' dormitory at the military post where he was stationed. He had hoped to see a nurse he was interested in, but was caught by an officer and reprimanded. Within an hour the skin lesion had developed.

What could be happening here? Are we dealing with a conversion symptom? When the skin is injured, there is a typical response of pain and inflammation. But this response involves not only the immediate effect of the injury, but a feedback system which maintains the inflammatory response. This feedback is mediated by antidromic – running the 'wrong way' – activity along the same fibres which carried the initial painful impulses (from the whipping), and it results in the formation of chemical substances at the nerve terminals in the skin which facilitate the inflammatory response and influence clotting mechanisms. Now, it is well known that the same feedback system can be mobilized by hypnotic suggestion of injury. The implication then is that the same would hold for conversions involving the *fantasy or unconscious thought* of injury to the skin.

This might explain the swellings and inflammation often found at previous sites of illness and injury, as well as rarer and more spectacular phenomena like stigmata. If these processes are linked with other bodily systems, imagine the possibilities in investigating disorders like eczema and dermatitis. The boundaries between conversion and other symptoms are thus not always going to be so clear. Tissue damage cannot be the criterion to differentiate them. If any part of the body has been injured, it will achieve mental representation, and so take on some meaning. Which implies that it can become the site of future conversion reactions. An illness in the past with *no apparent psychological roots can then become reactivated years later* either to express a symbolic message or simply as a response to a disturbing or psychically unpalatable event.

The implications of this simple idea are fascinating. It suggests that if we search for a psychologically disturbing event linked to the onset of a symptom or disease process and don't find one, it doesn't rule out the possibility of exactly those factors. In dermatology, for example, it is often observed that someone can work with a reactive material for years without any problem, and then suddenly develop a contact dermatitis coincident with an emotional upheaval. The reactive material suddenly becomes a 'cause' of the symptom, as if the body is being used as a pathway to express the disturbing changes. The temporal factor is crucial here. Just as the reaction may only emerge at this significant moment, so the same symptom may appear later on in the absence of the reactive material. A sceptic might see this as a 'have your cake and eat it' type of argument. But it is an important point which should not be ignored. What matters is the fact that a bodily process *achieves representation*. Once this has happened, once it is registered in the body, it may become activated at some time in the future. The *same* symptom or illness could thus have a *different* function at different moments in one's life. And isn't this something we see with the most common kind of symptom like an allergy?

The onset of an allergic reaction may be mysterious at one moment and clear at the next. Once the physical reaction has been mentally registered and encoded, it can then become operative at other times. Psychological factors may or may not have been significant in the first onset situation, but this will not always affect its future course in a predictable way. New wine can be poured into old bottles. This suggests that a symptom will not necessarily mean the same thing all of the time and, furthermore, that we should give up the idea that symptoms either mean something or they don't.

7. When the Body Replies

A physical symptom can serve many purposes. It may have started for reasons that have little to do with emotional factors, yet be resurrected in the context of psychological pressures. This may be months, years or decades after the initial recovery. Once a symptom has been mentally represented, it may in some cases become available for future use. This complicates the study of illness, since it suggests that if no psychological factors are found in the early appearance of an illness, further investigation may be discouraged.

The model we are exploring doesn't claim that every physical lesion is a conversion or a vegetative symptom, just that the *timing* and *site* of the lesion may be significant. This could be direct or indirect, linked only to an association in time that has no symbolic meaning. Once again, we have to confront a complicated process rather than a simple one. The boundary between conversion and vegetative symptoms may be possible to draw in some cases, but not in others. But are there further ways of distinguishing somatic symptoms that seem to have a link to unconscious processes? Could some symptoms be ways of asking a question? If we think back to the case of the nickel allergy in the previous chapter, was the symptom implicitly asking something – 'Am I unclean?' – or was it providing an answer, 'I am unclean', as we might suspect when we consider the exchange between daughter and mother when they were doing the dishes? Was the emergence of the symptom like an answer, a stamp or seal applied to the body?

Could a distinction between questions and answers be helpful here? Researchers in psychosomatic medicine have sometimes observed how a symptom, particularly one with a sudden onset, may function like a signature, a marker that pins down some aspect of the person's identity at a time when this is being challenged by external events. Let's take two examples. The first case is reported by a French psychoanalyst, with French the language of the treatment. The patient had been hospitalized for ulcerative colitis – a bowel disease involving inflammation and sores in the lining of the large intestine – and surgery was planned to remove a portion of his intestine. Believing that his problem was somehow linked to psychological factors, he contacted an analyst, and began to talk about his life.

The patient's family name embarrassed him, he revealed, as it sounded similar to a derogatory expression. To escape ridicule, he'd changed it by making a minor alteration, to produce a new name that evoked a village he'd seen on television that had been destroyed in war. The name change had taken place ten years previously, on meeting the woman who was to become his wife. He'd felt that it would be impossible to keep his real name, and around this time he'd met his future wife's family, striking up a close friendship with her father. Not long before the marriage itself, and after the change of name, he had his first episode of colitis, with significant loss of blood. He married, had a son, and life proceeded on a fairly even keel for the next ten years. But recently he had been losing blood, and the cortisone treatment which had helped him with the first episode was no longer effective. Hence he had been hospitalized and was awaiting surgery.

Now, a lot had happened over the previous few months. He had divorced his wife, on learning of her infidelity, and this separation had deprived him not only of his wife and home, but also his beloved father-in-law. The patient had never known his real father, and had only one isolated memory of him: at around three years of age, he was returning from school with his sister when a large, powerful-looking man hoisted him up and gazed at him. The sister told him not to mention this episode to their mother, as she was opposed to any contact with their father. He described how he would miss seeing his father again as he waited with his sister after school for their interminably late mother to collect them. At this moment in his story, the analyst broke her silence with the words '*Sans père*', which means, literally, 'without father'.

The patient then described a memory. As a child, he had gone into the kitchen at home one day and found a used sanitary towel soaked in blood lying on the floor. He assumed it was his mother's. At which point the analyst broke her silence again with the words '*Sang perd*', which means 'lost blood', and sounds, in French, exactly like *sans père*. It was through this intervention, the analyst argues, that the patient was able to engage with the question of his mother's desire that he have no contact with his father: that he be, literally, *sans père*. At the moment he'd changed his name – in other words, **at the moment he'd relinquished the one thing that kept him linked symbolically to his father** – the somatic symptom had emerged. The second episode, in turn, was triggered by the separation from the father-in-law. In each case, there was a *sans père*.

From this point on in the treatment, the patient showed an active interest in his real father. He tracked him down and met with him. As he explored this aspect of his life, the episodes of bleeding were significantly reduced. They stopped definitively after a dream in which he was about to be killed by a bandit, and which he interpreted himself as playing out his own death wish. Now, how did the analyst interpret this remarkable sequence? She saw the colitis as an appeal to a dimension of paternity which had been blocked for the patient, and which could be released and set back in circulation by her intervention '*Sans père*'. *The episodes of bleeding (***sang perd***) were transformed into a quest for the father*. And the dream, she thought, was about the patient becoming conscious of the death drive within himself.

Now, what status does the bodily symptom have in this case? We could see it less as posing a question than as a kind of response, a *designation* of the subject as *sans père*. We must assume here that these words were somehow arbitrary and imposed by the analyst, and that hence the colitis was not the symbolic expression of the phrase *sans père*. What the words did was offer a bridge between the symptom and the question of paternity, opening up an unarticulated dimension in this person's life. At the same time, the punning quality of the intervention invited him to choose words and language instead of the body. Although the illness was clearly not a kind of magic materialization of words, it functioned like a stamp or seal which fixed his identity. It was something quite literally inscribed in the body, going into the place of the problematic symbolic dimension of kinship. *The body responds here with an answer when the symbolic universe doesn't*. Unlike a conversion symptom, it isn't a communication, but quite the opposite: a kind of short-circuiting of communication. Like the difference between meaningful speech and the apparent meaninglessness of a proper name.

This case could be linked to earlier research on ulcerative colitis. In a series of important studies in the 1950s, George Engel described what he saw as a pattern. Sufferers would be involved in a highly dependent relation with one or two

people, showing an intensity lacking in their other relationships. The colitis would start or recur at moments when one
of these intense relations was broken off or threatened. Engel
also observed that, when in medical treatment, colitis sufferers
would follow the same model: they would either develop a
highly charged relation with their doctor or a cold, distant
one. Those who became close and dependent tended to fare
much better medically. It followed that their relations with
their gastroenterologists – or psychotherapists – should never
be broken off definitively.

Let's take another example. A patient suffering from asthma
began psychotherapy, his condition having grown significantly worse after he had moved to Britain for a new job.
Unable to spend time with the friends and family in the
foreign town he had come from, he complained that 'in
London no one treats me properly – I feel like a nobody'.
His doctor had attributed the exacerbation of the asthma to
the pollution of the big city. The history of his symptoms
was instructive, however. They had started in his teens during
a stay with his father, whom he saw very rarely, his parents
having separated when he was six. The next time it occurred
was when, in the course of a Saturday job he'd undertaken
some years later, his boss had shouted at him and a row had
occurred. When the patient was questioned about the details
of this fight, it turned out that the boss had employed an
expression very close to one that the father had used during
the summer he had stayed with him. They had argued, and
the father, a violent and bitter man, had shouted at the patient
that he was, to translate the expression literally into English,
'a waste of air'.

There was thus an immediate continuity between the insult
and the symptom, as if the father's words had been directly
printed on to the patient's body. When the asthmatic attacks

returned after he moved to London, it was at a time of separation from his social network. He was alone now, a 'nobody', and it was here that the symptom intervened to make him 'a waste of air'. The symptom was like a name, fixing his identity and pinning down his existence at the moment of being reduced to no one. This differs from a conversion symptom in that, as a direct inscription, it isn't asking the question *why* the father might have used that expression or *what he might have meant*. And it isn't a disguised expression of a sexual wish or a punishment for this. We could also think here of the case we discussed in Chapter 5 of the man haunted by his mother's prophecy that something 'dire' would strike him down. Her words were directly inscribed on him, rather than being repressed, forgotten or contested. Conversions tend to reveal hidden forms of questioning, whereas here the somatic phenomenon doesn't seem to be asking 'What does my mother or father want?' or 'What is my situation?' or 'Am I lovable?' It just echoes what has been heard, like a sort of reflex response – the salivation of Pavlov's dogs.

This sort of reaction is often found in the flaring up of physical symptoms. A lesion may appear quite promptly to mark a birthday, an anniversary, an encounter or a separation. It might give the impression of a sort of chronometric marker, simply fixing the event, like the severe eczema that would erupt on a boy's body at precisely the moment when he was about to see the mother who had abandoned him. There seems to be a continuity in such cases between the emergence of the symptom of illness and the precipitating event, which does not pass through the usual circuits of cognitive activity. It just happens. And researchers have been struck by the lack of mental elaboration or questioning concerning such moments.

This can have an effect on the way someone seeks help. When the symptom acts as a question, it tends to generate appeals towards sources of knowledge, be they medical or psychological. The patient doesn't necessarily want to know what the symptom *means*, but they want a label or diagnosis for it. The search for a label can also happen if the symptom is a response, but there is much less mental elaboration and sometimes even a silence. There are many published cases of people who find a suspicious lump somewhere on their body, yet fail to have it examined. Sometimes, they just assume it is cancer, and that this is a punishment for some betrayal or sinful act on their part. When they do receive medical attention years later and cancer is diagnosed, it is too late.

In one case, a woman discovered a lump in her breast when she was forty-five. Some two years previously, she had been kicked in the breast by her nephew, who had tried to force her into sexual relations. There had been considerable swelling as a result, and when the nephew committed suicide sometime after her discovery of the lump, she interpreted its appearance as God's punishment of her responsibility for the death. If she had initiated him sexually, she said, his suicide might have been avoided. She only consulted a doctor two years after finding the lump when it had ulcerated and she wanted to know what could be done about the odour.

As with the case of eczema we mentioned above, there is a continuity here between events. The link between the disease and the scene with the nephew was clear to her, even if other evidence might rule out any association. What matters is how the patient had given meaning to the events, and the silence that followed from this. In the boy's case, when he was first seen by an analyst at two years and nine months, he was completely expressionless, inert and uncommunicative. Attempts to engage him in play were fruitless, and he seemed to have no reaction at all to the events around him. And yet each time it was announced that his mother would be arriving, the eczema would erupt in the most severe form. Interestingly, the fading of his symptoms during a long period of therapy coincided with his ability to play out sadistic, violent games with a group of model figures, and to express more overt aggression to other people.

The somatic symptoms here bring into focus the ambiguity we discussed at the end of the last chapter. If we assume that the eczema was first an unequivocal mark on the body, a direct inscription of the distress at the idea of contact with and separation from the mother, could it later take on other functions? The analyst observed what he took to be traces of this process, as the scratching introduced an erotic quality to the symptom. Indeed, we could wonder whether *any* somatic symptom can fail to evoke responses which involve feelings of pleasure and pain, and thereby the shadow of sexuality. Freud's physician Max Schur drew attention to the way that medicine doesn't want to know anything about this. A GP might ask a patient whether they scratch their eczema or psoriasis, but they won't try to find out how much they *enjoy* doing this. And yet any activity involving friction of the body surface invokes this question of sexuality. A powerful strand of human pleasure, after all, comes about through stimulation of the body surface.

This shows how a symptom can function at several different levels at once. Let's say that some external agent causes a skin reaction in a patient, without worrying for the time being whether psychological factors were at play in the initial reaction. The patient takes medication to remove the symptoms, but at the same time cannot stop scratching. The scratching makes the condition worse, and the patient vows to stop aggravating it. Yet there might have been a disturbing pleasure in the scratching. And now the patient is confronted with a new dilemma: the conflict between pleasure and prohibition. The wish to scratch conflicts with the knowledge that scratching is prohibited, and this kind of tension will in itself introduce sexuality. Scratching the body surface may be a sexual activity, but prohibition will also evoke the sexual dimension. Prohibition, after all, creates desire. The battle between touching and not touching may well become associated unconsciously with problems concerning masturbation and illicit fantasies: should they or shouldn't they indulge? And so, as this terrible process continues, the symptom could start to function as both a source of pleasure, however repugnant, and the punishment for this pleasure.

These examples in no way warrant *generalization* about the symptoms we have discussed. It would be absurd to argue that any skin reaction would revive guilt associated with masturbation, just as it would be to see asthma or ulcerative colitis as always constituting marks of identity rather than forms of questioning, or indeed, other forms of symptom that we have not even discussed. What the examples show is the importance of detailed attention to individual histories. This should include an exploration of what *function* a symptom will have in each unique case. The same explanation cannot apply to all instances of asthma, colitis or indeed any other condition.

All we can conclude is that perhaps there is an interest in distinguishing somatic symptoms which seem to be the vehicles of questions and those which seem to be forms of response, of designation. And also, that there may be cases where a symptom appears in the place of a broken relationship. It is interesting to observe how the conversion symptoms described by Freud are built up around conflicts and questions, whereas other somatic symptoms seem sometimes to function almost like punctuation points in human narrative. When we find illness following a break in a relationship, the question is then to ask what role the relationship had in the first place. If it was *itself* a defence or a response for another relationship or dimension in the person's life that was lacking, the symptom may take over the job done by the relationship. In the case of the man with ulcerative colitis discussed above, the relation with his father-in-law protected him from the unsymbolizable question of the relation with his own biological father.

This may be linked to a particularly fascinating remark made by the analyst Joyce McDougall, a New Zealander working for many years in Paris who has specialized in somatic problems. Discussing the relation of conversion symptoms to other somatic ailments, she says that conversion symptoms tend to be linked to sexual and narcissistic themes, whereas certain somatic ones may be about the *right to exist*. If we add to this the distinction between the symptom as a form of question and as a response, an answer that comes from the body at certain moments in a person's life, perhaps this gives us a useful framework for thinking about some of the phenomena we have discussed.

Clinically, it would suggest that the doctor listen out to see if a symptom conceals an appeal to be heard. It is a familiar situation in which someone presents again and again with a somatic complaint to the same or different doctors. Sometimes, medical diagnoses are found and the symptoms treated, with further symptoms soon following in their wake. At other times, the doctor may insist that the problem is in the patient's mind, while they insist that, on the contrary, it is in the body. As this impasse continues, the patient may be sent on an endless series of medical tests and consultations. Some of these may pick up a recognized pathology and so the process will be diverted for a while. But what remains untouched is the question articulated in the patient's symptoms which may well have a link to common childhood preoccupations: 'Is there something inside me?', 'Am I a man or a woman?', 'Am I at risk of losing an organ?'

It would be interesting to find out what percentage of GP consultations deal with symptoms which could be seen as forms of these three questions. It is uncanny to realize that these basic human enquiries are also central to basic human diseases. Although they may never produce any somatic symptoms in the patient's lifetime, they will be closely associated with how that person's culture pictures illness. A child who spends hours each day worrying that there is something eating her up from the inside might be especially intrigued or terrified later on when she learns about cancer. And a boy nervous about what it means to possess a penis might be panicked to hear about illnesses which could lead to loss of a body part, like gangrene or even a simple dental problem.

We could think here of what will happen if someone with certain unconscious preoccupations contracts later in life exactly the disease that most chimes with their anxieties. Some illnesses, perhaps, may actually be ways of articulating these painful questions. A hormonal disorder in adolescence, for example, may be a way of asking to what sex the person belongs, even if this thought is never admitted clearly to consciousness. The interruption of periods may be part of a question about whether one can be a woman or not. When hormones are described as chemical messengers, we should ask where exactly the message is coming from.

These questions clearly resonate with some of the interests of medicine, and indeed with a wide range of actual diseases. But a sensitivity to this dimension of an appeal need not rule out all other approaches. The old distinction between conversion and vegetative symptoms may be useful in some cases, but not in others, and we have seen some of its limitations. Distinguishing between symptoms as the vehicle of a question or of an answer, or between the sexual and the right to exist are thought-provoking but by no means rigid contrasts. Although we would not agree with the exact form of all of these distinctions, perhaps there is an echo here of a profound difference in the function of somatic symptoms. These symptoms, as we have seen, can play very different roles in people's lives.

8. The Heart

Human culture has turned the heart into a symbol. Literature, poetry and everyday language picture the heart as the embodiment of states like love, joy, anger, fear or sorrow. We speak of having a broken heart, of wearing one's heart on one's sleeve, having one's heart in one's mouth or of one's heart skipping a beat. Could the fact that the heart is made to carry so many meanings actually have an effect on its functioning? If someone who complains of having a broken heart subsequently dies of heart failure, is this a tragic coincidence or a sign that the body is responding to mental despair?

The theme of conversion that we have discussed in the previous two chapters suggests that when a part of the body acquires a mental significance, it can in some cases become the site of physical illness. Would the many representations of the heart in language and culture then pave the way for the emergence of cardiac symptoms? This is certainly the conclusion of some medical anthropologists. Western doctors were curious as to the number of Cambodian refugees from the Khmer Rouge regime who complained of heart symptoms and what they called a 'weak heart'. Palpitations, trembling, shortness of breath and fear of dying were associated with this idea, even though it turned out that there was nothing significantly wrong with the heart itself.

As they studied the problem, it became clear that the physical symptoms were linked to a cultural representation of the human heart. This was frequently imagined as an automobile, which would need petrol when low on fuel and would rattle when the tank was empty. Breathing was pictured as a piston-like movement, and conventional Cambodian remedies consisted mostly of energy drinks, continuing the analogy with a car that needed liquid fuel. Anthropologists traced this relatively recent syndrome to the period of French colonization of Cambodia and the effect of French-language expressions like '*faible de coeur*' (weak-hearted).

This example shows how language can help to shape physical symptoms. The idea of the heart and its associated imagery was creating bodily disturbances. But if the Cambodian 'weak heart' is an example of a conversion process, what about the cardiac problems involving serious damage prevalent in Western society? Could these ever be shaped and mediated by words in the same way? Or are they, on the contrary, downstream effects of states of mental distress, tension and impasse which have little to do with our mental representations of the heart?

Heart disease is the single greatest cause of death in industrialized countries. In 2002, nearly 12 per cent of the British population were suffering from long-standing heart and circulatory illnesses, and each year there are more than a quarter of a million heart attacks and around 338,000 new cases of angina. In the States, one in five deaths is due to coronary heart disease, and over a million people will have a heart attack each year. A total of $242 billion will be spent annually on medical care for cardiovascular disease in the States, and €104 billion in the European Union. In Britain alone there are 180 million prescriptions for cardiovascular drugs each year. With these statistics steadily rising, heart disease is a huge, and ever increasing, problem.

Many of the early studies in psychosomatic medicine would generalize about the type of person likely to suffer from heart problems. They would be prone to anger, always in a rush, demanding of others and equally merciless on themselves. Beyond these stereotypes, there tended to be very little differentiation of specific kinds of heart problem. The heart, after all, can malfunction in a variety of ways, from arrhythmias, cardiac failure, ischaemic heart disease and valvular heart disease to infective endocarditis, hypertension and congestive heart disease. If personality mattered, should each of these disorders have a distinct personality type to go with it?

Some forms of heart disease are far commoner than others. It is estimated that coronary artery disease makes up around 80 per cent of cases, but there are several different causes of this disease. Diabetes and hypertension – chronically elevated blood pressure – can lead to coronary artery disease, as does atherosclerosis, which involves a thickening and stiffening of the arteries, with a reduction of their diameter due to the build-up of scar tissue and fatty deposits. These may grow from tiny tears in the artery walls caused by rapid increases in blood pressure. The body's sudden need for energy means that stores of fat will be mobilized so they can be immediately available, and the heart starts pumping faster. To find the 'atherosclerotic' personality, should we be on the lookout for the kind of person who experiences a lot of sudden demands for energy?

Arrhythmias present a different kind of problem. These are disturbances in the electrical impulses which cause the muscles of the heart rhythmically to contract. They come in a number of different varieties depending on the source and nature of the irregularity, how regular the beat is, whether it is speeded up or slowed down. Arrhythmias, such as ventricular fibrillation – an abnormal heartbeat producing ineffective contractions – are the cause of many mortalities from sudden cardiac death, and one trait significantly associated with them is the experience of anxiety. A study of male health professionals showed a six-fold increase in the risk of sudden cardiac death in those with high levels of anxiety. What seemed to be occurring was a loss of control of the heart as violent signalling pulses from the autonomic nervous system disturbed its rhythm. Should we be on the lookout then for people frequently experiencing anxiety to find the 'arrhythmic' personality?

Arrhythmias have been linked to those victims of sudden cardiac death who die from the terror of an earthquake, mugging, or, in the case of Cannon's 'voodoo death', discussed in Chapter 4, the witchdoctor's curse. A dramatic release of adrenaline and noradrenaline in the heart is brought on by intensive activity within the sympathetic nervous system. Cannon had been on the right track here. These two hormones drive heart cells to open their calcium channels, allowing such a quantity of calcium to flood into the heart fibres that they seize, bringing on a fatal arrhythmia. Yet although they were once seen as anomalies, technological advances that allow continuous monitoring of the heart show that arrhythmias in fact happen *throughout the day*, even in those with healthy hearts. Over-regular heart activity may be less robust than the occasional skipping or addition of a beat.

Despite the complexity of the clinical picture, personality profiling has had an enormous success in the study of heart disease. If much of the psychosomatic research from the late 1960s onwards prided itself on its rejection of the profiling model, it is ironic that by far its most popular and widely accepted finding involves personality types. This has led to the popularization of an apocryphal story of where the model came from: not the pioneers of psychosomatic medicine but the casual remark of an upholsterer.

Meyer Friedman and Ray Rosenman were running a busy cardiology practice in San Francisco, yet despite its success, they were beset by a continual, irritating problem: they were forever being forced to re-upholster the chairs in their waiting room. On one occasion, a new upholsterer showed up to assess the damage, and, casting his skilled eye over the furniture, asked what on earth was wrong with their patients. People just didn't wear out chairs like that, not even in the naturally tense environment of a waiting room. In particular, it was the front few inches of the seat cushion and of the padded armrests that were the worst affected. The patients must have been fidgeting compulsively, on the edge of the chairs, grating and scratching away at the armrests.

And so the cardiologists realized that they might be dealing with a very particular type of patient, one so nervous, impatient and restless that the furniture itself would bear the marks of their suffering. It turns out that this story is only partly true: Friedman has observed that he remembered the upholsterer's remark some five years after his research had started. This had apparently been sparked by the observation that accountants' cholesterol levels would shoot up around tax time. But the way the tale has circulated is significant. It suggests a kind of Eureka moment, with no link to the past, when it would be much more plausible to see Friedman and Rosenman's work as coming out of a long tradition of research in psychosomatic medicine.

What was the personality type they came up with? The Type A was aggressive, competitive, ambitious, restless and with a terrible sense of time-urgency – always on edge, always in a rush. It was no wonder they wore out the waiting-room chairs, or parked their cars facing outwards rather than inwards in the hospital car park. Photos of the parking area show how the cars of the Type A patients were positioned to allow them a quick getaway: no time could be wasted. With so many things to do in such a time-limited, finite day, they wanted to be able to leave as quickly as possible.

These subjects wanted an 'unlimited number of relatively poorly defined things from the environment in the shortest period of time'. Although the Type A concept was introduced in the early 1960s, this sort of description seems just as apt today as it did at the time to describe a certain type of behaviour, particularly in the big cities of industrialized countries. The fact that this behavioural style seemed appropriate to modern consumer societies even led some doctors to question the rationale of trying to discourage it, as this would risk upsetting the economy. As one doctor put it: 'Widespread reduction of such behaviour might have adverse socio-economic consequences of decreasing productivity and pressure to achieve.'

Good for the economy or not, one big question was seldom being asked. As Dean Ornish from the San Francisco Preventive Medicine Research Institute pointed out, the problem was less to find out whether hard work gave people heart attacks, than *why these relatively affluent subjects felt the need to work so hard*. What was pushing them? If it wasn't economic necessity, what kind of internal taskmaster did they have? The Type A concept caught on quickly. In one of the early studies, 3,400 men apparently free of coronary artery disease were rated for Type A-style behaviour solely on the basis of psychological variables. Two and a half years later, the Type As in the group aged between thirty-nine and forty-nine were found to have more than six times the incidence of coronary disease than the Type Bs (those who didn't have the Type A characteristics) in the same age group.

Many of these studies on the Type As had a worrying

disregard for variables like age, sex and socio-economic status, and it wasn't long before several more complex studies argued that, if these were taken into account, the Type A lost some of its specificity; the characteristics of a high percentage of the coronary patients proved more similar to those of the population strata to which these patients belonged than to those of other coronary patients from different population strata. A 1987 review of Type A studies found, in fact, that, after an explosion of positive results in the early and mid 1970s, negative results began to appear more often by 1978. Overall, it seemed that the links were weaker than originally surmised, but changing evaluation techniques may have had a hand in this.

There were fewer extended interviews and more paper-and-pencil questionnaires. Questionnaires are supposed to be more objective than assessment by interviewers, but they can only provide a shallow view of human life and are open to all the fallacies of self-reporting. Patients are often limited by a set number of responses and not being able to follow a train of thought to wherever it might happen to go. There was also pressure from the editors of medical journals to start publishing negative results. After countless studies claimed that the Type A was a valid concept, some doctors felt that there was a trend to bring on the negative press as a backlash.

Today, people have mixed feelings about the Type A categorization. Internet questionnaires can tell you if you are Type A in a couple of minutes, but what does this really indicate? Successive research projects have tended to try to isolate the different variables of the Type A (ambition, time-urgency, hostility, etc.) and then to test to see if one of these is the active ingredient of heart disease. This will run into the problems that result from assuming that emotions and affective states can be isolated, classified neatly and segregated. It is similar to the age-old quest for the philosopher's stone, with a pure, unequivocal and single affective state taking the place of the equally mythical quest for a way to turn base metal into gold. Could groups of people with ambition and time-urgency really be separated from groups with time-urgency but no ambition?

Some researchers have claimed that the only feature that really matters here, in the context of heart disease, is hostility, in particular held-back hostility. A more recent concept of the Type D personality has been proposed, characterized by the experience of negative emotions, termed 'negative affectivity', and the tendency to inhibit 'self-expression', called 'social inhibition'. A Dutch study at the Erasmus Medical Centre in Rotterdam of 875 patients undergoing angioplasty found that so-called Type Ds were at a five-fold greater risk of dying or having a heart attack nine months later. Type Ds, we are told, are at higher risk of cardiac problems and mortality.

Whether one is reading about Type As or Type Ds, the references to suppressed, repressed or over-controlled emotions are legion. Perhaps it was no accident that in the mid 1960s the Japanese Psychosomatic Society was the largest in the world. Study after study looked at the effects on the body from bottling up feelings like rage and anger. The research conducted by Richard Shekelle in the 1980s on a group of 1,800 middle-aged men, whose blood vessels were being examined by the X-ray technique known as angiography, successfully predicted higher disease rates among the more hostile patients. In another study of coronary-artery calcification – the formation of calcium deposits in the arteries – 374 people were rated for hostility, with significant correlations between higher hostility and degree of calcification, indicative of more severe atherosclerosis, measured by a CT scan.

Despite the technological advances of scanning techniques, anger and hostility have always been the usual suspects in questions of heart disease. When we get cross, we experience sudden increases of blood flow, and this will not only produce scarring on the artery walls but call on the body's energy reserves at short notice. When this happens, fatty acids will be released into the bloodstream, which may then clog up artery walls, forming the fatty plaques associated with atherosclerosis. If you not only get cross, but try suppressing your anger, things only get worse. This is likely to increase sympathetic nervous system activity, with adrenaline and noradrenaline being pumped into the bloodstream and so raising blood pressure.

More recent work has both refined and challenged some of these older ideas. 'Negative affectivity', or having an attitude problem, has been associated with increased production of pro-inflammatory protein molecules called cytokines, including one known as tumour necrosis factor-alpha. This acts locally to facilitate the development of inflammatory responses at the site of a lesion, and plays a role in each of the three pathogenic phases at the site of a vulnerable artherosclerotic plaque: plaque instability, plaque rupture and thrombosis, or clotting. This is bad news.

It was believed for some time that the most common cause of myocardial infarction (the death of heart muscle) was the build-up of these atherosclerotic plaques in a high-cholesterol environment. The rupturing of these plaques, followed by clotting and blockage of blood supply to the heart, would then provoke the infarction. But more recent work has drawn attention to the fact that, in at least half of heart attacks, the patient's cholesterol levels are no higher than average. The rupturing plaques, it is now claimed, are local sites of inflammation where huge numbers of immune cells have been drafted in. Where once the successful use of aspirin to reduce the risk of heart attack was attributed to blood thinning, it is now thought to work largely through its anti-inflammatory action. Cholesterol is not irrelevant, but it is part of a bigger picture.

More and more importance has been accorded to the single layer of cells that lines veins and arteries known as the endothelium. Its functions include allowing dilation and constriction of blood vessels, maintaining their tone and preventing the build-up of lipids and platelets, molecules carried by the blood which may stick to the vessel walls. Dysfunction can lead to atherosclerosis, as well as ischaemia and arrhythmia. The diseased vessels may constrict on exposure to a chemical which would normally cause them to dilate, a response associated with advanced heart disease, but just being in a difficult situation can produce this response in a healthy subject. In fact, more and more links of the endothelium to our mental life and how we register our experiences are currently being studied.

In healthy functioning, there is a balance between the dilation effects of the endothelium and the constricting effects which are signalled by the autonomic nervous system (ANS). The ANS acts on the smooth muscle cells of the arteries, and may have direct effects on the endothelium. The two, indeed, seem to be dynamically locked to each other. ANS disruptions can generate endothelial problems, encouraging certain immune cells and lipoproteins to attach themselves to endothelial cells. Any disruptions to the dynamically balanced interaction between the ANS and the endothelium can impact on a range of heart disorders, and this becomes all the more significant when we remember

the well-established effects of a person's emotional life on
their autonomic nervous system.

So we have a route here from emotions to heart disease.
Emotional life will impact on the autonomic nervous system,
which will then have significant effects on the heart. But
what kind of emotional effects are we talking about? Reading
through many studies on the mechanisms that affect cardiac
health, one variable that occurs again and again is the presence or absence of social contact. Loneliness and the feeling
of helplessness are seen as crucial factors which have a direct
impact upon the health of the body. Brigitta Bunzel from
University Hospital, Vienna, showed that support from a
spouse was crucial in predicting the survival rate of heart-
transplant patients, but the question of social networks is a
far wider one. Study after study has claimed that the fewer
one's social relationships, the shorter one's life expectancy
and the more devastating the impact of infectious diseases.
Surprising as it may seem, this is statistically a greater risk
factor than smoking or obesity, and even after taking these
latter variables into account, it makes someone two and a
half times more likely to die than someone of the same age
and economic status who has a network of social relations.

One of the first and most famous large-scale investiga-
tions of this phenomenon was known as the Roseto study.
This town in Pennsylvania had a population of around 1,600,
and was founded in the late nineteenth century by immigrants from Roseto Val Fortore in southern Italy. A health
study was conducted over several years, and comparisons were
made with neighbouring towns. Surprisingly, the death rate
from myocardial infarction was only half that of the neighbouring towns or the US in general. Yet their diet wasn't
particularly healthy, and their blood cholesterol was about

the same as that of their neighbours and they smoked a fair bit. But what struck the researchers was the cohesiveness of Roseto *as a community*, and the high levels of mutual support. The study showed how children of immigrants who stayed in this socially cohesive Pennsylvanian town shared the same good health as their parents, but those who left would tend to become as ill as others in the towns to which they migrated.

If it wasn't the diet or the smoking, the answer seemed to lie in the organization of social bonds. Other studies following in the wake of the Roseto research made similar findings. Rates of heart disease in Japan were very low in the 1960s and '70s, yet Japanese who moved to the States would develop the same morbidity rates as Americans. Those migrants, however, who remained closely linked to the Japanese community and followed traditional rituals would maintain their previous health even if they now ate an American diet.

Shying away from these important questions, much of the later research focused on forms of social contact that promised to be easily **measurable**. Groups and communities did seem to be beneficial. Heart rate, blood pressure and blood chemistry were all found to be altered by transient human interactions. This can be seen in the effect on electrolytes, such as sodium and chloride, and on hormones in matched menstrual cycles in roommates. In teams, people react biologically in different ways from isolated individuals, producing fewer fatty acids when under pressure, for example. Animal experiments were invoked to show how sustained competition for resources in difficult circumstances led not only to kidney failure, but to atherosclerosis, hypertension and stroke. Other experiments showed how social groupings could affect physiological response. In one study, the reaction of squirrel monkeys placed under stress measured in terms of cortisol levels was lowered by 50 per cent when in the company of another monkey, and reduced to zero when in a group.

As research on the links between social relations and health expanded in the 1970s, it was argued that relationships buffer one from the normal 'stressors' encountered by those living in industrialized society. They would encourage so-called 'adaptive' responses to the pressures involved in everyday life. But soon enough it dawned on researchers that social relationships were not just buffers to these pressures but that they had a much more *direct* impact on health itself. In one well-known study, 4,775 adults in Alameda County, California, were distinguished into four different classes of social bond, with each type predictive of mortality through the succeeding nine years. Adjustments were made for baseline health, yet still those low on the scale were twice as likely to die as persons high on the scale. This study had relied on the subjects' own reports about baseline health, so sure enough another study was undertaken involving thorough physical examination of all participants at the start: 2,754 people from Michigan were tested, with broadly similar results. When all the considered biomedical risk factors had been adjusted for, social relations proved once again to be predictive of health.

In another brave, and some would say foolhardy, study patients with myocardial infarcts were treated not in hospital but at home. The study concluded that the risk of death was no greater, and possibly a bit less. These results could be linked to the fact that cardiac arrhythmias were associated with people separating and the direction of a person's hostility inwards rather than outwards. George Engel tells the story of a canny medical student who saw what was going on when a patient suffered a cardiac arrest while already in a hospital casualty department. While staff members and patient were being congratulated on their good fortune that the arrest had happened while in casualty, the student noted that it had occurred after two house officers had unsuccessfully tried to insert an arterial line. The officers had then left, leaving the man alone in a cubicle, and he confided to the student that he had felt increasingly anxious and angry. Overwhelmed by his helplessness, he had blacked out.

Social bonds are important, but what exactly does 'social' mean here? It seems clear that people can have regular contact with other human beings without feeling that they are having a real or meaningful interaction. Studies of the elderly, for example, made the surprising finding that the amount of contact with the rest of the family is far less important than the expectation that someone is there for them. Knowing that family members are contactable and available may matter more in many instances than actually receiving regular visits. What we mean by 'other people' can thus include their physical or their potential presence. The physical presence of people is not always the same thing as participation in a social network.

Of even greater importance is the *political* dimension of these studies, despite the fact that most of the research fails to make this obvious point. What does the Roseto study imply? Isn't it suggesting that there will be links between the biological body and the community? Or, to put it in the terms of political theory, the body and the politico-social community known as the 'polis'. The implication here is radical: that physical health will be related to *the way the community is run*. And this, of course, is a political question. Wouldn't it become the *duty* of medicine, then, to debate the best ways to run the polis?

Many of these themes had been examined by the French psychoanalyst Jacques Lacan in the 1940s, decades before they were to become popular in the 1970s and '80s. Lacan had worked with a team of internists and surgeons in Paris on the question of heart disease, and came up with findings that prefigure many of the more recent studies. Lacan focused on hypertension, and argued that factors such as diet or smoking were of less importance in predicting heart disease than the relation of the individual to the social group.

He was specially interested in the mechanisms of *identification* that bind members of a group to each other. The link of the individual to the group would be woven into a rich and complicated fabric of relations of hierarchy and social structure, conditions which determined what he called 'an organic dependency'. This could be seen most clearly in the phenomenon of voodoo death. The fact that someone could die from a hex indicated a hard-wiring of belief systems and hierarchies of group knowledge and power in the very body of the individual. Ritualized forms of relationship were what held the human group together, and something like voodoo death was then less an anomaly than a sign of how successfully such beliefs and group knowledge had been internalized. It showed how group structures of this kind had been wired in.

Lacan believed that contemporary society was seeing a decline of these traditional group relations. There was less internalization of structure, and he argued that this explained the amazing popularity of theories of homeostasis – how an individual maintains an inner equilibrium – and self-regulation that were already receiving so much attention. Following the sociologist Emile Durkheim, he saw membership of social groups as more pertinent to health questions than the simple stimulus-response model. The more the individual was separated from the social group, the more he would be seen as an isolated unit **regulating himself from the inside**, rather than through a network of external relations. One of the powerful implications of Lacan's argument here is that the whole programme of research into stress, based on an individual trying to maintain homeostasis when faced with external stressors, **was itself symptomatic of social change**.

This led Lacan, decades before the Roseto study, to point out the low levels of hypertension among those immigrant parts of American society that had managed to maintain cohesiveness and the presence of cultural rituals. And now the theory grew more subtle. Lacan distinguished two kinds of identification: one in which a person identified with the image of their counterpart, trapping them in a cycle of jealousies and rivalry; the other which normalized these fruitless struggles by situating the subject in the symbolic dimension, governed by social laws and the assumption of symbolic positions within the family and the group. In the first form of identification, each person wants the other's place and so fights an endless battle without ever getting anywhere. In the second form, they take on a place within the social and familial structure and so transcend the battlefield of the first form of identification.

The first form of identification here would encompass the kind of model popular in American research at that time. The cycle of rivalries described by Lacan was exactly the phenomenon observed, for example, by the American analyst Jacob Arlow who studied the identificatory mechanisms in heart disease. Here identification would involve a hopeless struggle to supplant both one's friends and opponents, and material success would bring little satisfaction or relief from tension. The person would be continually drawn into new situations which recreated again and again the original competition, which the subject attempted to master by identifying with the rival. Identification with the father here was not a solution to the problem but its source. What Lacan added was the distinction between the different forms that identification could take. If it remained at the level of competition, the constant cycle of struggle and frustration would presumably produce both sharp increases in blood pressure and the other mechanisms we discussed which impact upon the endothelium, getting the atherosclerotic process going even in childhood.

Lacan saw human development at this time as involving a series of existential crises, which had to be overcome one by one. Key moments like weaning, the Oedipal period and puberty would consist of terrible crises of frustration, which would be resolved, if all went smoothly, by what he called 'sublimating identifications', setting the person on a new track and establishing a symbolic position for them within the family and the group. But given the period of frustration and aggression involved during these stages, which Lacan set at the ages of two, eight, eighteen and thirty-five, and given time for lesions to develop, they would then become predictive of the high points for hypertension. Surprising as it may seem, increased blood-pressure levels in the hypertensive range can already be found in childhood.

The modern emphasis on individualism and competition isolated the human being from social communities and rituals, with devastating effects. Lacan proposed as a remedy a society which would take into account the warnings of Plato in Book VIII of *The Republic*, on the assimilation of passions to the structure of the city. In that section of *The Republic*, Plato runs through the different forms of personality that are products of a badly run society. The first type is incredibly similar to, yet actually more subtle than, the Type A. The timocratic character, for Plato, grows up in a family where the mother complains that the father isn't a real man. The father is not ambitious enough and fails in the political and economic marketplace. The child soon picks up these reproaches, but will at the same time have learned to value the father's choice not to compete in what he sees as a corrupt society. The child is thus situated at a junction, torn between two incompatible messages, subject to a terrible conflict about how to evaluate the father. His solution is to act so as to acquire honour.

This strikingly modern portrait is just one of a series of character types that echo the figures described by today's personality profilers. But where modern theories see single causes, such as the desire for economic success, Plato sees conflicts, like the tension between the desire for economic success and its refusal. And he makes these conflicts the result of the identifications the child has with his parents: should he be like the father or the mother? Which imperatives should he follow? The parental figures, in turn, are understood as consequences of unsound forms of social structure. Their own personalities are in part determined by the socio-economic conditions in which they were brought up.

Lacan's message to the psychosomatics research of his time was to return to Plato. His emphasis on rivalry and its identificatory mechanisms has also been supported by contemporary research. A recent study from the Harvard Center for Society and Health of 12,643 subjects found that those who had what they called a 'rival' attitude had a higher risk factor for mortality than that given by smoking. Distrust and jealousy were the biggest killer, especially for men, and the best protective factor was neighbourhood cohesion. This suggests the need for a dialogue between medicine,

philosophy and political thought on the nature of social structure. Social problems lead to individual ones even at the level
of the body itself. And this, as we've seen, is exactly what
research into heart disease has shown.

But what of the links between society and the individual? Surely the way our existence is registered by our
caregivers and family at the start of life will have an effect
on how we respond to the social network? Both the experience of solitude and of competition are bound up with
our place in society, yet these will be determined to a degree
by our early interactions. So in what ways do we first become
connected to other people?

9. Two Bodies or One?

Our bodies start life connected to other bodies. We gestate inside our mothers, and then we depend on our caregivers for survival after birth. It is perhaps no accident that often the only thing adults remember from their school biology lessons is the concept of osmosis. The one idea that evokes a close, even fusional state is the one that stays with us. And in the womb and as infants, what happens to the mother's body will affect our own. Pregnant and breastfeeding women are instructed to avoid certain foods and activities, since it is known that they may adversely affect the body of their child.

Research into the relation of mother and foetus has shown how the two bodies respond and relate to each other. Exposure to bright light on the abdominal wall will result in changes in foetal position and heart rate, and taste and smell receptors will be stimulated by substances present in the amniotic fluid. Changes in the mother's heart rate will be followed about a minute later by changes in the heart rate of the foetus. Likewise, increased secretion of hormones like adrenaline and noradrenaline in the mother, which we have seen to be closely linked to psychological factors, will lower blood flow around the uterus, and this is significant as it may inhibit the transportation of many vital substances. At a physiological level, mother and foetus are very much in communication with each other.

It was once believed that an infant could only develop a relationship with its mother sometime after birth. But we now know that this starts much, much earlier. At a sensory level, while hearing was thought to begin in the infant's first weeks and months, it has now been shown that the foetus will respond to music listened to by the mother from about three to four months after conception. Newborns are even able to distinguish between a story mothers read to them during pregnancy and one not heard before. Kicking and a variety of intrauterine movements will also be closely linked to what the mother is doing, and researchers have claimed that foetal life involves a kind of dialogue between foetus and mother, with each party increasing or inhibiting their activities in response to the other.

It isn't just what the mother eats that will affect the foetus, but what she sees, what she listens to and what she feels. Amazingly, research has found that the foetus not only responds to tunes heard in the womb, but actually has a heightened reaction to the tunes that the mother herself prefers. This means that aspects of the mother's subjectivity are transmitted to the child. The same goes for her moods. Anxious mothers have been shown to have impaired blood flow through the uterine arteries. And several studies have claimed that depression in the mother will have chemical effects on the foetus, raising cortisol levels and impacting directly on the future functioning of the baby's brain cells.

There is thus a highly sophisticated series of interactions between mother and child that gets going well before birth. If a dialogue begins when the child is still in the womb, it continues in ever more complex ways later on. Each party in the dialogue may give a place to the other, allowing them to respond and react. Now, mothers and infants continue this kind of relation in a process that is known as *attunement*. As a baby reaches out to try to grab some object, the parent might raise their voice to mimic the child's effort. Once the child reaches the object, the parent's vocalization might stop, showing a synchrony between their activities. Or, as a baby taps the edge of a cot, the parent could make sounds or tap another object to match the infant's beat.

Everyday interactions between mothers and infants reveal a wealth of such synchronized activities. The baby's stretching out for some object may be accompanied by a muscular 'shimmying' of the mother that stops when the object has been reached. Or the shaking of a rattle may be matched by the mother's rhythmic nodding up and down of her head. Close observation of parents and children playing reveals that such attunements make up a very large percentage of the time spent together. Generally, parents are actually unaware of what they are doing, but their infants will react strongly when the rhythms of attunement are broken. When a mother is responding to her child via a video relay, if the sound transmission is delayed by a fraction of a second, the infant will notice and respond negatively.

Attunements can take place in many different sensory systems (of sight, sound, touch, etc.), and it is important that the adult uses a *different* sensory modality to that used by the child. When the child reaches out, for example, the proprioceptive (movement and positioning) modality is at play, while the parent's vocalization in response uses the sound modality. It would be an odd situation indeed if the parent were always to use the same modality. This would be mere mechanical repetition, matching behaviour without evoking the links between sensory systems and internal states such as striving. The child psychiatrist Daniel Stern found that only 13 per cent of attunements used exclusively the same modality, and argued that attunements across different modalities helped the infant to acquire the idea that mental states could be communicated to and registered by other people.

Attunements will help to establish the transfer of information from one sensory system to another. They show how systems of registering information exist which are functioning right from the start of life. Several experiments have shown that a very archaic system must exist for the registering and transfer of this information in the process known as ***intermodal*** transfer. If infants are shown a range of differently textured dummies after sucking on one of them, they can tell which one they have sucked on even though at the time they were not able to see it. The information gathered by the sense of touch had been transferred into visual terms. Other experiments have shown transfers from the visual to the auditory, and the visual to the proprioceptive. Objects explored by touch alone can be recognized visually later on in instances where touch itself is not possible.

Attunements show how such transfers operate not just within one person but between people. As an infant makes an increased effort to get to some object, the parent's vocalization gets louder, showing a matching of intensity. Such processes, we might think, bind people together. They may consist of imitation, but more often it is a matching that works in different sensory systems, as we have seen. It indicates that forms of identificatory behaviour are taking place very early on, where one party puts themself in the place of the other, or shows that there is a link between their experiences. And this can occur in a variety of ways.

More and more synchronies have been found between the behaviour of parents and their babies. There are moment-by-moment coordinations of cycles of verbal and non-verbal exchange, such as vocalizing and pausing and looking and looking away. Video studies have shown how even the infant's limb movements synchronize with the rhythm of the mother's speech from some twenty minutes after birth. Out of all the different ways in which parents and infants can be attuned, probably the most important is temporal matching. Thus, the adult's vocalization ends when the infant gets the object, or they stop shimmying when the infant stops stretching. This shows how the activities of parent and child relate to each other temporally, and how the temporal patterning of interaction takes precedence over the *modality* of the interaction. Time matters.

These rhythms are at play in all of the interactions between mother and infant, including those associated with feeding, sucking, sleeping, head movement, crying and body care. By the mid 1980s, many researchers had agreed that cycles of reciprocal interactions, attunements and these various forms of rhythmic exchange were important for the social development of children. Advances in technology made the study of the micro-rhythms of mother–infant interactions much more precise, and here at last was experimental 'proof' that mothers and infants were in very, very close contact from very early on, and that the rhythms involved could be indicative of the nature of the relationship between them.

This is where things get particularly fascinating. Although a wide range of the baby's activities and reactions can be tracked and monitored, can we ever really know for sure what the baby is feeling, even if certain broad categories like 'distress' or 'contentment' seem obvious? But, crucially, as caregivers, adults have to respond *as if* they did know. And this means something very precise: that all of the baby's physiological reactions are understood as *signs*, as expressions and *communications* of pain, joy or whatever state or need is attributed to them. And so the baby's body is caught up in a cycle of meanings and intentions, which have been transmitted and shaped by the caregiver. A cry is understood as a request to be fed, an outstretched arm as an appeal for the adult's presence. Vocal and gestural phenomena become differentiated into appeals for different objects, agents, acts and places. Sensations become signs, as they are understood to be signifying something.

Sceptics might object here that all we are really seeing is some sort of vague interactive cycle, and hardly a dialogue. If, for example, jiggling a feeding baby produces a temporary halt in sucking, and stopping jiggling generates a burst of sucking, we might be observing a rhythm, but does this have the dignity of human dialogue? The same point could of course be made for the various intrauterine phenomena we have mentioned. But the key here is precisely the fact that, even if these cycles are not a dialogue, the mother behaves *as if they are*. It is this belief that will help introduce the infant into the world of human interaction and, later, verbal dialogue. It will be an essential condition of human subjectivity.

What would happen if the caregivers failed to respond in any of these ways to the child? What effect would it have if the child's reactions were never interpreted as types of communication? This can certainly happen: for example, if the mother's own anxiety or depression prevents her from responding to the infant or if her own wishes are continuously imposed. In some cases, the baby may be brought up using an automated system, where feeding, sleep and excretion are expected to run on a schedule that has nothing to do with the child but with a system of rules established by the parent or some published advice. This idea might seem bizarre to many parents, but it happens with alarming frequency. As well as depriving the infant of the idea that bodily experiences are signs and modes of communication, this kind of automation also blocks the idea that the infant's

bodily and mental states can affect other people. The dimension of a dialogue is obliterated.

Back in the 1940s, the psychoanalyst René Spitz was one
of the first to emphasize the idea of dialogue between mother
and infant, and its importance in establishing a child's sense
of identity and of *being responded to*. An infant's bodily states
call for a response. Hunger, thirst and temperature regulation are all linked to other people. Spitz conducted some
very famous research on infants who had been abandoned
by or separated from their parents. Brought up in well-
equipped, up-to-date foundling homes, they still showed high
levels of feeding difficulties and developmental problems.
Holidaying later in Mexico, he noticed how the infants in
a run-down, filthy orphanage seemed to be doing much
better. He found out that local women would come every
day to feed and care for the children: it seemed to Spitz that
it was their attentiveness and warmth that was nourishing
the kids.

Spitz believed that, despite the up-to-date technology of
the foundling homes, children would languish, and in some
cases even die, when deprived of real attention or care.
Without these factors, susceptibility to infection and disease
was increased, as was mortality. Since the same children would
flourish when moved to more caring environments, the
conclusion seemed obvious: we need the love and care of
other humans to survive. These ideas were developed from
a rather different angle by John Bowlby and Mary Ainsworth,
who thought that infants have an innate biological predisposition to seek closeness and contact with the mother.

What do these conclusions suggest? At first glance, it might
seem that we need love in the sense of physical care: the
provision of food and shelter. These minimum requirements
need to be met for life to continue, but this isn't what Spitz

was getting at, and in fact he argued a much stronger thesis: that these requirements were *not* the minimum for survival. What mattered was not just food and shelter, but *the way in which these were administered* – hence some of the problems associated with schedules of caring for an infant which are imposed regardless of the infant's reactions, states and needs. Later workers showed the importance of these aspects of timing and temporal patternings for the growth of bonds between mother and infant, and the encouragement of the idea of a separate identity. The cycles of attunement that we have described were seen as central to this process.

This brings us to an intriguing divergence. British and American researchers have done a great deal to explore the relation of mother and child and to elucidate the rhythms of attunement, focusing on the mother–child unit and all the possible ways this could malfunction. On the Continent, however, Lacan was studying the way in which the relations of mother and child were affected by a third party: the father. This introduced an important difference. Where British and American research gave a positive value to attunement and even blamed developmental problems on its absence, Lacan suggested that the key to childhood progress was that the mother was not completely attuned to her child. This was the split between love and desire.

As Spitz had shown, the mother's love was obviously vital. But beyond this love, and all the degrees of attunement that went with it, it was crucial that she desired something else, something beyond her child. Through her absences, distractions and preoccupations, the child would realize that the mother's world was broader than the unit they formed with her. The focus of these attentions could be the father, but also anything else that the mother focused on beyond her offspring: work, a career, friendships. This would introduce the dimension of a 'beyond' into the mother–child relation, and so allow the child to separate gradually from the mother. What mattered was not total attunement but precisely not being attuned all the time.

If the mother fails to transmit this dimension of a beyond to her child, what are the consequences? In some cases, the child can try to do it themself. There may be phases where the father, or someone else in the family entourage, is suddenly elevated into an omnipotent figure, despite their manifest lack of importance for the mother. The child is trying to create a third party that would function as a 'pole' beyond the mother. In other cases, a phobia can fulfil the same role: the child's world becomes reordered around the fear of some animal or vehicle. In all of these examples, the child searches for ways to find a horizon beyond the imme-diate relation with the mother.

Could a physical illness have the same function? It is often observed that excessive closeness between mother and child can generate or exacerbate symptoms like eczema and asthma. It is tempting to interpret such cases as a direct bodily response to the proximity of the mother, as if there was no other way of registering the sense of threat or anxiety. But could some illnesses also be ways of appealing to a third party, emerging where the dimension of beyond has not been established by the mother? We could think here of the coli-tis case we discussed in Chapter 7, where the symptom reappeared each time the link to the patient's father was put in question, and also of the teenager we discussed in Chapters 1 and 4 who had knotted together the idea of her father and her diabetic illness. The French psychoanalyst Jean Guir has suggested that, in some cases, the physical symptom may be like 'an organic filiation', compensating, as it were, for the absence of the paternal dimension.

The complexities of this approach are often missed in the work which focuses exclusively on the mother and child, without including the question of how the mother gives a place – or doesn't – to the father. If there is a real third party present in this sort of research, it is less likely to be the father than a laboratory animal. Curiously, theories about the mother and child often seem to doubt their own legitimacy until outside proof has been acquired though rats and chimps. For a researcher like Bowlby, this made sense since he was trying to fit his ideas into an evolutionary perspective, stressing the bonding experience between mother and newborn shared by animals and humans. If the data seemed to match for both animals and humans, the theory would be confirmed. But such methods introduce a number of confusions. To start with, which animals should we concentrate on?

As the psychologist Jerome Kagan has pointed out, we have too much choice here. If you want a model of how mothers care for infants, point to rhesus monkeys; if you see the father as the primary caretaker, point to titi monkeys. If you believe that surrogate care is closer to nature, point to lionesses. If you are certain that men should dominate harems of women, point to elephant seals; if you believe women should be in positions of dominance, point to elephants. If you wish to sanctify the institution of marriage, point to the pair bonding of gibbons; those who think infidelity is more natural can point to chimpanzees. If you believe that people are naturally sociable, point to baboons; if you think they are solitary, point to orang-utans. If you believe sex should replace fighting, point to bonobo chimpanzees.

And this is not the only problem. Even those with no time for evolutionary theory turn to the animal results, as if everyone needs persuading that relationships are important for human development. Do these experiments give the psychological theories a scientific gloss? Or is something else at stake, something perhaps more hidden? Many of these experiments were, and still are, unspeakably cruel. Harry Harlow at the University of Wisconsin conducted a number of studies in the 1950s, separating monkeys from their mothers at birth. The bereft chimps developed poorly, and they would cling to dummy mothers made of cloth, only leaving them for feeding periods. This proved, it seemed, that touch was more important for the chimps than food. Countless other animal experiments separated mothers from their children, and endeavoured to quantify the effects of such deprivation. In one experiment, a research team were interested to measure how many shocks a mother rat would endure to try to reach her young when separated by an electrically wired-up space.

These studies won't tell us anything about human psychology, but they may sometimes generate hypotheses concerning the body's physiological mechanisms. In some very careful studies, Myron Hofer, a physiologist at Columbia University, has explored how the bodies of the mammalian mother and her offspring are enmeshed. Every organ system so far studied has been shown to suffer when the offspring is separated prematurely from the mother: heart and respiratory rates fall, control of body temperature is lost, levels of neurotransmitters in the brain, nucleoproteins and enzymes like ornithine decarboxylase – an important agent in the body's defences against cancer – diminish, and physiological development is impeded in many areas. Prematurely weaned rats are more likely to die of disease, and rats that have been socially isolated get more infections, ulcers and bigger tumours. There is a general increase in later susceptibility to infection and abnormal tissue growth.

Although some of these experiments have provided significant biological results, why is there so often the need to support pyschological research into humans with research into animals? Obviously there are things that can be done with animals that would not be permitted or even possible with humans. But these are by no means the only reasons. Do such experiments provide an added legitimacy? And can the vocabulary for emotional and subjective states be applied to animals at all? It is curious that female primatologists tend to attribute more complex mental states to the gorillas they study than male psychologists do to human beings. In general, animals are assumed to lack subjectivity. What would happen if someone proposed that the rat's swift ulcer development after being separated from the mother was due to the physiological effects of *blaming her* for the separation? Or, to make it more complex, the result of *suppressing* the angry feelings of blaming her? But aren't these exactly the features that we should aim to investigate in humans?

The problem here is a failure to distinguish between separation and the *meaning* of separation, just as we saw in our discussion of the life-event scales in Chapter 3. How could we tell whether it's the loss of physical contact with the mother that matters so much or the rat's distress at the thought that the mother wanted to abandon him? And isn't it exactly this kind of question that characterizes the mental life of human beings? Separations and losses have meanings, and we perpetually ask what it is that the other person wants. The biochemistry of the body of an adopted child can be studied, but how could the question of *why* they had not been kept by their biological parents be factored in?

We have asked why it is that anyone would want the evidence from animal experiments in the first place. Could it be that some people – animal experimenters included – are so cut off from the realities of interpersonal relationships and the emotions involved in them that they need the 'distance' of animals to be able to think? It is well known that when young children are bereaved, there might be little reaction until, sometime later, a pet dies. This generates a vast outpouring of grief, and many cases indicate that feelings and thoughts linked to humans have been displaced on to animals. Animals often provide us with the means to distance ourselves from thinking about what we feel towards humans.

The child who tortures an animal may be playing out what he feels he has experienced himself, or what he would like to do to a sibling or parent, just as the child who lovingly nurses a pet may be enacting how he himself wishes to be treated by his parents or perhaps once was. As we examine the realm of animal experiments, it is difficult not to notice that so many of them are really giving results not about the laboratory animals *but about the experimenters themselves*. What does Harlow's experiment with chimps show, for example, about his early relations with his mother? John Watson, one of the founders of behavioural 'science', spent much of his solitary childhood with only rats for company, training them in various tasks. It seems likely that he was playing out with his rodents relations he either had or wished to have with humans: and that, at some level, *he identified himself* with these poor creatures. The rat or the monkey is the experimenter himself.

This is bound to have an effect on the way in which humans are then studied. They become little more than substitutes for the animals which once, perhaps, had replaced them. Development and love are reduced to finite ingredients which can be monitored and measured, added and subtracted. This was precisely the approach that Spitz had been struck by. As love was confused with physical care, the body could in some cases start to shut down, and this is where the biology became interesting. Chemical changes would occur which were not simply the consequence of lack of nutrition. In a pioneering study, George Engel was able to observe a young child hospitalized at fifteen months in a depressed and inert state. Her young mother was also suffering from depression, and it was difficult for her to relate warmly to her child. The child, Monica, had a congenital defect, oesophageal atresia, a condition in which the oesophagus is formed with a blind end. This meant that she could not be fed via the mouth, but only through a gastric fistula, a surgically constructed passage into her stomach.

Monica became attached to some of the hospital staff, yet when she encountered strangers, rather than crying she would become unresponsive and detached. This would be accompanied by a loss of muscle tone and by changes in the levels of her gastric secretions. The fistula allowed the researchers to monitor these secretions, and they were studied carefully over a five-month period. They found that hydrochloric acid levels would increase not only when she was being fed but when someone she knew and liked was approaching her. Her muscle tone would also return swiftly at these moments.

It seemed as if Monica's digestive apparatus was joining in the conversation. Acid secretions would fall when she was depressed, and were even unresponsive to histamine, which ought to have increased them. This suggested that nothing was to be taken into her stomach, yet when her favourite experimenter arrived, the secretions would increase once again and the histamine would produce its usual effect. The body was responding biologically to human relationships. Monica's stomach was reacting to situations involving human contact, which were affecting her basic physiology. This could have significant consequences. If acid secretions are continually being activated in the absence of food, the lining of the intestine may be damaged, setting the ground for a condition such as ulcer. Engel felt that these results should encourage a new field of study: a physiology based on the early somatic accompaniments to our first relationships with our caregivers.

What the Monica study showed so clearly was how the very fabric of the body was involved in the dynamics of human relations. Thanks to the fistula, some of the biological changes taking place when her psychological situation changed could actually be tracked. And this could affect the growth of the child in a quite literal sense. As more precise methods were introduced for the measurement of growth hormone in the blood, it was found to be highly sensitive to psychological factors. Growth-hormone disorders are quite rare, but several studies have shown that psychological variables affect its secretion. Gerald Powell and his colleagues from the Johns Hopkins University School of Medicine reviewed the cases of thirteen children in 1967 with growth failure, all of whom had been brought up in very disturbed family environments. When the children were moved to a more caring environment, there was a significant rebound in growth, and growth-hormone test results returned to predicted values. Growth increases of up to 10 cm were seen in a period of only six months.

In another well-known study, Lamont and his colleagues hospitalized children allergic to household dust. The team then collected copious amounts of house dust from the children's homes and distributed it liberally in their hospital rooms. In nineteen out of twenty cases no asthma ensued. Many other similar studies claimed to show that it was never just the dust, but the dust plus other factors – and in some cases, not even the dust. The relation with the parent, particularly the mother, seemed the key variable. It was observed that the high frequency of asthma starting around age three coincides significantly with the time at which a child may be experiencing conflicts around establishing some degree of autonomy and separating from the parents.

Engel believed that psychosomatic research had been severely limited by its reliance on the fight-or-flight model with its emphasis on the autonomic nervous system and Selye's general adaptation syndrome (discussed in Chapter 3) with its emphasis on the hypothalamus–pituitary–adrenal axis. Both of these models could be useful at times, but they were inadequate when considering the physical effects of early relations of the child and mother and the complicated effects of past experience. Fight-or-flight mechanisms were interesting, but weren't human babies characterized by precisely the fact that they couldn't fight or flee in their early life? Humans, after all, are unlike most species here in being helpless and dependent in the first stages of life. Confronted with inevitable losses and separations, the biology of withdrawal becomes fundamental, in Engel's view. Since losses and separations so commonly precede the onset of illness, how could feelings of despair, grief and sadness be ignored?

In a series of studies developing this line of thought, William Greene at the Rochester Hospital explored cases of leukaemia and lymphoma in children, arguing that they often develop in settings of depression and loss. But rather than seeing the child as an isolated being, Greene emphasized relationships. What mattered was how a child's parents had responded to loss, and how the child themself would be affected by this mental state in the parent. As study after study examined stressful events in the life of the patient, Greene asked not only what was happening with the patient but also *what was happening at that time in the life of the patient's parents*. He found that there could be significant effects on health when the child was made the site of an unconscious projection on the part of one of the parents (for example, being identified with a dead child or adult) or when a well-established projection (for example, being identified as a replacement child) was suddenly removed.

Although Greene's ideas about how this might happen biologically may seem far-fetched today, his work had the great merit of focusing on the dynamic between genera-tions. One person's health was linked with a constellation of people around them in both the present and the past. This suggested that difficulties in mourning may be important for disease onset. When a recent congress on leukaemia discussed the apparent correlation between sleeping with a night-light on and the disease, the immediate explanation seemed to be in terms of daily or circadian rhythms. As we will see in Chapter 11, at night levels of melatonin need to peak to spur the cell-mediated wing of the immune system. Light distur-bance to this peak might therefore compromise the immune system's surveillance of damaged cells, and so increase the possibility of the disease. But why did no one ask the obvi-ous question: what made these children – or their parents – have to keep the light on at night?

Several subsequent studies of other diseases argued that loss and grief might prepare the ground for bodily illness. Feelings of helplessness and hopelessness would weaken the body and set the stage for an attitude of giving up and a sense that one had been given up. This would involve a sense of fail-ure and the belief that no help would be forthcoming. Engel argued that helplessness would affect the biological systems dealing with obtaining and conserving supplies, and it is important to note how these ideas imply relations with other people. Helplessness means that someone else won't be responding to you, and hopelessness that someone else gives up on you since you have failed to satisfy them. Both of these perspectives evoke the childhood situation where the infant realizes it cannot control the will of the parents.

This is a way of asking what value we have for other people. We have seen how lack of social recognition may contribute to our falling ill. Perhaps beneath this social question is the personal question from our childhood, revived by social interactions, of how our existence is registered. What are we for others? What value does our life have for them? Since we start life with our biological systems linked to others, changes in our relations with them are bound to have an effect. If the mother does not manage to transmit the message 'Live!' to the child, what paths are left open? Won't the feeling that they have given up on us affect the very will to live? Or at least have some effect on our biological systems.

We could think here of perhaps the mildest example, the child who daydreams about how their parents would respond to their absence. Or, more extremely, a woman who has a serious car accident after learning that her mother had wished to abort her during her pregnancy. In both instances, what matters is how one's existence is registered by someone else. In the second case, the mother's apparent wish to cancel out the unborn child's existence is dramatically played out. What we imagine we are for someone else can affect our very sense of self-preservation.

Let's take another example. Several studies of rheumatoid arthritis in women have claimed that patients went through a period of 'masculine protest', the refusal to accept their femininity, the insistence on masculine identification and a resentment against men. Now, whether we believe this or not, what matters is how the various studies *fail* to factor in the significance of **relationships**. They assume that the protest is the person's own problem, yet given the importance of other people which we have been discussing, don't we have a richer theory if we add that the person may have problems with their body *because they perhaps assume at some level that a parent wanted them to have a different one*: a boy's body? Or, if the mother values the father, that the daughter may be drawn to an identification with him? Could the impingement of someone else's desire have effects on the body itself?

This is not as strange as it sounds. We need only think of hormonal changes in the body at puberty, for instance, and the common problems people experience at important moments like the first period, ejaculation or departure from home. Such moments are symbolic as well as biological. Changes in the body entail new symbolic positions like manhood and womanhood. Initiation rituals in many cultures will mark the body at these important times with tattoos or incisions. And bodily illness may sometimes involve a similar process. Faced with an impossible situation or a conflict, the body is marked by illness or functional disturbance.

When endocrine (hormonal) disturbances emerge here, such as the absence or arrest of periods, there is often the question of how the person unconsciously perceives the desire of a parent. If there's the idea that the parent *won't allow them* to become an adult, they may have great difficulties with the biological threshold of womanhood or manhood. Anything linked to the idea of being a woman or being a man may cause problems, affecting issues such as fertility, potency and even growth. The conflict around the symbolic position generates problems at the physical level. Hence it is crucial to determine whether somatic illness coincides with a symbolic moment, one at which the person has to take on a new position in the world. This could range from giving a speech to becoming a mother to retiring.

Parents are often affected here at the moment that children leave the nest. All moments of symbolic separation matter. We could think here of the parents who become ill or have an accident on the day of their child's wedding. This is incredibly common, and it is testimony to the fact that a wedding makes separation from the parent a symbolic act. In many cultures, the rituals employed in wedding ceremonies are similar to those used at funerals, suggesting that the ceremony functions not only to enshrine the new union but also to **establish the separation** between generations. It may be very difficult for a parent to see their child move on in this way, however happy they are at a conscious level about the match.

But there is nothing simple about a mother losing a son or a father losing a daughter, and the further such thoughts are from consciousness, the more likely it is that they will reveal themselves in the disguised form of illness or accident. Whether it is a sudden onset of flu or a domestic accident resulting in immobility or fracture, we see how emotional states are often hidden from conscious awareness. Endocrine and other disorders are astonishingly common here. Their emergence may coincide with the sudden emptying of the family home once the children have moved out. Physicians too keen to find medical remedies for their patients' suffering often miss this important trigger. What gets lost here is what it means to the mother to lose her child. Once again, it is the way the person has responded to a change in their position or way of life that matters.

We see the effect of these symbolic thresholds with perhaps the greatest regularity during pregnancy, in which the question of becoming a mother, and hence *distancing oneself from one's own mother*, must be confronted. The psychology of a pregnant woman's relation to her mother will have critical indications for her physical health during pregnancy and child-birth. It also gives us a clue as to why a woman who has not been able to have children might become pregnant immediately after she has been approved for adoption. Being given the green light after the highly significant process of assessment is a *symbolic acceptance*: and it may be exactly this that allows the biological processes necessary for pregnancy to get under way – as if the Court of Appeal had overruled the fantasized prohibition on pregnancy. Sadly, medicine has little time to study such processes. It is interested in one body, not the relation between two.

Yet this relation can be vital. We need only think of the response of incubator babies to human care. These infants are more likely to survive if they are held and spoken to than if they are simply serviced for their bodily needs. They will also grow almost 50 per cent faster than babies who have not benefited from this care and have a reduced risk of mortality from respiratory failure. Although published studies have spelled these points out quite clearly, it is amazing how much variability there is from one neonatal unit to another. In some of these, we have seen staff anxious to keep the parents away from the machines containing their children, or grudgingly encouraging them to handle their children, as long as they would then make themselves scarce so ward life could continue uninterrupted. In other units, contact and care were warmly encouraged and facilitated.

Taking these clinical details seriously might change our attitude to some apparently outlandish practices. An American surgeon was ridiculed for his habit of speaking to his patients during surgery, yet is this really so preposterous? If we add what we know about incubator babies to the fact that a very simple experiment can show that someone waking up after an operation will react more strongly to music they have heard while anaesthetized than to other tunes, the idea of a talking surgeon seems less absurd. We might expect that a surgeon will perform better if they treat us like a machine rather than a person, but a human voice may be of great importance. It may be a crucial thread that links a person to life itself. For some astronauts, simply hearing a human voice on their radio was the one thing that kept them from giving up.

10. Identification

When Monica grew up and became a mother herself, she held her children in a very peculiar way during bottle-feeding. Although this felt perfectly natural to her, it struck her doctors as odd until they realized that she was replaying exactly the same gestures used to hold her as a baby when she had been fed through the fistula. One person was identifying with another without having any idea that they were doing so. We saw in the last chapter how our bodies are fundamentally affected by our relations with other people, and identification is one of the most important ways in which this happens. But what exactly is identification? And how might it affect our physical health?

At the simplest level, identification means that we become like another person. The endless TV programmes which involve people swapping roles with each other show how captivating this process can be. A farmhand becomes a lord, a prince becomes a pauper, a shy student becomes a glamorous playboy: all of these transformations involve one person doing their best to imitate the manners and customs of someone else. Identity is seen as fluid and changeable. We can become whoever we like given the right props and circumstances. But identifications with others operate at a much deeper level. Most of the time, they take place outside our conscious awareness. We become like others without knowing it. And it is these unconscious identifications that will matter when it comes to our bodies.

Identifications develop in many different ways. Children

will identify with aspects of their parents from the very start of life, mimicking their facial expressions and, later on, their tone of voice, their style of speaking or their opinions and tastes. As their own identity is forged, different traits are borrowed from the parents. These traits are like building blocks, basic constituents of who we are, yet which originally come from someone else. Such archaic forms of identification with a parent are often described as cannibalistic: just as an infant tries to put external objects in its mouth, it also incorporates the traits and details of those around it.

A further kind of identification occurs at those moments when an intense emotional relationship is broken or put in question. Imagine a child who speaks proudly of the fact that one day they will marry Mummy or Daddy, or who enjoys a specially close bond with one of the parents. When they realize that life will in fact hold out no such reward, or when the beloved parent seems to distance themself, the child may start to adopt some trait or behavioural detail of precisely the parent who disappointed them. It is as if identification has taken the place of a special emotional bond. The pain of the disappointment or frustration is dealt with by incorporating some aspect of the other person into themself.

Spitz and others analysts had noticed that when a child is left by someone they love, they will often identify with the actions of that person. They thought that this could explain specific problems like rumination, or 'mercyism' – the compulsive regurgitation of food by a baby. The ruminating child was identifying with the nursing mother, bringing food back into their mouth as if they were both ingesting food and feeding themselves. They were two people at once: the feeder and the fed. In many cases of rumination, there has been a sudden separation from the mother or interruption of breast-feeding. The compulsive rocking that infants sometimes display could be understood in a similar way. They were playing out the rocking once received from the caregiver and then lost.

There is little doubt that identificatory traits or behaviour will become more pronounced if the mother's care is suddenly withdrawn. At such moments, the infant *becomes* both mother and child, as if a very primitive form of defence is being implemented. The child defends itself against loss by becoming the lost person. Yet rumination and rocking cannot be reduced to just these factors. Rocking causes the production of endorphins and so may sometimes be a form of self-drugging. Pain is kept at bay by the rhythmical activity. Spitz's idea of mercyism is also questionable, since there are plenty of cases where the psychological situation does not seem so neat. The advantage of such explanations is that they draw attention to the many identificatory processes at work in the nursery, ranging from mimicry of someone else's behaviour to the adoption of a particular trait, such as the way in which another child cries.

These childhood identifications play a role in the formation of our personalities and the actual mastery of our body. The first months of life are, to use the expression of Claude Bernard, a time of 'physiological misery'. An infant has little power over its motor functions, and we can often see the painful spectacle of a baby trying to reach out or change its bodily position unsuccessfully. Babies tend to become more and more fascinated by the motor agility of adults that they themselves are unable to attain. The visual sense is crucial here, and babies will often stare captivated by the movement around them. Lacan thought that there was a tension here between the undeveloped physiological state of the newborn and what it saw as the wholeness and apparent self-sufficiency of the visual image of other people. This would include the mirror image of the child itself, and it is well-known that at around six months babies start to become intrigued by their reflection, investigating the mirror with laughter and joy.

This 'mirror phase' initiates a pattern in infants in which a visual image is perceived as a kind of *way out* of a physiological state. The more an infant can identify with the image and become like it, the more the child will be able to transcend the vulnerable and uncoordinated situation they find themself in from birth. Captivated by these images, they may start to master their own motor functions, as if the images held out a template for what they ought to become. This process will lay the foundation for our relation to our body image: images outside us, like those in the mirror or those of other people, will captivate us and lure us with the promise of a completeness which we do not possess. At the same time, the mirror phase shows that such images do actually help us to improve our coordination of our own bodies. Is it an accident that the first thing most people do each morning is to look at their reflection in a mirror?

This brings us to another kind of identification, revolving around the desire to be in the same situation as someone else. To adapt Freud's example, take the case of a coughing epidemic in a girls' boarding school. One girl receives a letter from her secret lover, perhaps giving her occasion to be jealous. She starts to cough, and very soon everyone is coughing. They are not coughing, Freud argues, because they are especially interested in this girl. They have no particular sympathy with her. But they do want to be in the same situation as her, having a secret lover, and so identify with the cough even if this brings them some suffering into the bargain.

Perhaps this serves as a price to be paid for their guilty wishes.

This form of identification is different from the others we have discussed since it doesn't necessitate any real emotional bond between the parties involved. There might be one, but the key is that the person who identifies wants to be in the same situation as the other person. In one study, researchers looked at the behaviour of men who seek medical help before, during and after their wives' pregnancies. More than 20 per cent of the husbands sought help for nausea, vomiting, abdominal pain, abdominal bloating and similar pregnancy-like symptoms. Anthropologists call this identificatory behaviour 'couvade'. The husband, as it were, becomes the wife, or identifies with particular traits of her situation.

These sorts of unconscious identification are a basic part of human life. Surprisingly, they do not only involve positive qualities and attributes. We might expect that a child will identify exclusively with the valued characteristics of a parent, but this is far from the case. They will often fix on moments of discontinuity, when the image of a parent is suddenly put in question: the benign parent who becomes angry, the healthy parent who falls ill, the confident parent who suffers an accident. The child will frequently identify with the very point of change here: the raised voice of the angry parent, the physical symptom of the sick parent, or some detail linked to the context of the change. *It is as if they are caught at the moment a rhythm is broken.* Since illness generally disrupts the patterns of family life and relationships, it becomes a privileged point for the child to identify with.

Analysts have repeatedly shown that if an illness appears in different generations of the same family, identifications may be the underlying mechanism. If a patient is told that they have a disease because their parent or grandparent had it, or that this would increase its likelihood, couldn't this just fuel the very identificatory process that ought to be explored and put in question? If identifications can change the actual material of the human body, then they should be taken very seriously. We would do well to consider the possibility of identificatory processes rather than jump to the conclusion that if we see the same symptoms in a family it is because of a *genetic* transmission, even if this may be a significant factor in some cases. Children don't just inherit their parents' genes, they inherit their parents. Invoking genetics usually serves to banish the dimension of human subjectivity, although the more that we know about genetic factors, the more it becomes probable that their expression may depend on psychological questions – exactly like that of identification.

Although identificatory processes were once a standard topic in psychosomatic research, today they are increasingly ignored. A recent study, for example, found that when subjects were placed in the proximity of someone who was yawning, they were more likely than a control group to start yawning as well. Similar findings have been reported for nearly a hundred years now, with actions ranging from yawning to blinking to stuttering to bodily movement and even heartbeat. But where the early studies were interested in the mechanisms of unconscious identification, the modern research tends to force it in completely different directions. Media articles on the yawning experiments proclaimed that they had shown that yawning is *contagious*. In other words, *the unconscious dynamics at work had been replaced by the bacterial model of infection*. Relations between people were redrafted as relations between an organism and a germ.

*

What are the physiological effects of someone 'becoming' someone else? Bodily changes can be observed in even the most everyday example of human development, as we saw with the example of the mirror phase. Parents know that if their toddler spends time with slightly older children who are already walking, this will speed up the mastery of those motor functions necessary for locomotion. As the toddler identifies with the other children, their own body will develop. This identification with the image of another child will also often be accompanied by new jealousies and demands: once they put themselves in the place of the other child, they will want what the other child has.

Other forms of identification will affect the body in different ways. Many studies have found significant changes at both autonomic and endocrine levels linked to identificatory processes. Female roommates, for example, can synchronize their periods – a quite common phenomenon believed to be mediated by a pheromone. Significantly, such endocrinological identification is much more likely if the parties concerned either like or dislike each other. If the roommates have little emotional contact, the synchronization of periods is less likely. Putting themselves in the place of the other person means that endocrine functioning is altered. The anniversary reactions we discussed in Chapter 4 are further examples of identification. One person puts themself in the place of someone else, an illness acting as the common link between them.

We might also think of the depressive states following bereavement. Endocrine and immunological changes have long been associated with the time following loss of a loved one. Yet these are also times where identificatory processes are acting powerfully. The bereaved may unconsciously identify with the lost loved one, taking on characteristics of the one they have lost, such as a tone of voice or a way of walk-ing. They may also submerge themselves totally in an all-encompassing identification: it is as if they become the dead person. They refuse to go out, they isolate themselves, they don't eat, they wear the clothes of the dead person and they long to join the dead.

This may also be visible in the self-reproaches that follow bereavement. A bereaved person may blame themselves endlessly for the loss. They will accuse, chastise and punish themselves with a vigour that baffles family and friends. This becomes clearer when we realize that the person they are attacking and blaming so persistently *is in fact the dead person*. The image of the deceased has engulfed their own ego. As Freud argued, a careful attention to the exact form of the self-reproaches often illustrates this. The accusation 'You're never there for me' can be reversed into the self-reproach 'I was never there for you'. Although this process is probably a part of any response to a loss, it can become magnified to eclipse the bereaved person's life completely.

When someone dies soon after the death of a loved one or special friend, the same identificatory processes often play a part. Whether the apparent cause of death is due to illness or suicide, that person has gone into the place of the one they have lost. The medical researchers here may be study-ing the body's reaction to loss, while the analysts are looking at the way in which someone may 'become' the lost person without knowing it consciously. The medical researchers tend to shy away from thinking about a person's wish to die, which is why the euthanasia debate has always proved so difficult to handle. But the question of the wish to die follow-ing a bereavement cannot legitimately be ignored. When the actress Billie Whitelaw sat at the bedside of her seriously ill son, she kept a bottle of pills with her so that she could join him if he died. Thinking through these issues may throw light on the life situation of a patient in a way that measurement of data and statistical tests never can.

Identifying with another person can involve questions of life and death. When a recent study of heart disturbances found that emotional shock appeared to trigger cardiac problems, the most common precipitating cause was hearing news of someone else's death. The investigators duly tried to posit a mechanism, involving a flood of cathecholamines to the heart. But what they didn't explore was how exactly the news of the death had been conveyed. If the patients described their attacks as starting with chest pains, it would be important to know whether the deaths described to them also involved chest pains. Was the heart problem just a downstream effect of emotional shock, or, on the contrary, something mediated by words and language? Was it, in other words, a form of identification?

Some of the heart problems we discussed in Chapter 8 also involve identification. What seems on the surface to be the rivalry and ambition of the Type A character could be analysed more subtly in terms of two different forms of identification. On one level, if someone identified with a rival, remaining caught in a cycle of competitiveness, the sense of frustration and impasse would be accentuated. What one person wants would be defined by what another person wants in an endless battle for prestige. By contrast, as we saw in Chapter 8, identifying with a particular role within a social structure would temper the effects of competition. Occupying such a symbolic place means there would be less of a pull towards identifying with the images of other people.

This second form of identification can provide a crucial point of reference. It could even be considered a vital component of physical health. In the film *Castaway*, Tom Hanks plays a man stranded on a desert island after his plane carrying Fedex packages goes down at sea. As he strives to build a world for himself in this inhospitable and barren place, he has none of the tools that we take for granted in urban living. Yet curiously, one reminder of civilization survives: a Fedex packet from the plane that has washed ashore with him. When he is eventually rescued and returns to civilization, he feels alienated and estranged. His fiancée has now married someone else, and after an emotional scene with her, he takes his leave. Yet his past life is not totally behind him.

After the painful scene with his ex, we see him driving through a deserted landscape. The car radio plays 'Return to Sender', and we realize he has taken it upon himself to deliver the faded and battered Fedex package he'd kept with him all this time. After leaving it at the recipient's home, we see him at a crossroads, confronted now with true freedom for the first time. What can this tell us about identification? At the start of the film, we see Hanks eager and zealous in his role as a Fedex employee. And after returning from the island, he still delivers his package. Rather than seeing this as a mere piece of celluloid product placement, why not acknowledge its central function in Hanks's survival? Despite being a castaway, he still retained his symbolic identity as the messenger, the deliverer of Fedex goods. This was the one symbolic mantle that he could hold on to in the absence of all the paraphernalia of civilization. Perhaps, at some level, this is what kept him alive. Hence, after delivering his final package, his facial expression is a mixture of dread and liberation: he has gone beyond the identification that had sustained him. There is no longer any reference point for him, and he is finally free for the first time.

★

Strange as it may sound, identification may not always be with people or with symbolic roles. It can also be with parts of the body. Let's take the example of transplant surgery. In its early years, physicians noticed that the chances of organ rejection after transplant increase dramatically when a significant relationship is broken. In this case, the transplanted organ may come to be felt both consciously and unconsciously *as* someone else, an alien presence. In one case, a man felt persecuted by his transplanted kidney. In another, a boy died when he learned it had been donated by his estranged father. When an important relationship is lost or put in question, feelings linked to this might then play themselves out, tragically, in the person's own body. The internal organ is rejected, echoing the experience of the break with the other person.

The contents of the body can also be equated with other people. If someone experiences diarrhoea or constipation when their lover has left them, their bowel contents may have been made representative of the other person, who is then stubbornly held on to (constipation) or excreted violently (diarrhoea). At the start of life, what are our first possessions? We are encouraged to think of our bowel contents in precisely this way: we are coaxed to release them or retain them during potty training. For this very reason, they can become equated with other people, whom we want to be able to possess. Children often think of birth as an anal process, and that babies are made out of faeces. Parts of the body are thus connected with other people. And the actual ways in which we inhabit our bodies are influenced by this connection.

Our body surface is first of all given a value by our caregivers. Certain areas will be touched more than others, and with greater or lesser love, attention, repugnance or hostility. Our bodies only come to have their parts divided up and represented through the actions of other people: as our body receives attention and care, some bits become differentiated from others. And the same goes for the inside of the body and its functions. Adults might worry about what's going on inside, look for signs of illness, scrutinize excrement, or employ medical procedures. The facts of the parent's own history may determine where the sources of their interest lie. If a grandparent, for example, suffered from a particular disease, a parent might be especially attentive to that part of the body which they associated – rightly or wrongly – with the disease in question. And this will usually take place *without the parent's conscious awareness*.

In one case, a man became a regular visitor to casualty due to a series of minor fractures. He eventually began psychoanalysis, although for entirely different reasons, which revealed an identification with his maternal grandfather. All the man knew about him was that he had been a good sportsman if rather accident-prone: the only photograph of him in the family home showed him with a bandaged arm. Although the man had never met his grandfather, the minimal scraps of information he'd gathered had been combined to make a symptom. In this case, the mother's relation to her father had been crucial for him, and his series of fractures put him unconsciously in the place of this ancestor he'd never known. Needless to say, as he was growing up, the mother had paid particular attention to her son's minor injuries, without linking them explicitly to those of her father. So much more is transmitted in families than we are aware of.

One could take juvenile-onset diabetes here as another example. Studies have shown how depressions in the mother will have an effect on the sugar metabolism of some diabetic children, as maternal mood swings are reflected in the child's body. This may be mediated through a specific chain of ideas in some cases, but not in others. In one case, a child linked the idea of 'blood' with the idea of lineage: it was through one's blood that one's identity was established. Blood, for this child, meant the networks of kinship, and in her case it had a very specific sense. Blood evoked for her what she saw as her only link to her mother. It was only through this that she was, as she put it, her mother's daughter. In other words, blood was an identificatory link to the mother, and so, as her treating doctor was to find out, the fluctuations in her diabetic condition proved to have clear links to changes in her thoughts and fantasies about her mother.

A sensitivity to these factors will have many consequences. For example, as part of ongoing work on skin disorders in the 1950s and '60s, there were several experimental studies that measured how an infant's skin reacted to a wide range of stimuli. These tests missed a crucial point, however: that before seeing what could cause a reaction in the baby, it was worthwhile studying how important skin was *to the mother*. If, in certain cases, the mother touched the skin of her baby affectionately, then that baby might use the skin as an unconscious way of remaining linked to her, like a memory trace inscribed in the body. René Spitz believed that if the mother caressed the baby's skin, the baby might continue to stimulate its own skin in some way, in the absence of the mother, even through a skin disease. Paediatricians have also argued that, when a child tears at their skin, it may in some cases represent an attempt to give themselves a bodily frontier or limit, at the point where the mother's absent caresses failed to do so.

Parts of our own bodies, as we have seen, are linked to other people. In some cases, a mother will attend to the infant's *body* yet be unable to respond to any kind of *psychical* or *emotional* need. The body and its complaints may then become the only language between them. Keeping the infant fed, warm, clean and quiet may be priorities for the parent as if human existence consisted only in these. The parent's relation to the child's body may then set the stage for the child's relation to their own body. A mother who obsessively cleans her child's body might do so in order to lessen her own anxiety or because of an unconscious fantasy of being dirty herself. This will mean that parts of the child's body will be connected to the mother's mental states. Parts of the body may then be felt unconsciously by the child to *belong to* the mother. And don't we often rage at a part of the body if it is unwell, exactly as we might a person? This opens up a number of new perspectives on identification, and on what happens when a part of the body becomes ill.

In a ground-breaking book published in 1933, Virginia Woolf's sister-in-law, the psychoanalyst and physician Karin Stephen, developed her own model of this type of identification. The organs linked to nutrition, excretion and respiration – the mouth, the anus, the urethra and lungs – and the organs of smell, sight, touch and hearing will all be involved in our earliest emotional relations with our care-givers. As well as this, of course, they serve the biological functions of nutrition, respiration, excretion, and so on. If the emotional relationship between child and caregiver is disturbed, this may then affect the biological functions. For example, if the mouth becomes the site of a conflict between pleasure and pain, such as the frustration of waiting to be fed, this may have an effect on appetite. Whenever dis-pleasure and frustration become mixed with satisfaction, the organ or bodily function may pay a price.

Since every infant will experience frustration of this kind, the very zones of the body which are sources of pleasure are simultaneously potential sources of pain. And with pain comes fury and rage. Stephen's idea is that it is these body zones rather than the caregiver which become the first enemy. They are hated, and this hatred antedates all future hostility to 'outside' enemies. The first real displeasure is thus displeasure at one's own pleasure zones. These have been transformed into an internal enemy by disappointment. And so the biological side of these areas of the body and the functions associated with them may suffer, even putting one's life at risk. The best defence against this is to deflect hatred outside, to create external enemies.

The body is thus a site of conflict, in which hatred and hostility underlie our own unconscious relation with our body and its parts and processes. These will then have a rela- tion with our experiences of others, both in relation to our unconscious representation of our caregivers and in our rela- tion to people around us. Even if one is sceptical as to whether this might play a role in the causation of illness, it is surely at work in some of our responses to it. As we will see in Chapter 12, people are actually taught to see diseased parts of their body as deadly enemies and to imagine their destruction. For this reason surgery is sometimes effective in removing a symptom that was not targeted in the surgical procedure itself. By removing part of the body, a form of revenge or excision has taken place.

There is one further form of identification often met with when tracing the history of a patient's illness. This is not an identification with a person or a body part, but with an imaginary role in human relations. We have noted how people often become ill when a relationship they have maintained for years is broken, through separation or bereavement. This may not be immediately visible, and it may take several inter- views to find out what the relation consisted of. We might discover how the person needed a spouse, a family member or even a neighbour to be there, falling ill when threatened with a break in this relationship. As well as the obvious issues of love and attachment, we sometimes find that the relationship allowed the person to assume a particular role. Or more precisely, it allowed **each party** to assume a role: for example, one could be the martyr or the helper, and the other the helped.

This is different from the kind of symbolic identification we discussed with the example of Tom Hanks in *Castaway*. Hanks was assigned a role in a broader social structure, which he willingly assumed. He could maintain this role even in the absence of the accompanying paraphernalia of his job, as if it was hard-wired into him. Imaginary role identifications, on the other hand, tend to require the presence of surface cues and other people. They are less hard-wired, and that is exactly why they can be disturbed much more easily by changes in the person's circumstances. Similarly, it is less a question of accepting a place assigned to one than of inventing a place for oneself. In a general sense, imaginary role identifications could be described as surface imitations of symbolic ones.

As we explore these role identifications, we find that they may have been at work throughout someone's whole life. They are like a kind of formula that people live by, even if they are usually not conscious. In place for decades, they are like a lifejacket or safety belt that has organized the person's existence. These role identifications have perhaps filled a gap in someone's psychical life. Faced with unbearable family situations and traumatic experiences that cannot be symbolized, the only possibility of safety lies in the role.

In one case, a woman who had grown up in a strained and violent family spoke of her special attachment to her dog. She would see herself as the dog's saviour, encouraging him in learning new skills and protecting him from threats and dangers. After leaving home, she began a relationship in which her boyfriend had a similar role. Using exactly the same vocabulary and formulations that she had used of her beloved pet, she described the way he would encourage her, protect her and teach her. It seemed clear that the relation of loving teacher-protector to student was what governed both relationships. The formula itself had been installed as her way of defending against the violence and neglect in her family. When the formula could no longer be maintained after separating from the boyfriend, she fell ill with an auto-immune disorder.

The formula gives the person a role *in relation to* another person, and thereby fixes a place for them in their world. This could even be the place of a victim in relation to a persecutor. What matters is that it provides a structure. When a role identification is removed – often due to external factors such as one's own relocation or that of the significant other – the formula breaks down and illness may ensue, though not necessarily in the body. A sensitivity to these questions may be useful clinically. If the patient has, for example, lost the role of 'helper' to a particular relative or friend, and this seems to have had a special importance to them, they might then be asked to become the doctor or the hospital's 'helper' by providing monthly information on their health or some other topic. This could be used as a working strategy which would also contribute to establishing some form of social recognition for them. It might seem a rather simplistic exam-ple, but it gives a good indication of the kind of consequences one might deduce from the theory of functional roles.

All of the forms of identification we have discussed so far have something in common. They all involve some kind of attachment, be it to an image, a role, a body part or another person. Psychoanalysts call the strength of human attachment 'libido', and its presence can be inferred in a wide range of individual and social activities: falling in love, sexual preferences, hobbies, drug addictions, sports enthusiasms, and all the drives and interests that make up our daily life. Libido does not have to be directed to a person, but may attach itself to almost any aspect of our existence. This allows us to channel and shape the experiences of excitation, unease, distress and passion that make up our early life. They become set into particular patterns that will be unique to each of us.

So what happens when such a pattern is disturbed? Libidinal investments, as they are known, may be challenged and undermined. If we lose an identificatory support or are suddenly forced to put in question some meaning or an image that has been important for us, where does the libido take refuge? These moments will involve *reinvestment*. They are frequently associated with times of separation and loss. Something in the patient's world has changed, upsetting the pattern of libidinal investment. And this may produce a strange response in the body in the form of a physical illness.

Let's take an example. A man lives for thirty years with a woman who always, he says, has the answers. As well as being the major breadwinner, she is always self-assured, calm and in control. Although he had complained from time to time about her omnipotence, it clearly suited him. But when she fell ill after an accident, his world was thrown into disarray. Everything he had invested in her image – with a good deal of fantasy – was put in question. Now she was a woman who needed help to carry out her everyday activities. An image of weakness had replaced the image of strength. When he subsequently fell ill himself with heart problems, one might suspect that the libido that had been invested in the image of the strong woman had to be channelled somewhere else. Perhaps taking advantage of a pre-existing cardiac weakness, it rerouted itself to a part of the body, in this case the heart.

This is certainly not the only way to interpret the case, but the question of libidinal investment is significant. We see it also in the odd pendulum that swings between love and hypochondria. It is quite common for hypochondriacal types to stop worrying about their bodies when they are in love. When the relationship with the other person is broken off, the worries reappear. It's as if the libido that was invested in love now flows back to reinvest the body, to generate the worries which are, after all, a form of interest. When the other person is 'disinvested', the body itself becomes an object. We tend to cling to our libidinal investments, and are loath to give them up. One example of this would be the reaction of the child to the illness of a parent. Amidst the love and concern the child feels for the parent there may also be fury, suggesting that the image of weakness that has come to mark the parent may be intolerable to the child. The challenge to the child's investment in the image of the parent is too much, just as we saw in the above example of the man whose wife fell ill.

What might happen to the fury unleashed when an investment is put in question? Is it possible that it can become directed to one's own body? Either as a kind of deflection, to protect the other person we love as well as hate, or because our own body includes a representation of the other. The attack on ourselves may involve an attack on the other. We could think here of the case of a young woman who stopped biting her nails when she realized that this activity was always more pronounced when she was in the company of her mother. She understood that what she really wanted to bite was her mother and, unable to do this, the person she bit was herself.

How far could such processes go? Is it possible that a deflection or reversal of aggression could actually have an effect at a cellular level? Could something as intricate and opaque as the immune system be caught up in the dynamics of identification? It is intriguing to observe how the body is often described as treating itself as if it were someone else in autoimmune disorders, attacking 'self-cells' as if they were dangerous invaders. Is this kind of vocabulary justified here? Do the concepts of 'self' and 'other' have any purchase at the cellular level of the immune network? This is one of the questions we turn to in the next chapter.

11. The Immune System

The immune system is a vital line of the body's defences. Cartoon images sometimes portray it as an army, moving around the body and mustering troops whenever the threat of invasion looms. Although some immunologists have tried to substitute the image of an orchestra for that of an army, the military vocabulary always prevails in popular imagery. The body is seen as a battlefield under threat from bacterial enemies, and the immune system as a patriotic defence unit. Medicine long considered it an autonomous fighting force, operating independently from the brain and nervous system. But this view has changed dramatically.

Early research on the immune system often took place *in vitro*, where white blood cells, the body's defensive workers, could be put through their paces in a controlled environment. These experiments revealed a great deal about how immune cells lock on to damaged cells or foreign bodies and destroy them. But they tended to assume that the immune system did its work more or less on its own. Research in the 1970s, however, showed how immune cells were very closely connected with the nervous system. Receptors for peptides (signalling molecules crucial for regulating bodily processes) active in the brain were found to exist on the surfaces of cells of the immune system. And tissues of the immune system found in places like the spleen, the gut and lymph nodes turned out to be connected to the brain by a complex network of nerves.

The brain was thus potentially communicating with the

immune system. This was taking place via the electrical pathways of nerve connections and also via chemical pathways using hormones. These chemical messengers were found to be actively at work linking the immune system, the nervous system and the endocrine (hormone) system. It was no longer possible to see the immune system as an isolated entity, cut off from any dialogue with the rest of the body. This meant that our mental life could be having a continual effect on our immune system.

Why is the immune system so important to our physical health? Its primary function is to rid the body of antigens: dysfunctional cells and invaders like bacteria, viruses and parasites. Without it, we would rapidly succumb to infections and diseases, and we would die. As befits something charged with such a vital task, the immune system is fabulously complicated. It operates along two main axes, known as *cell-mediated* and *humoral* immunity. Cell-mediated immunity acts on damaged and infected cells. It will destroy a cell in one's own body that has already been infected by a virus or bacterium. The job of humoral immunity, meanwhile, is to prevent damage from extracellular microbes, like non-invasive bacteria and fungi, and their toxic products.

The lines of defence of the immune system also fall into two classes. Immunity is either *innate* or *adaptive*. Innate immunity is about blocking intruders from entering the body, or rapidly getting rid of them once they've done so. Enzymes in saliva, for example, can destroy bacteria, and little hairs called cilia can stop foreign particles entering the body's orifices. In the blood, certain groups of white blood cells such as eosinophils also work to get rid of unwanted bacteria and emit chemical messengers to call in other parts of the immune system for help.

Innate immunity is by and large there from birth, and it doesn't seem to involve any process of learning from its encounters with intruders. Its defences do not change after battling infectious agents. The immune cells known as phagocytes, for example, rely on recognizing the difference between an invading microbe and one of the body's own cells, and are not altered by the encounter. Other important cells here are the natural killer (NK) cells, which act against virus-infected self-cells and some tumours, and mast cells, belonging to the humoral wing, which bind to allergens and release inflammatory substances such as histamine, as those who react badly to insect bites will know.

Adaptive immunity works in tandem with innate immunity to produce a highly intricate system of defences. In comparison to innate immunity, adaptive immunity is capable of much more subtle discriminations of what belongs to you and what doesn't, and it can learn from its experiences. An example of this is the antibody-producing *B cell*, which develops in bone marrow and which is active in humoral immunity. Each B cell is designed to lock on to the surface proteins of a foreign body. Countless millions of these B cells are produced with different receptors to cover the whole range of dangerous microbes threatening the body. The diversity of these B cells is generated by a kind of shuffling of the pack of relevant genes. This random process naturally leads to the production of cells whose receptors neatly match proteins on the surfaces of the body's own cells, the very things which need protecting. So, before they are allowed to emerge into the bloodstream, B cells are put to the test and those found to latch on to self-cells are made to self-destruct.

When a B cell meets up with the protein of some foreign body that matches its receptor, it starts spewing out huge numbers of daughter cells. Some of these clones will then rapidly produce large amounts of antibodies, which are mole-cules that can lock on to other copies of that foreign body. Once attached to their targets, further cells of the immune system are called in to eliminate the invaders. The rest of the clones remain in the body as memory cells. The first time you are challenged by an invading microbe, the immune response may take some time to mount an adequate defence, but because of these memory cells, a second infection by the same type of microbe produces a much faster reaction.

While B cells mature in the bone marrow, *T cells* mature in the thymus, a small organ situated above the heart. T cells come in three varieties. Cytotoxic T cells are capable of destroying cells of one's own body that display proteins which reveal that they are damaged or infected. The other two vari-eties of T cell are helper cells of types 1 and 2 (Th1 and Th2). As their names suggest, these cells assist other parts of the immune system to perform their duty. Th1 cells play a role in cell-mediated immunity. They help cytotoxic T cells and the mopping-up macrophage cells associated with innate immunity to act against infected cells. Th2 cells, on the other hand, play a role in humoral immunity. They encourage B cells to produce antibodies. Again, the extraordinary diversity needed to recognize the vast array of potential invaders is achieved by genetic shuffling, and a similar process of weed-ing out cells which would latch on to self cells will take place.

As with B cells, when a T cell is called into action, memory cells are produced. These two types of memory cell provide the basis of immunization. Non-toxic antigens whose surfaces resemble those of potentially damaging microbes are injected or fed to a person to stimulate an immune response. When the real thing comes along, the body is then prepared to deal with the danger very rapidly. This is what happens when you get vaccinated against diseases like polio, typhoid or mumps.

The T helper cells use messenger molecules known as *cytokines* as their signals. Not only do cytokines act as signals to call in reinforcements, they also steer some types of immune cell away. Indeed, recent research has discovered that the two wings of the immune system use messengers to regulate each other: a cell-mediated response will inhibit a humoral response and vice versa. So there is a dynamic balance between Th1 activity and Th2 activity, and this balance fluctuates through each 24-hour period, driven by changes in circulating hormone levels. Typically for women, Th1 activity is stronger than in men, and as we age our immune profile shifts in the Th2 direction.

Type of immunity	Cell-mediated	Humoral
Targets	Damaged and infected cells	Parasites, toxins, some bacteria
Types of cell:		
Innate	Natural killer Macrophage	Mast cells Eosinophils
Acquired	Cytotoxic T cells T helper type 1 (Th1)	B cells T helper type 2 (Th2)
Regulating hormones	DHEA and melatonin	Cortisol
Circadian peak	Night	Day
Overreactions	Multiple sclerosis Rheumatoid arthritis Type 1 diabetes	Asthma Allergy

A very schematic table of immune system properties

The immune system has to work quickly enough to prevent infection by dangerous intruders, while not overreacting to harmless foreign bodies or attacking the body's own cells. The hayfever symptoms brought about in response to pollen are an example of this type of overreaction, as are other allergic and asthmatic reactions. These responses shouldn't be happening. Allergic sensitization is the down side of memory cells. So-called *atopic* individuals for whom Th2 activity is stronger tend to suffer from these conditions. The defence against external challenges has become exaggerated. In contrast, the cell-mediated wing of the immune system has its own way of being over-officious. Driven by Th1 activity, it can attack the body's own cells in a number of diseases such as juvenile-onset diabetes and rheumatoid arthritis. Many of these autoimmune disorders are more common in women with their stronger Th1 activity.

One of the decisive results that showed the link between immune response and mental states was the discovery that the functioning of immune cells could be conditioned. The immunologist Robert Ader and his colleague Nicholas Cohen mixed a drug that suppressed immune responses with a saccharine drink and gave it to a group of mice from a strain with an overactive immune system. The result, predictably, was a lowering of immune functioning. But when they gave the mice just the saccharine drink *without* the immunosuppressant, their immune systems responded just as weakly. This showed how immunity could be learned, and later experiments reinforced and refined these same results. A simple demonstration of this can be seen in the heightening of immune functioning in people with hayfever. Hayfever involves the immune system's response to pollen. Yet when presented with a picture of a hayfield or with an artificial flower, some sufferers get worse. The fake stimulus creates changes in immune functioning because of the associated connection. If the immune system can be taught to react in such ways, could suggestion cause it to malfunction permanently?

Despite these significant results, many researchers chose to ignore or even deny the possibility of links between the immune system and the central nervous system. Writing in 1980, Robert Ader noted how immunology itself was reductionistic, basing an understanding of immune processes on *in vitro* analyses rather than on the complex environment of interacting systems and processes outside the test tube. Ader also pointed out how the nervous system's influence on immunological reactivity had been actively studied by Soviet scientists from the 1930s, yet Cold War barriers blocked scientific dialogue. In fact, already by 1926 Metalnikov and Chorine had produced inflammation in the lining of the abdomen by warming and scratching the skin, having conditioned the response earlier by pairing this stimulus with fragments of a microbe. It is interesting to note how during the Cold War some issues of the journal *Psychosomatic Medicine* carried subversive little adverts for free translations of Soviet journal articles, and one wonders how frequently these offers were taken up.

The immune system is a dynamic network, constantly operating on different levels and with other systems. Like an ecosystem, there are rhythms to its functioning, and some of these are driven by the hormonal system. The body has many rhythms operating over different periods. A woman's menstrual cycle, for example, has a period of roughly four weeks, and animals have well-known annual rhythms to their hormone levels. There are also daily or *circadian* rhythms, operating over roughly 24-hour periods. Products of the immune response to infection can make you want to go to sleep, but even without being challenged by viruses, the immune system naturally swings to the Th1 axis at night-time, when melatonin and DHEA production peaks. Then at around the time you wake up in the morning, a sudden boost in the circulating levels of cortisol occurs, peaking around thirty minutes after you wake up. This kicks the system in the Th2 direction.

The immune system messengers – the cytokines – play a subtle role in modulating our sleep patterns. And sleep in turn modulates our immune efficiency. Deep sleep, a state adults typically enter two or three times a night, triggers the release of two hormones, growth hormone and prolactin, which enhance several aspects of immune functioning. Interference with sleep patterns can thereby impair the immune system's efficacy. Partial sleep loss during a single night may influence the cortisol cycle, resulting in higher levels the following evening. In view of the fact that the shift to Th1 dominance in the early hours of the morning comes about through suppression of cortisol levels, it is not hard to see how disturbance to sleeping patterns can impact on the Th1/Th2 balance. This may play a part in the higher incidence of breast cancer among female night-shift workers, for reasons we will discuss in the next chapter.

Our body clocks are affected by time signals, or *zeitgebers* (literally, 'time givers'), one of the most important being early-morning light. Freed from the effects of these zeitgebers, in a sensory-deprivation chamber, the major pacemakers of the body run at a period of about twenty-five hours. After a few days of this treatment, the major oscillators become out of synch and rhythmic biological functions fluctuate out of phase. Intriguingly, besides the hormone-triggering effects of morning light, social cues are important in regulating daily

rhythms. Subjects kept alone in a room where a light came
on at the same time every morning experienced disrupted
circadian rhythms, which were only restored by the introduction of a bell to signal a demand for their urine sample.
This is a very significant detail, as it shows that light itself is
not enough to set the body's clock.

Aircrews have also been thoroughly studied to determine
the symptoms of changes to the body clock. Anyone who
has flown long distance, especially from west to east, knows
the effects of time difference, including daytime tiredness,
sleep difficulties, loss of concentration, headache, irritability
and gastrointestinal problems. Yet it seems as if social cues
help to speed up the resetting of the body clock. Jetlag
sufferers fare better if they have to engage with other people
on arrival in a new time zone. It's not just light, but language
and interaction that matter here.

The absence of this aspect of human life may be particularly pronounced in the situation of a bereaved person. The
normal moments of interaction and exchange may vanish,
and this loss of social contact may be significant in the weakening of the immune levels often found in the months after
loss. This can be affected by many factors, including loss of
sleep with its restorative function. Yet we should be cautious
here of falling into the trap that we warned of earlier in this
book. The more that detailed knowledge of a body system
emerges, the more we lose sight of the whole picture and
the person. A bereaved person hasn't just lost a daily pattern
of interaction involving stimuli; they have lost someone they
love. There seems little reason to shy away from using this
kind of language in favour of a more atomizing approach.

Taking circadian rhythms into account, it is not surprising that a person's defences vary through the day. This goes
for other mammals too. Herbert Weiner found that mice

injected with pneumococci at 4 a.m. fare much better than those injected at 4 p.m. Now, given that protection by inoculation depends on the body's immune response, the timing of beneficial injections must also be significant. Recognition of the part played by the body's daily cycles has, indeed, led to medical treatments being administered at the most suitable time of day. This *chronomodulation* has been applied to the chemotherapy given to children with leukaemia. It has been found that survival times are improved by a factor of between two and eight by timing the administration of high doses of anticancer agent to coincide with periods of the day when they will be most effective and least toxic to the rest of the body. Chronomodulation thus opens up vast prospects as to how to achieve the best results from immunization, surgery and drug-based therapies.

Differences between individuals are of great significance here. Our bodies don't all neatly follow these circadian rhythms. Many people have flattened or exaggerated peaks. Some rhythms become shifted out of phase with each other, the length of their cycles may change, and sometimes their peaks and troughs become erratic. There are many possible causes for these disruptions, but the most important one is thought to arise from dysregulation of the HPA axis via cortisol and other hormones, which has been linked to such psychological factors as chronic worry and the experience of trauma.

This brings us to a crucial point. These results suggest that our immune system may be affected not only by infections and antigens but by our experiences of situations and other people. The beneficial effect of social contact after air travel compared with the detrimental effect of social isolation and grief after a bereavement or loss demonstrate this quite clearly. Mental distress will impact on the functioning of our immune system, disrupting its rhythms and swinging it in particular directions. Some theorists have argued that there is a correlation between depression in mothers and increased cortisol in their infants, and we have seen how cortisol will influence immune functioning. If the mother fails to respond or responds negatively to the child's demands, the child may give up. Rather than articulating their distress, they withdraw, and this behaviour has been linked to an increase in cortisol levels. Would this suggest that being able to articulate mental pain would benefit immune functioning? Could this be why asthma sufferers fare better if they are encouraged to write about their troubling experiences?

We should remember here that writing always presupposes that there is someone to *write for*. The voicing of distress always needs an addressee, and the experiments in which asthma sufferers are encouraged to write introduce not simply the function of writing but also that of this addressee: the experimenter who wants the subjects to keep a journal or describe their difficult experiences. Once again, we recognize the importance of the place of the interlocutor in human life. Just as we saw in earlier chapters how experiences could not be easily processed if they were passed over in silence and excluded from any dialogue, the asthma results show how the presence of a listener matters. It would not seem unreasonable to conclude, therefore, that human dialogue – and its abolition – can have an effect on immune functioning.

One of the key discoveries made by recent researchers in immunology has been in the area of inflammation. Michael Balint had predicted in the 1930s that one day all major diseases would be seen as varieties of inflammation, and today it seems that conditions as diverse as arthritis, many cancers,

Alzheimer's, diabetes and coronary heart disease all involve inflammatory responses of the immune system. If we prick ourselves on a thorn, the skin around the point of contact will rapidly turn red and there will be local soreness and some heat. This is the immune system in action, working to stop microbes from infecting us. Once it has done its job of killing the microbes, designated immune cells send out a signal to turn off the inflammation. Other immune cells come along to mop up the debris and the emergency is over.

Although this is inflammation at its most visible, it is actually a process that mostly takes place inside our bodies, in arteries, nerve endings, bronchioles of the lung and in the brain. Problems will emerge if signals are not sent to shut down the inflammatory process. For example, in rheumatoid arthritis, where a healthy knee joint will have a synovial lining a few cells thick, if it is diseased hordes of immune cells will be clumped together in frond-like patterns. The command to stop has not got through, and the defence mechanism has not been turned off. Like the enchanted broom in *The Sorcerer's Apprentice*, a potentially beneficial action has been started which just doesn't stop, with catastrophic effects for the person.

This becomes all the more interesting when one considers how some psychologically difficult situations are very likely to result in a flaring up of autoimmune symptoms. Marital failure, separation from loved ones and frictions in a relationship have all been observed to aggravate the symptoms of arthritis. But how could this be possible? How could a thought or a situation or an emotion result in such a complicated process in the body? And if the brain can make symptoms flare up, could it also play a part in the actual genesis of those symptoms?

We have seen in earlier chapters how autoimmune disorders are often clearly influenced by psychological situations.

The man with rheumatoid arthritis we discussed in Chapter 3 would experience significant aggravations in his condition whenever the theme of his relation with his father emerged. Hundreds of case studies have mapped such convergences in detail, not just with arthritis but with other autoimmune disorders such as diabetes. A recent series of studies in Sweden confirms the link of diabetes with separations, losses and other significant events. Type 1 diabetes is associated with autoimmune destruction of the insulin-producing beta cells in the pancreas. Several factors, including psychological difficulty, may cause an increase in insulin demand, since distress is known to decrease insulin sensitivity and so extra stress is put on the beta cells, which may then lead to an autoimmune reaction. The stressed beta cells may look different to the immune system, which may itself be perturbed by the difficult situation, leading to the autoimmune reaction.

These questions about the exacerbation of symptoms are complicated by the issue of pain. What might appear medically to be the same level of symptoms can generate differences in pain. When it is said that a symptom flares up, what exactly is flaring up? Is it the pain or the cellular changes that result in pain? It was once believed that pain was a peripheral sensation, mediated by pain receptors and transmitted to pain centres by pain fibres: increased pain meant worsening symptoms. But this view can be modified so that pain is seen more as a feeling or emotion. This means that once pain has been represented psychically, it can be activated internally without any peripheral stimulation. The tissue damage might remain unchanged, but the pain would increase. The brain could thus turn on or off the experience of pain either as a response to a sensory input or independently of it.

This might help to explain those remarkable increases and reductions in pain which seem to defy medical knowledge. But what happens when the tissue damage itself gets worse? The most likely way in which psychological factors affect the immune system to create such disturbances is via the two stress-response systems: the HPA axis and the autonomic nervous system, both the sympathetic branch studied by Cannon and its parasympathetic counterpart. The immune system must vigorously attack infective agents. There's no point in it being cautious. Often it is better that parts of the body's own tissue be damaged than that an infection be allowed to take hold. The TB scars that used to turn up on chest X-rays testify to this kind of action: the body has reacted to the infection with an inflammatory response and the scars are the traces of this. The body has damaged itself rather than allow infection to take hold.

On the other hand, there need to be mechanisms in place to stop this aggressive defence action going too far. By the release of the steroid hormone cortisol into the bloodstream, excessive inflammation is eventually controlled by the HPA axis. Given the fact that so many diseases, including cancer and heart disease, involve processes of chronic inflammation, psychoneuroimmunologists have focused on ways in which activity in the HPA axis can be disrupted by the mind, and so prevented from switching off the inflammation.

This opens up a number of questions. Medicine understands the anti-inflammatory activity of steroids, but its interventions pay little attention to the mind, and at times such treatments can seem dangerously clumsy. How wise is it to treat those suffering from asthma or eczema with long-term use of steroids? Prolonged steroid use appears to shift the Th1/Th2 balance over to Th2 dominance. But it's the kind of patient who suffers from these conditions who already has an imbalance in this direction, so the medication could end up eventually making the situation worse. The integrated network formed by the nervous, immune and endocrine systems is at least as intricate as an ecological system. Treating patients simply with steroids over a long period might turn out to be like trying to improve the climate through adding carbon dioxide to the atmosphere. This may have the beneficial short-term result of giving us pleasanter weather, but end up producing exactly the opposite effect. Overloading the atmosphere with carbon dioxide may warm us up initially but eventually precipitate the disappearance of the warming Gulf Stream, making the climate locally colder.

The HPA axis is by no means the only pathway between brain and immune system. Cannon's so-called fight-or-flight mechanism is another. A huge amount of evidence points to the conclusion that sympathetic nervous system activity also promotes a shift in the Th2 direction, partially mediated by beta-adrenergic (sensitive to adrenaline and noradrenaline) receptors on many cells involved in Th1 activity. In effect, sympathetic signalling is dampening down cell-mediated immunity, allowing its humoral partner greater leeway. We may know of someone taking beta-blockers to provide a barrier to the excessive impact on the heart of the sympathetic nervous system. Well, these drugs also block its interference with Th1 activity and the resulting promotion of Th2 activity, and so are used to control congestive heart disease, which is partly caused by the accumulation of Th2 cells.

A good illustration of these effects of the sympathetic nervous system on immunity comes from research carried out on a group of people suffering from facial herpes who had reported that they found the sight of dirty glasses and dishes so distressing as to bring about an outbreak of symptoms. Ten patients were shown slides of dirty glasses and then asked to handle and inspect the actual glasses, while another ten were shown slides of 'neutral' objects and allowed to handle them. Four of the first group had developed herpes symptoms within forty-eight hours, and none of the control group. No signs of HPA activation could be discovered, as the experimenters had expected, but it was noticeable that most of the first group showed typical characteristics of sympathetic nervous system activation, such as sweating, flushing and trembling hands. The Th1 activity was presumably reduced, allowing the dormant virus to generate symptoms.

Recent research has complemented this exploration of the sympathetic nervous system with a new emphasis on the parasympathetic. It has been known for some time that the sympathetic nervous system plays a role in reducing inflammation, but it now appears that the parasympathetic can perform a similar function. What is so intriguing about this finding is that where the sympathetic nervous system acts systemically – diffusely through areas of the body – the parasympathetic can also act much more locally. This takes place through the vagus nerve, which allows the brain to detect information about what's happening in the body, and to send out instructions to organs such as the lungs, heart and gut, as well as the immune system. Disruptions to parasympathetic activity, usually associated with a relaxed state, could have serious effects on inflammatory responses in all of those areas. Study of the parasympathetic system promises to be one of the most exciting avenues of psychosomatic research, opening up the possibility that the brain might be contributing to illness or recovery in specific, chosen parts of the body.

*

Dirty glasses can usually be avoided, but what of people caught in difficult long-term relationships? Research carried out on ninety newly wed couples explored the way they coped when asked to discuss points of conflict in their relationship. Strong associations between negative or hostile behaviour and impaired immune functioning were found, especially in women. A woman who experienced her husband's emotional withdrawal could expect to have twice the level of cortisol in her blood, compared to a woman with a responsive husband. And this, as we have seen, will interfere with immune functioning by disrupting the Th1/Th2 rhythm.

The classic example of impairment to health brought on by a deteriorating relationship is caring for a spouse with Alzheimer's. One study found that the wounds of Alzheimer's carers took nine days longer to heal than those of a control group, and not only do many immune measures decrease during the period of caregiving, but even years after the spouse has died immune function remains impaired. Indeed, it has been suggested that this kind of chronic problem ages the immune system prematurely, bringing about the typically more vulnerable state of the elderly. The many studies which suggest adverse health effects for the caregiver tie in with those that examine the role of hostility and anger. Although it may at times be difficult to admit how they feel, caregivers often experience a massive rage towards those they love and care for.

The caregiver may feel enraged that the person they are caring for is no longer the person they used to be or were once imagined to be. Their image has changed, and we discussed some of the possible effects of this in Chapter 10. There can also be rage that the person can no longer be relied or depended upon. Such slow-burning resentment may be very difficult to accept at a conscious level. It will conflict with an individual's sense of love and duty. And this conflict is likely to impact adversely upon health. When immune responses are found to slump during long-term caregiving or after bereavement, these factors should be taken very seriously. The extent of the pressures entailed with caregiving becomes clearer when we recall that there are an estimated 24 million homes in the US in which a chronically ill person is being cared for. We could add to this figure the number of people who cohabit with a depressed person.

Social support is enormously important in helping to address this problem, and caregivers should have the opportunity to maintain dialogue with others outside their home. But much will also depend on the way the carer perceives their charge. Interesting work is now being done to show that even in patients seriously affected by Alzheimer's, their sense of identity remains less compromised than we might expect. Tape recordings of their speech show that if the long pauses between their utterances are removed, a listener will judge them to be much more coherent than they appeared to be at first. If carers could be taught to listen with greater tolerance, allowing more time for the patient to respond, they might remain healthier.

We have seen how developments in immunology hold out many promises for charting the impact of psychological factors. But how far should we go here? When immunologists talk about the immune system recognizing self-cells and destroying outsiders, could these ways of speaking be taken literally? The language of self and non-self, recognition and rejection, identity and foreignness, suggests that the terms of psychological theory have been transplanted right into the cellular structure of the body. Is it all about differentiating self from non-self? And when things go wrong, as in the autoimmune disorders and instances of chronic inflammation, isn't there a kind of self-destruction at play, enabled by the immune mechanisms? What better example of the Freudian death drive than an autoimmune problem? The self is attacking the self.

We should be wary of the metaphors that get grafted on to theories of immune functioning, but we should also not forget that exacerbations, and possibly the onset, of a wide range of autoimmune diseases can be triggered by psychological events. To give one example, a man in his thirties was diagnosed with the autoimmune version of vasculitis, an illness that affects blood-vessel walls to produce a variety of symptoms including lumps on the skin. After preliminary consultations, he went to see one of the world authorities on the disease, who was delighted to find such a pronounced case in which the symptoms – swellings on the skin – were to be found in an area of the body not usually associated with the disease. He took a sample of the patient's blood, and duly injected it into him a week later. The reaction was as predicted: an allergic response to his own blood cells.

After further study, and the unsuccessful trial of a couple of drugs, the patient was told that he would have to take powerful immunosuppressant medication for the rest of his life to control the disorder. Checking up on its side-effects on the internet, he read some research which showed that this medication would increase his chances of getting leukaemia by some 25 per cent. Shocked, he decided not to take the drug. And soon enough, his symptoms were gone. The disease did not follow its predicted course, and it seems likely that the effect of what he learned contributed to the disappearance of his symptoms. Later on, he would suffer recurrences of the symptoms only when he was anxious or emotionally distressed in very particular situations, and so was able to take appropriate action with a weaker form of medication. Since the dramatic change in the pattern and severity of the symptoms would have involved immune mechanisms, we have a good example here of an interaction between mind and immunity without having to go as far as to posit that the patient was 'allergic to himself' in the sense of a concept or image of the self operating at a cellular level.

But the idea is still intriguing. Researchers have found almost adhesive links between a patient and someone close to them in several autoimmune cases. The French analyst Marie-Claire Célérier noted how illness frequently may follow a period when the person is confronted with their difference from this significant other, perhaps due to a conflict, a separation or some other event. She found a similar difficulty in separating in allergy cases. We can perhaps see an illustration of this in the response one dermatologist received when she suggested to a patient suffering from the autoimmune disorder lupus to embark on psychotherapy to deal with her anxiety and insomnia: 'I don't need to. My sister already sees a psychiatrist.' In other words, the identity between them was so strong that if one of them did it, the other didn't need to.

These themes of identity should certainly be explored in autoimmune disorders, even if we don't have to accept that cells use concepts like self and other. But it may well resonate with certain clinical details, such as the frequency with which autoimmune patients show up for hospital consultations *with someone else*, even if their physical condition does not require this. Or, to take another example, a curious association has been noticed between left-handedness and autoimmune problems. This is tentatively explained in terms of testosterone and other endocrine influences affecting brain development, handedness and immunologic development.

Yet why not look at the way that handedness may have a link to identificatory processes? These may be based on the visual relation to a human image. It is known, for instance, that babies imitate the facial expressions of those in front of them within two hours after birth. Similarly, as adults, we will blink or stutter more when faced with someone who blinks or stutters excessively. These examples show how we are captured in visual images in an unconscious way: we don't decide to blink or stutter more, we just do.

Psychoanalysts have studied in detail the way that infants are caught up in their own mirror image or the visual images of other people from the very start of life. If this is indeed the case, surely the question of handedness will, in some instances, be linked to the way that such identifications occur. If you identify with the person facing you in the sense of literally seeing them as a mirror image, your left will be their right, if they are right-handed. But if you identify with *the point from which* they are looking at you, left and right are preserved. The human dynamic of identification may be useful here to make sense of some of the many claims made about handedness. Sadly, those who work on these questions in medicine and psychology tend to be unaware of the research and the mathematical models developed by analysts.

Let's make one more point here about autoimmune disorders. In the previous chapter we saw the importance of processes of identification. If someone has identified at an unconscious level with someone else and feels hostility towards that person, what will happen next? Given the identification, it would seem logical that the hostility would be directed back towards themselves. Without having to hypothesize that cell attacks cell, there may well be other routes by which this perturbation of one's unconscious identity impacts on processes which, in turn, generate the downstream effect of the cellular recognition problems.

Work in psychoneuroimmunology has shown quite convincingly that psychological factors can affect immune function, our susceptibility to immunologically sensitive illnesses, the sustained response to such illnesses and the reactivation of latent infection. The studies of temporal rhythms and immunity indicate that the importance of basic forms of human interaction cannot be overestimated. We should remember here that the biological rhythms that are established for us in the early weeks and months of life take place within the context of a close relationship with another human being. To speak of sleep rhythms or feeding rhythms as if they were autonomous processes is to obscure their link with the role and impact of the caregiver.

How these will affect the intricate workings of the immune system is a rich and potentially revolutionary area of medical research. As psychological factors are taken into account rather than ignored, some of the mysteries of immune functioning may become clearer. What was once seen as a bodily system completely removed from the mind has now been persuasively shown to be linked to it through a number of pathways. Psychological factors have proved to be present where they were once least suspected. Might the same go for other processes and dysfunctions of the body? Could there be a psychological input, for example, in a disease like cancer, a set of illnesses that seem to continue their destructive course regardless of one's mental state?

12. Cancer

Cancer currently claims the life of one in four people in the developed world, and the World Health Organization predicts that this will rise to one in three by the year 2020. It is estimated that by this date one in two people in Britain will develop a form of this disease, the most common of which are currently breast, colon, lung and prostate cancer. Cases of lung cancer and malignant melanoma have been rising, due presumably to the smoking and holidaying habits of Western nations in the twentieth century. While these causal factors are by now well established, what about the role of psychological processes in the initiation or exacerbation of the disease?

This question never fails to incite the fiercest and most passionate debates. Hundreds of books and self-help manuals tell us how we can avoid cancer, not just by eating the right foods and exercising but by thinking positively and expressing our emotions. For those who suffer from the disease, a vast range of products are on sale that claim to affect its course, and many therapies are available that offer alternatives or complements to conventional medical treatment. Some of these are recommended by oncologists, while others are actively discouraged and dismissed as quackery.

Attitudes tend to fall along a spectrum here. At one end, those who insist that hope, faith, belief and fighting spirit can genuinely protect against cancer; at the other, those who see these psychological factors as desperate defences against the brute reality of cancerous growth. Terror at the threat of cancer, according to this view, spawns an appeal to anything that holds out the promise of a cure, or that at least provides an explanation for the dreadful biological lottery of disease. These extremes are more complex than they may first appear. Blind acceptance of biological reality, for example, could in some cases be the same thing as religious faith. There is a belief in a higher power to which we submit. Similarly, confidence in a self-help guru for one patient might be identical to confidence in a conventional doctor for another.

What these extremes have in common is a way of relating to the world. There's the idea of something beyond us which we have no power over: fate for one person, biology for another. In between are those who think that we can have an effect on what happens to us, and that we are perpetually engaged in the process of shaping our lives. Can we learn anything from cancer research about the consequences of these beliefs? Do they really have an effect on our health? Can the course of cancer be altered by our psychological state or even our attitude towards the disease? And could a cancer in some cases actually be initiated by our mental life?

In the history of medicine cancer has frequently been linked to mental states. In the second century, Galen observed that depressed women were more prone to cancer than cheerful ones, and several eighteenth- and nineteenth-century studies evoke long-term grief and depression as exacerbating factors. James Paget wrote in 1870 that 'the cases are so frequent in which deep anxiety, deferred hope, and disappointment are quickly followed by the growth and increase of cancer that we can hardly doubt that mental depression is a weighty additive to the other influences favouring the development of the cancerous constitution'. And Walter Walshe, in 1846, claimed that 'mental disquietude' was so clearly connected with some cases 'that I decided questioning its reality would have seemed a struggle against reason'.

By the mid 1950s, several research teams had tried to find evidence for this sort of anecdotal correlation. Were there links between psychological factors and cancer, and if so, what were the significant psychological states? The most common claims were about the life situation of those who would develop cancer and about their way of relating to others. Cancer sufferers were described as martyrs, eager to help others and unable to express hostile feelings. They had invested enormously in some role or relationship in life, and when this was removed or threatened, the risk of falling ill would increase dramatically. Breast cancer patients, according to many studies, were often incapable of the outward expression of anger, an 'inner turmoil' covered over by 'a facade of pleasantness'. It was observed how the people who seemed to do best were the more 'bizarre personalities', compared to the polite, acquiescent patients with rapidly progressing disease.

These early studies are rarely taken seriously today, due to their poor methodology and small patient samples. Yet the basic points have been reiterated again and again by later research. In one of the first large-scale studies, Caroline Thomas and Karen Duszynski at the Johns Hopkins School of Medicine assessed the health of 1,337 medical students, noting that the clearest psychological profiles were of those students who later developed cancer. The students they tracked from 1948 had all been in good health at the time of the initial assessment, and they were checked in 1972 for health problems. Although the researchers had not looked for correlations between cancer and emotional expressivity, the cancer sufferers, they argued, had as children experienced little closeness with their parents and were unable to display strong feelings.

These retrospective results were echoed in predictive studies. Several projects in the 1970s tried to use psychological testing on patients entering hospital clinics to see if biopsy results could be predicted in advance. A study by Horne and Picard in 1978 claimed that psychological risk factors were just as significant as a history of smoking to predict diagnosis. With a group of 130 subjects with chest pathology, psychological testing could correctly predict 80 per cent of those with benign disease and 61 per cent of those with cancer. Reviewing research, they found the most consistent result to be the loss of an important relationship, together with the inability to express emotions and a lack of closeness to parents.

In another sample of nearly 1,000 doctors, researchers at Johns Hopkins found that those who were emotionally inexpressive were sixteen times more likely to develop cancer than their peers. And in a number of well-known studies from King's College Hospital Medical School in London, Steven Greer and his colleagues have argued for correlations between emotional inexpressivity, in particular the over-control of hostile feelings, and survival time in breast cancer patients. Of 160 women interviewed prior to biopsy, extreme suppression of anger was significantly linked to cancer diagnosis, and, in patients over forty, suppression of other feelings was similarly linked. Again and again, such subjects are claimed to suppress awareness or expression of their own feelings in favour of service to others.

In one case, a terminally ill patient whose cancer had spread throughout his body insisted on eating shark cartilage every day, but not because he believed it would cure him. He hated the smell and the taste, yet explained that he still had to eat it. It turned out that this man had been the chief executive in a company that marketed shark cartilage as a treatment for cancer. Although he despised the product, he thought that his business partner would feel let down if he gave up the faith. Thus, even as his life drew to a close, his wish to keep other people happy took precedence over the rest of his well-being.

As research continued, two other factors began to take centre stage: depression and fighting spirit. A University of Illinois study, for example, tracked more than 2,000 middle-aged men, and found that those who were prone to depression were more likely to develop and die of cancer in a twenty-year period. In another detailed study, Brenda Penninx and her colleagues assessed depression levels for 4,825 people on three occasions at three-year intervals. While depression levels recorded at the final measurement did not predict cancer incidence, the 146 people who were depressed on all three occasions were significantly more likely to develop cancer. After carefully controlling for smoking habits – since it might seem obvious that depressed people will smoke more – they actually found that the chronically depressed non-smokers were more likely to develop cancer than the smokers.

The concept of fighting spirit has also been much discussed in psychologically minded cancer research. Greer found that patients with fighting spirit or denial were more likely to be alive and relapse-free five years after diagnosis with breast cancer than those patients who displayed helplessness or stoic acceptance. This is interesting as one might have expected denial to be a negative sign. Yet like fighting spirit, it is seen to indicate an active relation to illness in contrast to the passivity of stoic acceptance. Denial is supposed to involve an active rejection of any evidence about one's diagnosis, including the very facts of breast removal. As one patient put it, 'It wasn't serious, they just took off my breast as a precaution.'

In the Greer study, those patients in denial apparently showed no emotional distress. Fighting spirit, by contrast, involved an optimistic attitude and a greater search for information about breast cancer. 'I can fight it and defeat it,' were the words of another patient. In a further study, women with malignant melanoma with stoic acceptance and men with more feelings of helplessness and hopelessness had significantly worse disease progression at follow-up 18–20 months later. Study after study came up with similar findings, and it wasn't long before this convergence of features was moulded into a profile of the cancer-prone personality: the Type C.

The Type C personality has come to be associated with the following traits:

1) Stoicism, niceness, industriousness, perfectionism, sociability and conventionality.
2) Difficulty in expressing emotions.
3) An attitude of resignation or hopelessness/helplessness.

Unlike the Type As of cardiovascular research, discussed in Chapter 8, the Type Cs will fit in quite well, won't bother other people and generally won't cause any trouble. In fact, they'd make ideal patients. Type Cs, we learn, have the remarkable tendency to see the world as a benign and welcoming place. Unlike the hypertensive subjects who supposedly see other people as dangerous and untrustworthy, cancer-prone personalities are much less likely to make trouble, answer back or interpret social situations in a negative light. Even if they are depressed, they aren't depressed in the right way: something is blocking their registration of significant events and situations, so they are unable to take on board the core

of their depressed feelings. Would this also suggest that para-
noid people are less likely to get cancer?

Lydia Temoshok and her colleagues reported that Type C
features correlated with faster-growing tumours and poorer
lymphocyte response in some forms of cancer, and many
subsequent studies have made use of the Type C model. In
one project, women were interviewed prior to biopsy after
having found a suspect lump in their breast. Using the Type
C criteria as a guide, the researchers were able to predict
with 80 per cent accuracy which women would be found
on biopsy to have a malignant rather than a benign tumour.
A similar British project screened 2,000 women undergoing
breast examination with psychological tests, and found that
those who were deemed to hold in their emotions, and who
had experienced more difficult events in their lives over the
previous two years, were more likely to have cancer.

Things get very tricky here. No one seemed to mind
blaming Type As for their heart problems, and condemning
the ruthlessness, ambition and striving that seemed characteristic of that profile. Yet this was hardly the case for the
Type C. It seemed unacceptable even to suggest the faintest
idea of blame when it came to cancer. Yet curiously, in everyday life it is precisely the Type C traits that we are continually
encouraged to correct in ourselves, our friends and our
acquaintances: 'Be more assertive!', 'Don't let people walk all
over you!', 'Don't suppress your feelings!' have all become
cultural imperatives.

So is being a Type C a health risk? Can the personality profile
really tell us much about susceptibility to a particular disease?
Listing personality types is open to much criticism. Like hand-
writing styles, different groupings can certainly be made, but
do they really map so neatly on to different illnesses or groups

of illness? In the heyday of personality theories in the 1950s, one patient with ulcerative colitis even complained to his physician that, according to the current profile research, he ought to have peptic ulcer instead. Where features like conformity and self-control were once associated with rheumatoid arthritis, they would also become linked to patients with hypertension, osteoarthritis, Parkinson's and multiple sclerosis. Did all these illnesses share some common personality structure, or was the search for specificity just an illusion? How could personality be classified? And what made the observers' classificatory labels so reliable?

Interminable disagreement has stalked rival personality theories since their inception. While many of the early psychosomatic researchers began with personality models only to move away from them in later work, today's studies seem to have gone full circle and many now embrace the concept of personality type once again. The other major difficulty here is that even if such studies come up with factors like depression, resignation, lack of closeness and emotional inexpressivity, these cannot be correlated with a single disease. Plenty of depressed or emotionally inexpressive people don't get cancer, and simplistic correlations of character traits and illnesses cannot really provide an exhaustive explanation for falling ill. Too many counter-examples belie this quest for one-to-one correlations.

The other important point to be made is that if a personality profile indicates you are cancer-prone, which cancer are you supposed to get? The word cancer evokes a single, monolithic entity, yet it comes in quite a number of different forms. According to some classifications, there are more than 150 varieties. Although we often associate it with the uncontrolled growth of cells, and exposure to carcinogens such as asbestos, UV rays or nicotine, what is less well known is that about 15 per cent of cancer cases result from infections. Cervical cancer, for example, may be initiated by the human papilloma virus. Likewise, some forms of cancer – such as certain types of breast cancer – are much more hormone sensitive than others, and so the question of the role of the endocrine system becomes particularly important.

Scepticism about personality types and also about single factors like depression or emotional inexpressivity does not mean that the search for links between mental states and cancer must be abandoned. On the contrary, the more that is known about cancer, the more these seem pertinent, but not in the simplistic sense of one-to-one correlations. How a tumour develops and how a human being resists tumour growth involve several processes that clearly have some links with our psychology. The aggressiveness of a tumour is partly determined by the tissue affected, the robustness of a cell-destroying mechanism called apoptosis, DNA repair mechanisms and the tumour's ability to divert blood supply. The resistance of the host will involve immune competence and the functioning of the endocrine system. All of these factors can be affected by one's mental states. This does not mean that certain mental states will lead inevitably to cancer, and we should remember here that the psychosomatic approach just means an openness to including psychological factors in an understanding of how disease has emerged in the life of an individual.

The body has several lines of defence against the growth of cancerous cells, and immune functioning has been much studied by those exploring the influence of psychological and social factors. Animal experiments here greatly out-number studies of humans, and some of the results have been suggestive. Animals injected first with 'killed' tumour cells and then with viable tumour cells tend not to grow any

tumours, while these will grow in the non-immunized creatures. Such inoculation shows the role of the adaptive immune
system in the prevention of at least some forms of cancer.
As for innate immunity, a massive amount of research has
been done on how natural killer (NK) cells involved in the
immune system's surveillance of new tumours are affected
during troubled periods in life. An NK cell's ability to kill
– its cytotoxicity – is reduced during times of mental upheaval
or intense pressure. Medical students about to take exams,
lonely young people and isolated carers with little social
support have all been found to have poorer NK-cell functioning than others.

There are also other mechanisms at play in defending
against cancer which can be affected by psychological forces.
In one experiment, X-rays were fired through blood samples
taken from a group of depressed subjects and a control group.
It was found that the blood of the depressed subjects had a
reduced capacity for the repair of cellular DNA. Likewise,
there is evidence that in times of personal difficulty cells may
be less successful at apoptosis, the process of programmed cell
destruction triggered by certain kinds of cellular damage. It
was found that this process was less likely to be taking place
in blood taken from medical students during exam periods.
In an animal experiment, it was found that methyltransferase,
an enzyme which responds to carcinogen damage to DNA,
was much lower in the lymphocytes within the spleens of
stressed animals compared to their less stressed controls.

Do such studies provide sufficient evidence to implicate
psychological factors in the inception of cancer? Things are
far less clear than some researchers once believed them to
be. Immune-suppressed patients, such as those afflicted with
AIDS, do not necessarily get cancer, but when they do, it
will generally be one of the virally induced varieties. This

supports the idea that for these factors to operate via reduced immune effectiveness, the viral cancers would be the most prevalent. But now recent research has suggested another scenario relevant to many more types of cancer.

The major factor here, once again, is inflammation, which has been found to play a vital role in many forms of tumour growth. Sites of chronic inflammation provide the ideal conditions for tumours to grow. This link may seem surprising, as we often associate cancer with genetic mutation caused by radiation or chemical pollution. But inflammation is crucial. Asbestosis and chronic bronchitis may lead to lung cancer, inflammatory bowel disease may lead to colon cancer, inflammation from *Helicobacter pylori* infection may lead to stomach cancer and sun-damaged skin inflammation may lead to melanoma. Even in the case of hormonally influenced cancers, mastitis increases the risk of breast cancer, and inflammation of the prostate gland makes prostate cancer more likely.

A good way to understand the mechanisms involved is through the so-called scar cancers, which develop from scar tissue that never heals. Cancers, indeed, have been described generally as 'wounds that do not heal'. For healing of a wound to occur, cell proliferation needs to be encouraged to form new tissue, and cell-mediated immunity and apoptosis must be suppressed to protect this tissue. New blood vessels must be formed to provide nutrients such as glucose. But if the wound fails to heal, inflammatory conditions will prevail, causing damage to the DNA of nearby cells. In this kind of situation, the last thing you want is for humoral immunity to be dominant in the locality, when it is cell-mediated immunity which has the capacity to kill off the body's own damaged cells. All the conditions would then be right for tumour formation.

It now seems that this scenario is common to many kinds of cancer formation. Typically, it's not just through the mutation of a single gene that a cell turns malignant. Chronic inflammation produces the conditions for significant damage to many of the genes belonging to nearby cells. Understandably this is bad news. First, DNA repair and cell-destroying apoptosis are inhibited. Then, as the tumour develops, it gains a stronger grip on the way the immune system behaves in its vicinity, fixing things so that the humoral wing dominates locally, and diverting the blood supply to feed itself. The big question then is whether the brain could have any input in this process.

If we consider the model of cancer as a non-healing wound, findings that psychological difficulties impact on the speed with which a wound will heal may prove to be very significant. In one experiment, holes were punched in the roof of the mouths of a group of dental students, once during a vacation period and once just before exam time. A wound in the same individual took an average 40 per cent longer to heal at around exam time. If this exam-time stress can have such an effect on wound healing, imagine the effects of long-term chronic human misery. As the Canadian doctor Gabor Mate pointed out, some people spend their whole lives as if under the gaze of a powerful and judgemental examiner, whom they must please at all costs.

Animal experiments have suggested that even short-term 'stressors' can make a difference here. Mice showed a poorer ability to rid themselves of sarcomas produced by the injection of a virulent virus after a cruel series of electric shocks. Where in 80 per cent of mice their immune system normally cleared the resulting growth, applying electric shocks to them for three days before injection significantly reduced this success rate, while shocking them afterwards increased it. This might suggest that disturbance of the immune system at a vital moment may have profound effects on the course of a cancer.

How relevant is this to spontaneous cancer formation in humans? We have seen in Chapter 11 how psychological troubles can affect HPA-axis activity and disturb circadian rhythms, resulting in a blunting of cell-mediated immunity in favour of increased humoral immunity. If someone suffering in this way is not made more likely to get cancer, at the very least we can say that the conditions in the body standing in the way of cancer have been compromised. If the danger here is that the immune system gets locked locally into the less effective kind of immune response, we might expect that those more resilient to the disease will have a steadier oscillation between the two poles of immune functioning. By the time that cancers like breast, ovarian, prostate, stomach and colon have developed, the rhythm of immune functioning has been disturbed, with a flattening of the daily variation in neuroendocrine activity. But much of the research we have mentioned indicates that these perturbations may facilitate the emergence of the disease in the first place.

Some studies have suggested that the stress hormone cortisol may encourage cancer growth, allowing tumour cells to better extract glucose from the blood by inhibiting its uptake in neighbouring cells. This mechanism suggests further potential ways for the mind to influence cancer growth through the control of blood flow. We can be aware of blood flow changing at moments like blushing, yet some of these changes can actually be brought under voluntary control. A rabbit was taught by a method known as biofeedback to control blood flow locally to one ear to such an extent that it appeared that the single ear was blushing. This kind of control may have a certain relevance to the question of blood flow to tumour sites in cancer. Although there may be nothing voluntary about it, there is the possibility that psychical registration of the body's pathways may, in some cases, have some effect on local activity there. When we read about a seven-year-old girl who developed a tumour in the eye with which she had regularly watched her mother's adultery through a keyhole since she was five, such questions of localization seem especially pertinent.

The role of the so-called stress hormones like cortisol and adrenaline is being closely studied here. We have seen how these may encourage disturbances to the immune system, and this may in turn weaken resistance to cancer progression. Besides cortisol, a product of the adrenal gland known as DHEA has been shown to be associated with breast cancer. High DHEA levels were found in one study to be predictive of the incidence of breast cancer in women who had donated blood to a blood bank nine years earlier. Since DHEA is linked to the activity of the HPA axis, it could well be affected by psychological variables. The difficulty in processing mental experience will result in raised levels of certain hormones and a greater likelihood of disturbances to immune functioning.

There are clearly suggestive links between psychological factors and the body's resistance to cancer, through both the immune and the endocrine systems. Yet the methods of exploring these factors have descended from the earlier work of the psychosomaticists into a reliance on oversimplistic models of personality, and the assumption that any relevant variables will be susceptible to measurement. Yet if we agree, for example, with the King's College studies that point to the importance of 'fighting spirit', how can this be theorized, let alone quantified? Could such a concept really be taken seriously in a medical landscape which focuses on intricate phsysiological processes like immunity?

The medical anthropologist Arthur Kleinman has observed that whereas every other medical system in the world has some notion of 'life force' or 'energy' or 'will', modern Western medicine is distinguished by its failure to acknowledge these. Hence what sense could most Western oncologists make of references to 'fighting spirit', aside from scoffing at it? Western medicine, indeed, relies on the exclusion of such concepts and, in particular, the ones that so obviously can't be measured. But aren't both doctors and patients losing out here? If everyone agrees that there is such a thing as life, surely there is also such a thing as *a relation to life*? When this is positive, isn't it what we call fighting spirit?

Despite its apparent simplicity, fighting spirit is a complicated idea. Discussing themes in the mother–child relation, Joyce McDougall offered an interesting interpretation of the state, often observed, in which it seems as if an unwell person has just given up. She pointed out that giving up may also be experienced as a giving in, the attitude of abandoning one's defences against the unconscious image of an invading, controlling and colonizing force, identified with the mother. Rather than fighting back and resisting, as many children do when they feel threatened, there is a giving in which submerges the person in the mother's world, as if controlled by her. McDougall thought that this may be either due to love for the mother, or sheer exhaustion. But the giving up could only be understood in relation to someone else.

If Joyce McDougall is right in her suggestion that giving up is about *giving in to*, it would suggest that fighting spirit is tied up with our mental representation of another human being (for McDougall, the mother) or some aspect of them. This implies that our most basic, vital position is linked to *how we feel others relate to us*. Do they value us? Do they want to swallow us up? Do they want to deny our existence? These questions might seem strange, but they are part and parcel of our childhood world, as we saw in Chapter 9. Is it an accident, then, how often patients in a hospital setting will develop ideas that they are being persecuted by staff, especially in post-operative situations? Here there really will be the question 'How is my existence registered?', which will inevitably stir up and exacerbate the anxieties of our childhood.

When descriptions of the disease process in cancer rely on an 'us' and 'them' terminology, it perpetuates this kind of situation. On one side are the factors that determine and influence the growth of a tumour, such as the type of tissue affected, the DNA repair mechanisms and the diverting of local blood supply. On the other are the factors linked to the resistance of the host, which are primarily immunological and endocrinological. It is significant how this implicit differentiation is often framed: tumour and host are kept separate, a splitting that mirrors the way that cancer is conceived culturally as an enemy that invades our personal space and must be battled and conquered.

These images and personifications of disease are likely not only to reflect but to reinforce sets of psychological tensions. We could think here of a note that Gene Wilder found after his wife Gilda Radner's death from ovarian cancer. Entitled 'Right-Hand Questions, Left-Hand Answers', the questions were written with Radner's right hand, the answers with her left. On the right, there was the question 'Is cancer your mother inside you?', and on the left the answer 'She doesn't want me to exist'. Now, without having to suppose that these thoughts led to her cancer, we could still ask how this way of personifying the disease may influence its course or the way help is sought or followed. It shows how a disease may be felt as an external agency, one linked to the presence of another human being whose own subjectivity is crucial ('She doesn't want me to exist').

The fury patients often feel towards a diseased part of their body could then be linked to the fury they feel towards another person. There is little doubt that cases we encounter in psychoanalytic practice sometimes bear this out: as analysis deepens, the hatred is shifted away from the body to another source, such as a parent. Cancer may be experienced by some sufferers not just as a surrender or giving up, but as a surrender to another person's will. This will not necessarily be a conscious thought process, and it might seem logical to encourage a patient to try to bring such ideas to the surface and elaborate them. If we believe those studies that claim that many cancer sufferers put others before themselves, this will clearly not be easy. This frequently mentioned trait of service to others may have little to do with the inception of cancer, but once cancer has been diagnosed, could a personification of the disease process then produce an attitude of giving in, as if it were a sacrifice to someone else? It is of course also possible that the mechanisms which block the person from following their own desires – as opposed to those of others – will be the same mechanisms that prevent such material from being questioned and explored. Couldn't this give us a clue to the question of religious faith, fate and destiny that researchers have noted in their observations of cancer patients?

To elaborate the concept of fighting spirit, rather than trying to measure it, it would seem logical to study the relational dynamics we have discussed. Instead of just trying to assess the fighting spirit of the patient, it would become crucial to learn something about the fighting spirit of the patient's former or present caregivers and *how this has been perceived*. It might then be possible to explore the question of how the patient senses that they were wanted or not wanted by other people – and this, as we have seen, leads into much of the research on health and links to society where there is the question of how one's existence is registered. We should remember here that our entry into the world is marked by the value accorded to us by our mothers from birth: how they transmitted to us the message 'Live!'

This would also allow a new way of understanding the many references to lack of closeness to parents in the medical literature on cancer. We may learn that certain patients lacked a sense of closeness to their parents, but what about whether their parents felt a sense of closeness towards them? The relational factor could be included here to open up the bigger picture and to introduce the many subtle questions of how the relation of human beings to each other – and how these are interpreted unconsciously – may have an effect on health.

The fact that fighting also implies that one is fighting against something helps to explain why so many people personify their disease, seeing it as a sort of witch or invasive demon that they must do battle against. Although this may have absolutely nothing to do with the inception of a cancerous process, there is no reason why it won't come to overlie it, and this is often encouraged by the media and our culture generally. There is indeed a continuity, at times, between the way a patient imagines the disease and the way they respond to medical staff, with both perceived as malign persecutors. When we ask the question why people get ill, this aspect of human experience has to be taken into account: not just how we relate to others, but how we have internalized the way others have related to us, or, more precisely, our interpretation of this. The ways we imagine our existence is registered by others will be crucial to our physical health. Yet most of the time, we will be unaware of this at a conscious level.

Losing sight of these ideas means that studies of the impact of psychological factors in cancer will simply generate personality-type models which obscure much more than they illuminate. What gets neglected here is the unconscious relational life of the patient, and, as we will see in the next chapter, the more general issue of symbolization and how we register experience. The question of the mind and cancer shouldn't receive an either/or answer. Instead, research should be open to the possible contribution of psychological factors and alert to the drawbacks of personality-type models and confused talk of emotion. If emotional expressivity is in any way relevant here, it is not so much to do with candour and disclosure than with the basic mechanisms of how we process our experience.

13. Health Risks of being Normal

How will our way of expressing ourselves affect our bodies? Study after study tells us that how we articulate our anger, distress or sadness will predict which illnesses we are most likely to get. Suppress your rage and up go the chances of arthritic disease, let it all out and risk heart problems. Although research work has become more sophisticated than such thumbnail correlations, there is still an emphasis on our personal styles of expressivity.

The eagerness to find emotions behind illnesses has often led researchers to suppose that feelings are unequivocal and transparent. Fear, rage and anger could supposedly be differentiated so neatly that experiments could match each emotion with a specific physiological state: rage could be produced when a subject's hand was suddenly immersed in a bucket of ice-cold water, anger when they were insulted, and fear by applying a mild electric shock. Such experiments involve the belief that a specific feeling can be elicited by a specific stimulus. Life is reduced to a sort of mechanical process in which the stimuli we receive will have well-defined emotional responses.

But are feelings really so clear-cut and neatly distinguishable? Everyday experience surely indicates that we are often confused about *our own* emotional states. We might oscillate between widely disparate poles of positive and negative feeling, or be prey to a whole mix of emotions. If we sense hostility towards someone we love, we might try to avoid this feeling, generating a strange state in which tenderness and resentment jostle with each other. Our failure to understand our own moods and feelings has in fact generated a whole industry of advice. Media articles and TV programmes often instruct us to interpret our feelings as consequences of foods we have eaten or neglected to eat, exercise we have taken or neglected to take, or other factors that have little to do with unconscious mental life.

Yet feelings are complex and their genesis usually needs to be studied carefully. If we are depressed or anxious one afternoon, we might review the events of the day for a clue to explain why we feel this way. We might hit upon some incident at work or just the vague idea that we are under a lot of stress. Finding a concrete cause might make us feel a bit better. But what if this is a mere smokescreen? Closer exploration might reveal that the feelings began not long after a phone call in the morning from a parent or sibling. We block out the disturbing aspect of the contact because we don't want to know anything about it. Instead, we have the depressive or anxious mood. And then we search for an alibi. Moods, in fact, often take the place of memories and connections between ideas that we cannot access.

The writer Rebecca West would be overcome by an inexplicable feeling of sadness whenever she saw the profile of a mountain range on the horizon. It was during her analysis that she suddenly realized that this matched exactly the form of the graphs showing the rise and fall of copper share prices that her father would anxiously scrutinize every morning at breakfast when she was a child. The feeling she experienced consciously was thus determined by forgotten memories and the emotions that had been linked to them. Since finding these connections is generally the result of lengthy analysis, it is highly improbable that they will just pop up to please the researcher conducting psychological experiments in the lab.

The words the patient uses will be vitally important here. They matter not because they designate some universally knowable and shared mental state, but because they will resonate with aspects of their life and history. If the patient says 'I felt let down', this might echo how their mother or father once described some situation they were involved in themselves. The quality and the intensity of the patient's emotional state may be determined largely by such unconscious connections. Words aren't simply conduits to emotional states, but are linked *in networks* to other words, images and attachments, as the story of Rebecca West shows. What we feel at a conscious level may often be the result of links being made in the *unconscious networks* which connect words and feelings with the past.

Several of the cancer studies we looked at in the previous chapter tried to distinguish emotions from the *suppression* of emotions. This is echoed in the popular idea that there will be consequences if you bottle things up. Suppressed emotions are generally equated with negative ones, and they have been linked to just about every disorder the body is capable of, from cancer to heart disease to arthritis. One review of research claimed that bottling up was responsible for a greater 'all cause' mortality than any other factor. But what is it that matters here? Is it the actual valence of the emotion or how it is expressed?

Emotions and the expression of emotions cannot really be distinguished so easily. Emotions involve patterns of communicative display, and so link us to other people. When we learn to smile or frown as infants, our physical expressions are given a meaning and responded to by our caregivers. If someone shows no emotion, does this mean that they are detached from any kind of social link to others? Or could it be that the expected emotion is absent because there has been some problem in registering the situation which that person is in? For an event to matter, after all, it needs to be understood as meaningful. A painful separation, for example, must be recognized as a painful separation, which implies that we have a mental idea of both what separation consists of and the value to us of the person whom we have lost. To speak about a loss, it must be registered as the loss *of something*. In other words, it means that we have *symbolized* our situation.

This might sound obvious, but symbolization should never be taken for granted. We do not always know what we have lost, and it is often unclear what it was that someone we have lost represented for us. A separation or a death might appear to be met with no emotional reaction, yet almost immediately afterwards there may be intense feelings of love or hatred towards someone new: a friend, a lover or a work colleague. These apparently fresh attachments may represent displacements of the feelings directed to the one who has been lost, yet they won't have been experienced consciously. Registering a loss, likewise, requires some system of inscription, whether it is a gravestone in a cemetery or the words of human speech. Many workers in psychosomatic medicine have been struck by how some patients seem completely unable to speak about their losses. They describe their lives as if nothing significant has happened, remarking blankly that someone has departed or died, before changing the subject. No emotion will register.

Is the person just too shocked to speak? Or, could it be that the impact of the loss, conspicuously absent at the level of ordinary language, has been situated *somewhere else*? Could it be that it has been recorded in the body? Or in a memory system inaccessible to conscious or unconscious thought? There seems to be a kind of deficit here: a complete lack of response at exactly those moments in life when we would expect the most powerful reactions. And this is one of the features that investigators have always been amazed at: the way that some physically ill people seem unable to access their emotional life.

There is a danger here of imposing normative views of how human beings should feel: people are supposed to react in set ways, and if they don't, there must be something wrong with them. We've already seen how generations of psychosomatic researchers would come up with strangely similar profiles of their patients: the arthritis sufferer who couldn't express their emotions, the cancer-prone subject who never articulated their anger, or the multiple sclerosis patient who was so incredibly nice. These resemblances worked against the thesis of any kind of specificity, and it seemed as if each time a character type was proposed for one illness, the same personality could be found in another. The features proposed for rheumatoid arthritis, for example, turned out to be more or less the same as those for hypertension, osteoarthritis, Parkinson's and multiple sclerosis.

In the 1960s this apparent problem became a solution. Perhaps those people who were cut off from their feelings were simply those more likely to fall ill – not from any one particular illness, but from illness in general. Pierre Marty and Michel de M'Uzan in Paris developed the concept of *operative thinking*. Operative thinkers were brilliant at the operations of everyday life: they could function better than most of us precisely because they were so cut off from their feelings and fantasy life. In fact, these people were perfectly normal. They were so normal that they became 'hyper-normal', extremely well adapted to any situation. Whatever happened, they would pull their socks up and get on with things. The only problem was that these people were also the most likely to become seriously ill at the organic level.

These descriptions struck a chord with clinicians in many countries. They were familiar with patients suffering from somatic illness who, if you asked them what their parents were like, would answer with the most minimal facts, as if these reductive and formulaic replies were an adequate response. No more information, they assumed, was required. When Joyce McDougall asked a patient what his mother was like, he replied, 'She's tall and blonde.' To her question 'What was your reaction when you learned of the death of your parents and your fiancé in a car crash?', another subject replied, 'Well, I thought I'd have to pull myself together.' When a patient was asked, 'Were you upset when you ran over this woman with the baby?', the reply was, 'Oh, I was insured against third-party accident.' In each of these three cases, the patient was being questioned about circumstances which seemed to be closely associated with the onset of their somatic illness. And yet it was *as if nothing had happened.* All emotional reaction had been drained away. No links were made between the violent events and the emergence of illness.

Where the interviewer expected detailed answers to her questions, there was just a void. McDougall noted the 'psychotic resonance' of these patients' use of language, marked by a particular detachment and lack of emotion. The subjects she described were all closely attached to facts and things in external reality. This sort of pseudo-normality was, for McDougall, a danger sign: 'Individuals who use such escape devices to an exaggerated degree tend to give an appearance of normality in that they are symptom-free [in the sense of neurotic symptoms] and often, because of the stifling of affect, appear able to cope with adversity in all circumstances.'

McDougall's observation is immediately interesting from many points of view. To start with, it complicates a very common take on the mind-body problem. For years, clinicians hostile to psychological approaches to organic illness would point to the good mental health and well-adapted nature of their patients. When Alexander argued that psychological conflict had a bearing on diseases like ulcerative colitis, critics cited the lack of neurotic symptoms like compulsions or anxiety states in patients with ulcerative colitis. This proved, they claimed, that it couldn't be based on unconscious dynamics like conflict or guilt. But according to the new theories of operative thinking, *it was precisely good adaptation that signalled the possibility of a mental route to a somatic problem*. Distressing emotional states would not be suppressed, to produce neurotic symptoms, but literally abolished, as if they had no existence. They would bypass thinking processes to go directly into the body.

Ask an operative thinker if anything untoward or disturbing had happened recently and they would say 'No'. Ask if anything had been bothering them and they would say 'No'. And if they said 'Yes', they would use 'pre-packaged' language, adapted perfectly to the expectations of an interlocutor. If they expect that the person interviewing them will be interested in terms like trauma or stress, they may then use these terms with great fluency. Inversely, this would explain the apparent paradox that, in some cases, *the presence of neurotic symptoms has been associated with a lower risk of certain somatic diseases*. Neurotic symptoms often involve disturbing thoughts that invade a person's life. But here the disturbing thoughts have been completely eradicated.

This brings us to a crucial point: there are different ways of pushing things out of the mind. It might seem complicated enough to suggest that most of our mental life isn't conducted at a conscious level, but beyond the basic distinction between conscious and unconscious, there may also be *other levels of psychical functioning*. In fact, many of the theorists we have discussed ended up with some version of this view. Repression was the mechanism that acted on thoughts and ideas, barring them from consciousness. Sexual or hostile currents of our mental life would be deemed too disturbing for us to deal with, and so rendered unconscious. They might then reappear in slips of the tongue, dreams and some forms of symptom. But it seemed that there were also even more powerful forms of defence. An idea could be repressed, but it could also be abolished as if it had never existed.

This would mean that the usual means of accessing repressed material wouldn't work. The psychoanalyst's traditional interpretations would be useless, and all the careful probing and exploration of a patient's history would fail to release repressed material. Instead, this material could return in another form, such as a hallucination or, indeed, a physical symptom. The fact that these phenomena so often seemed completely alien to the patient, imposed on them from the outside, indicated how powerful the defence mechanisms were: they had succeeded in distancing the material so far from the patient's mind that it appeared to be entirely cut off from their subjectivity.

The unconscious was made up of repressed material. But what about the material that had been pushed even deeper? Where was it registered? Could physiological patterns of response provide an answer here? An emotional reaction would not be registered in the unconscious but pass directly into the physical body. This explained, according to these theorists, why attempts to find unconscious conflicts and fantasies in many physically unwell people had been relatively fruitless: it wasn't the unconscious that mattered here, but precisely the failure to register an experience, a conflict or a separation *in the unconscious*. Those researchers who had been exploring the patient's unconscious mental life had been looking in the wrong place.

Marty's concept of operative thinking was given a new gloss in America with the concept of *alexithymia* – derived from the Greek *a* (without), *lexis* (speech) and *thymos* (emotion). This was introduced by the Boston analysts John Nemiah and Peter Sifneos in the early 1970s to designate the difficulty many physically unwell people had in accessing and describing their feelings or fantasy life. Their communicative style was notable for its flatness and limitation, and they seemed unable to articulate their feelings. Their cognitive style was 'stimulus-based' and externally oriented, and they had a limited capacity for imagination and fantasy. As Graeme Taylor says, 'They follow a robotlike existence, going through life in a mechanical way, almost as if following an instruction manual.'

The psychoanalyst Rosine Debray had noted many of these features in her work with diabetic patients. Despite the fact that the disease would begin not long after important events like separation, loss of a loved one or some other life change, no connection would be made between them. Instead, this coalescence of dates would be described as a coincidence, and emotional life would be described in a flat, detached manner. In one case, a man developed diabetes simultaneously with the birth of his second child. He had not wanted his wife to have the baby, yet saw no significance in the fact that his first hypoglycaemic episode took place at the exact moment of the birth.

Several studies that have bought into the concept of alexithymia claim that it is correlated with high levels of bodily symptoms, especially following difficult experiences. Although those who coined the term do not believe that there is any simple one-to-one correspondence between alexithymia and somatic illness, it has been associated with cases of ulcerative colitis, peptic ulcer, asthma, skin disorders and heart disease. Other studies question the link, and there is some disagreement about assessment methods. This is further complicated by the fact that an alexithymic subject may respond in exactly the ways expected, showing great adaptation to reality, which may include the 'reality' of assessment methods.

Whatever we make of this, an important question here is whether to see alexithymia as a defence mechanism or as a basic deficit. Where most of the American and some of the French researchers understand it as a sort of biological deficit, something missing in the brain, McDougall sees it as a very primitive defence mechanism, in which traumatic events cause pain that is too disturbing for the person to bear. Getting rid of such feelings would be a desperate way of avoiding an unspeakable pain. Alexithymia would not be a pre-ordained biological fault, but a mechanism introduced as a last resort – the most extreme escape route possible.

What would allow such a mechanism to operate? Psychoanalysts had long observed that for a child to begin separating from its mother, it needs to develop fantasy activity during her absence. This could involve such basic games as throwing an object and then pulling it back, or any play involving making something absent and then present again. Such processes allow a representation of the mother's absence, which can then be elaborated and woven into our unconscious mental life. Although several different ways of theorizing these activities have been proposed, there is a general agreement that processes of thinking and representation are developed around the experience of absence and frustration. It's the space left by the absent mother (or part of her) that will form an important platform for these processes to get going.

But what would happen if the infant had a problem in accessing this empty space? The mother, in some cases, might inadvertently prevent her child from thinking by refusing to let anything take her place. She might not want the baby to do without her, and even block the child's vital search for substitutes: toys, bits of cloth or any object that could start to replace or represent her. There would be no possibility for play and the fantasy activity linked to it, and so no sense of developing a space built up around her absence. The mother here might offer herself as the sole and unique object of satisfaction for the child, as if nothing else could even be thinkable. Developing these ideas from the French analyst Michel Fain, McDougall found that such factors were quite common in the background of her patients suffering from somatic illnesses.

In these situations, the child sometimes makes the decision to dissociate from the mother, as if her mental state did not and could not exist. She becomes a distant, external figure, more like a biological organism than a human being. Hence, later in life she can be described completely flatly, with no feeling. The mother won't necessarily fit the picture we have described above, as she might be all too ready to allow the child to live without her. She may be deeply depressed or absent in other ways, so that engaging with her becomes too much for the child, who is forced to make a kind of 'all or nothing' choice to block out not only her mental state but the very idea that she – and other people – could have a mental state. If this choice has been made, there may be an astonishing inability to be aware of the fact that other people have feelings.

We often find an accompanying phenomenon here: a particular passion for *sensations*, be they materials, colours or any other sensory detail, even a tone of voice. It is as if these detached sensory fragments have gone into the place of the missing interpersonal dimension linking child and mother. The child fixes on these details, as if the sensory feelings generated by a material substance or visual or kinaesthetic object can act as a point of reference or anchor. This may follow from either the excessive absence or excessive presence of the mother and the infant's desperate decision to do without other people's mental states. The person will spend their time glued to this one particular sensory dimension and the objects that are associated with it.

French researchers have developed the idea here of what they call 'essential depression', a very primitive state in which the link to life seems to be given up. There is no hope of response and no hope of moving forward. Every pathway seems blocked, and the person gives up. This is different from more conventional models of depression. According to the psychoanalyst Gérard Szwec, a classical depression might involve representations of the loss of someone important to us, but an essential depression involves not the representation of loss but the loss of representation. There might be a rejection of the very idea of a representation of the mother, for example. In a case discussed by Szwec, a boy developed eczema at exactly the moments when he was about to see his mother. Unable to think about her, he responded directly in the body, as if thought and the process of representation had been short-circuited.

Other analysts have argued that the lack of response from the mother or her excessive attention to bodily care of the child may produce a defence whereby perception of external reality takes the place of affective relations. If everything is about bodily care, what place is there for the child's feelings and desires? And what can the child learn about what might be missing from the mother's world? Without that, won't she remain in the position of an all-powerful and hence menacing presence? It is always a crucial moment when a child realizes that, although the mother is in charge, she doesn't have everything: she is herself lacking something.

In some of the situations we are discussing, it is as if the mother has failed to transmit any idea of this lack to her child. The overinvestment in perceptions and sensations by the child can then be understood as a defence against the feelings of unbearable proximity to or distance from the mother. Real bodily sensations will take the place of internal feelings. Hence such children may have no stranger anxiety. When they encounter someone new, they will behave as if that person has the same status as everyone else. Adaptation to reality here is less a developmental success than a desperate defensive measure. Reality can be brilliantly dealt with since it has been disconnected from any emotional life.

A 52-year-old man described his childhood as happy and uneventful. Nothing had really happened, they had stayed in the same house, and schooling and social life had just been 'normal'. His parents were depicted as nondescript figures, leaving for work and then returning with regularity, preparing meals and watching TV. He had two younger sisters, both of whom were described as pleasant, and no conflict or tension was reported. Detailed questioning at first revealed no real inconsistency in his account, as if he had grown up, in a sense, without a history. He had only made his appointment to see the therapist on the urgings of his wife, who was worried about his growing reliance on sleeping pills, a dependency that had now become quite dangerous.

It turned out that his history had been, in fact, more complicated. Completely absent from his initial narrative was the fact that, during her pregnancy with him, his mother had been hospitalized with an infection. The doctors had been very worried about her, and had told her there was a risk that the baby would not survive. Although she responded well to medication and the birth was unproblematic, she had become convinced, after the doctors' prognosis, that the child would be born dead, something that had actually occurred in her own family history: her mother had delivered a still-born child some years before her birth.

When she gave birth to a healthy baby, the patient's mother behaved as if he had in fact been born dead. Unable to engage with him, she sank into a deep depression and with-drew from family life. She would hardly speak to him and serviced his needs coldly and mechanically. The patient was left to grow up more or less on his own, and he described his interest in certain shapes and sensations, such as the feeling of a cold metal spoon being put into his mouth and the way that high-contrast lines could be made to form grids and patterns. These memories took the place of those involving interactions between members of his family, as if the interpersonal dimension had been emptied out. The sensations and patterns were still described dispassionately, as if they were details in the life of someone else. They emerged in the therapy sessions only after repeated questioning about specific aspects of his early years.

When the patient eventually began work, it was in the field of graphics, and the grids and patterns that he had been so captivated by as a child now became a feature of his design projects. As for the sensation of cold metal, this also left its traces in his life. Sometimes, he would press a metal object like a steel business-card case against his wife's naked body and ask her to do the same to him. Yet these practices produced no real associations for him. They were not linked to any other memories of situations or feelings, as if they had been cut off from the rest of his mental life. The rhythm of life he had maintained over decades had only been upset, it seemed, when he had been forced to stop work due to the closure of his company. Unable to find another design job at his age, he had started to blank out his days and nights with sleeping pills.

On paper, his life until then had been a healthy one. No real frictions or fallings-out with other people, diligent at work and no great traumas or turbulence. Yet his distanced, uninvolved relation with the world around him and his view of people as little more than animate bodies suggested that his early years had involved a decision on his part to cut himself off. Rather than try to enter into some sort of relation with his severely depressed mother, he had separated himself, focusing instead on certain isolated sensations, like the feel of metal, or the sight of the grids and patterns. When he was no longer able to elaborate this latter thread through his work, rather than becoming anxious, depressed or angry, he simply responded in his body, using the sleeping pills to obliterate his physical feelings.

This would be one example of the way in which the experience of loss is not processed and thought about but passes into the body. Instead of forming neurotic symptoms, the subject develops either somatic illness or, in other cases, a reliance on some substance that changes bodily sensation. McDougall argues that ideas and feelings are not repressed or reacted against here but 'foreclosed' from the psyche. They are 'thrown out of the psyche, to be discharged instead through the body and its somatic functioning'. 'Foreclosure' refers to a defence mechanism more extreme than repression, literally abolishing some element from the psyche. Having no inscription in the unconscious, it may return as a hallucination, or, as McDougall argues, as a somatic symptom. We could think here of the diabetic patient we discussed whose hypoglycaemic episode coincided with the birth of his daughter. Troubling perceptions are denied meaning and psychic existence. And so they cannot be thought about and elaborated in verbal chains.

One implication of this idea of a radical mechanism like foreclosure is that the material caught up in a somatic illness bypasses the unconscious. The unconscious, after all, is made up of repressed thoughts and desires. But here the material is not *repressed* but *abolished* from the psyche. This would chime with the old observation that somatic illnesses don't mean anything. With such material cut off from the networks of meaning and symbolization that characterize the unconscious, there would be no point in trying to find complicated hidden meanings or symbols. If anything, there would be a more direct inscription of some element in the body. And this would also indicate the failure of classical old-fashioned psychoanalysis as a clinical treatment.

Do these models of child development illuminate how and why people fall ill later in life? The danger here, as with so many of the other theories we have examined in this book, is to search for one-to-one correlations between specific situations and specific illnesses. Most of the researchers who developed the idea of operative thinking and of alexithymia came to see it as significant in some but by no means every case. What mattered would be the study of individual histories, to see if the capacity to think about events had any effect on whether that person fell ill or not. Would they be able to symbolize what was happening to them, or would they, on the contrary, deny the reality of a situation that concerned them?

When McDougall's colleagues published their first important book on psychosomatic illness in 1963, Lacan made a few comments that allow a fresh approach to these questions. Although he had himself elaborated the concept of foreclosure, he chose not to use it, opting instead for the term *holophrase*, which was then developed by some of his students. This concept, taken from linguistics, is used to refer to single words or phrases used by a child before it can articulate more complex verbal structures. One word would be used to designate a whole situation in a kind of 'word-sentence' often associated with moments of requesting or greeting. To say 'Toe', for example, might be understood as standing for the sentence 'Bring me my shoe'. It suggests a kind of compression or condensation of language.

A holophrase involves a reduced form of linguistic expression. Rather than several words or phrases, there is one word or phrase. This might suggest that what has been abolished is the gap between words, which is necessary, after all, for human speech. Language relies on the fact that words are differentiated from each other and then combined to make larger units. As we add words to a sentence, the meaning will become clearer and human dialogue is established. So what would happen if the process of combining words was blocked? Let's expand our use of the term 'word' here to apply to any representation or memory trace. Then let's remember the point emphasized by Karin Stephen that all of the body's zones associated with biological survival are also linked to our *relations* with caregivers. If a zone or function is stimulated (say, the mouth or lungs), this will lay down a memory trace of the stimulation which combines the traces of the physiological activity with the traces of our feelings linked to the caregiver (say, anger or pleasure).

Now, this is where the holophrase idea gets interesting. Let's assume that this complex memory trace, or bundle of traces, can then become linked to others to form associative chains and networks. This might be similar to the way that children may learn to name the crescent-shaped object in the night sky 'moon', and then apply this to grapefruit segments, geometrical shapes and then to other images that are not even crescent-shaped. As representations are taken up into networks, they lose their link to their original referents and start to function autonomously. This is what human language is largely about. Words are connected to other words in complicated systems that rely on difference rather than direct association with the original context of their use. This creation of linguistic networks is one aspect of the unconscious, which takes up the original memory traces of bodily activities and links them to other memories, hopes and trains of thought.

But what would happen if this process of linking traces were compromised, if there were barriers to the creation of networks of associations? This might mean that the original trace remains isolated and unconnected, linked only to rudimentary circuits. The trace could be understood as a neural circuit or a certain pattern of physiological response. To say that a situation cannot be symbolized or thought through would mean that such a circuit cannot be connected to others and so may be reactivated directly, as if the body registers a situation without the buffer of mental elaboration and the unconscious network of ideas which could otherwise give it a framework. There would not be a sequence of other traces to take up the initial record of innervation. In other words, there wouldn't be the gap between representations necessary for human speech. Instead, there'd be a holophrase.

Let's take an example. An eleven-year-old boy was seen by paediatricians at the University of Chicago Hospital after episodes of bleeding inside his right elbow. No precipitating trauma could be found for the bleeding although he was known to have suffered from haemophilia from his early childhood. The bleeding continued to affect his right elbow, and more than fifteen episodes took place over a two-year period. The mother consistently denied that there had been any family problems or upsetting situations that might have worsened her son's condition.

As the paediatricians worked with the boy, they found out that in fact the first elbow bleed had occurred when the father was away. A part-time racing-car driver, he frequently lived away from home and had little contact with his son. The boy's symptoms, apparently, brought the father back, and it turned out that they had begun some time after he had witnessed a serious racing accident involving his father. For a time, it was believed that the father would have to lose his right arm, and he was left with limited mobility of his right elbow. After a family therapy started, the bleeding episodes more or less stopped. When it was discontinued, he bled inside his right elbow once more, and was then free of bleeding for several months.

Reviewing the case, the paediatric team considered his frequent bleeding unusual given the moderate nature of his haemophilia. They argued that the sustained location of the bleeding in his right elbow could not be accidental or explained properly on a purely biomedical basis. The symptoms, they thought, were triggered by the father's leaving home, and they aimed to make him return. They also echoed the symptoms associated with leukaemia that another son had died from about four years before his own birth.

How might these symptoms be understood? They didn't seem to be expressing forbidden wishes and punishments like conversion symptoms. Neither did they seem rich in fantasy activity or concealed meanings. There was something minimal about them, and they appeared to copy the image of the father's injury. This might be an example of a holophrase, a single isolated signal that takes the place of a more articulated expression of thoughts. The boy's symptoms marked moments of separation from his father, and perhaps played a part in making him return to the family home. If that was the case, they functioned like 'word-sentences', punctual and abbreviated signals that send out a single message.

This seems strikingly similar to the patient with ulcerative colitis whom we discussed in Chapter 7. There is little mental elaboration or questioning process, just a call or appeal to the father, which is inscribed in the body. And isn't it exactly this minimal characteristic that has made so many theorists talk about breakdowns in symbolization and processes of representation? Rather than an articulated dialogue or questioning, there is just a direct inscription. The body replies with a time-specific and isolated message.

Would this mean that a somatic symptom is an attempt to say something? A message is not necessarily a communication, especially when the whole process takes place beyond the realm of conscious intention. Let's take another example here. In his autobiographical memoir *Lead, Kindly Light*, the American reporter Vincent Sheean describes the terrible moment of Gandhi's assassination. After hearing the shots, and realizing what had happened, he experienced what he described as 'a storm inside my head', which continued for a few minutes. Then he became aware of two sensations: a stinging and burning in his eyes and in the fingers of his right hand. In the eyes, there were tears, but when he looked at his hand, he saw that the third and fourth fingers were covered in blisters that had not been there before the shots.

Sheean interpreted this strange phenomenon as an almost intentional act. The blisters appeared, he thought, as evidence of his 'connection' with the tragic event: it should have been him who died instead. He remembered a trip to Vermont the previous summer where he had dreamt repeatedly of trying to interpose himself between Gandhi and the inevitable murderer. Despite this rationalization, he was stunned by the fact that it was physically possible for the blisters to appear within the space of a few minutes.

What might we make of these blisters? Could they have signified that the injury should have been felt by Sheean and not by Gandhi? Or could they have symbolized at a darker level that unconsciously Sheean wished to be the man holding the gun himself? If we interpreted them as a conversion symptom, they could be articulating the forbidden thought of wishing to harm Gandhi, or take his place, together with a symbolic punishment for this wish. The fact that he became so curious as to where the blisters had come from indicates that he was involved subjectively with his symptom, rather than seeing it as something external and alien to himself. These are all characteristics of a conversion symptom, but they are not enough to settle the question.

If, on the other hand, we introduce the idea of the word-sentence, do we have a better framework for explaining the symptomatic eruption? The blisters could be understood as a kind of *response* to the situation and all the conscious and unconscious currents that might have been at play. As a condensation or compression, the process of thinking was short-circuited (Sheean's 'storm in my head'). All that could emerge with clarity was the blisters, as if they, rather than a thought process, *marked the event*, like an improvised memorial or *concrete memory trace*.

But surely this is also a characteristic of the conversion symptom? Sheean's response to the symptom does suggest it is connected to unconscious processes and conflicts. Other symptoms, however, could share the feature of marking an event without having to pass via unconscious pathways. This would suggest a very early form of inscription of experience, and also that a *situation has been reduced to a single element*, as if there is only one marker for it. This might explain the absence of meaning, together with the significance of the timing and location of the symptom. It is suggestive here that linguists describe holophrase as a *border* phenomenon: it marks the start of what we recognize as speech, yet seems very close to the cries and gestures that precede this. This directness might also be seen in the way infants convert disturbing experiences *directly* into somatic responses, like crying, screaming or spasmic reaction, before they are able to use other sign systems, like speech or drawing, to indicate their distress, and before they are able to use the process of displacement to distance themselves (for example, by becoming afraid of a character in a story).

The fact that the symptoms we have discussed so often seem to mark points of separation and loss should make us pause for a moment. The bleeding in the boy's elbow, Sheean's blisters and the eczema of the child we mentioned in Chapter 7 all occurred at times when a relationship was broken. Unable to process or symbolize the terrible events, they were reduced to a mark or signal in the body. And doesn't this invite a return to Engel's project of studying the physiology of early experiences of separation?

★

Whether we favour operative thinking or alexithymia or holophrase or foreclosure, these mechanisms all suggest that a somatic problem may result when there are problems in the *symbolization* of a situation. The fact that so many new terms – and there are many more! – have been coined in this context by researchers is itself intriguing. Doesn't it imply that we are dealing with a process that escapes traditional models of psychical functioning? The invention of all this new vocabulary occurs at precisely the point where researchers are trying to explain how psychological reactions may be registered neither consciously nor unconsciously, but in the body.

But rather than simply claiming that this is due to the person being cut off from their emotional life, we are finding that there is a deeper, more basic problem here. Confronted with situations which require complex mental processing, there is a direct response in the body rather than a psychical elaboration. So what could stop something from being elaborated mentally? We have already looked at some of the scenarios linked to the mother–child relationship proposed by Continental analysts. Many of the British and American writers believe that these problems are due to the failure of having established a good internalized representation of a 'soothing mother' and of a maternal care which would help the infant to process disturbing feelings and experiences. The idea is that to care for oneself one has to have internalized the image of an environment that cares for one and that can turn experiences into mental representations. The mother who treats her child's cries as communications would be furthering this process. Rather than ignoring the infant's distress, she responds as if the cries, grimaces and bodily contortions had meaning.

This is a linguistic process, since it involves meanings and signs. The infant is being taught to see its bodily states as signs of meanings like the wish to be fed, clothed, changed or held. But language is working here in other ways as well. In a complicated developmental process, we internalize representations of fundamental human questions such as gender, mortality, procreation and identity. These enigmas may never be entirely resolved for us, yet a scaffolding of ideas and images can be constructed around them to allow us to make sense of them in a basic way. But if these frameworks aren't properly established in the first place, what would happen when someone is forced to confront a situation which involves reference to them?

A birth, a death or a physical change like that of puberty will leave such a person with no ready response, no way of making sense of and symbolizing what has happened. We have observed previously how all human societies mark such moments with ritual and ceremony as if to help the individual symbolize the transition. The symbolic moments of baptism, confirmation and marriage marked by the sacraments of the Anglican faith, for example, have profound effects on people's lives, even if they are usually unable to say exactly how this has happened. It is exactly at the times when we are called to take up a position with regard to our gender, mortality, procreative place or identity that bodily illness may appear, and we can see the similarity of this model to the holophrase idea. If we think of the mental frameworks as networks of unconscious trains of thought, their absence means that there is no possibility for mental elaboration. Rather than an unconscious chain, there is a single, isolated trace or bundle of traces in the body which don't succeed in becoming linked to unconscious mental life.

These problems with symbolization can be linked to the question of disease onset. Where Engel and his colleagues

had emphasized the experience of helplessness and hopelessness as setting the ground for disease, this should be
distinguished from the *representation* of these states. Isn't it
significant if a child manages to find a way of articulating
their sense of failure? Feeling helpless and without hope are
one thing, but being able to give a voice to this experience
is another. There must be a difference between the situation
of someone who believes they will be able to represent their
plight and that of someone who is deprived of any means
of doing so. Doesn't it follow that one's susceptibility to
illness might actually increase if one hadn't found a way of
articulating the feeling of impasse and failure?

We saw in Chapter 4 how studies of bereavement have
found an often dramatic increase in illness in the period
following loss. But what anthropologists and medical
researchers have also observed is that the rates of somatic
illness are reduced in those areas where mourning rituals are
present within the social group. Rather than being left with
their grief, the mourner shares their loss with the community. Like the Roseto study (Chapter 8), this indicates the
effects of social cohesion. The rituals allow the bereaved to
represent their state. Without such shared outward forms of
expression, the chances of falling physically ill increase. The
individual is forced to deal with the loss on their own, and
the internal resources to do this may well be lacking.

There is a difference then between an experience and
the inscription or registration of an experience. In her semi-
nal study of diabetes, Rosine Debray argues that onset may
be linked to what she calls 'non-integration' of an important conflict. Juvenile-onset diabetes peaks at the ages of 3–6
and 10–14, with only 25 per cent of sufferers developing
the disease after twenty-one. The fact that these peaks coincide with the ages of the Oedipal conflict and puberty

are not only due to hormonal changes but also to the flaring up of problems of sexuality that need to be worked out, but cannot be. Onset here involves a problem of symbolization, and suggests that it may also occur when someone faces a similar impasse.

How might this link to bodily processes? The nervous, endocrine and immune systems are all continuing to mature well into our twenties. For example, the adrenal cortex matures from the age of around five until adolescence, when adult levels of the hormone DHEA are produced, a mild androgen responsible, among other things, for the development of pubic hair in adolescents. Broadly speaking, DHEA acts in an opposite way to cortisol to stimulate Th1 functioning, a feature of cell-mediated immunity. Both cortisol and DHEA are manufactured in the body from cholesterol. While cortisol is produced on demand, DHEA in the form of a compound is readily available to provide a balance control to the fluctuations the HPA axis exercises on the immune system by means of cortisol. Juvenile-onset diabetes is increasingly seen as a result of the destruction of insulin-producing cells by a complicated malfunctioning of the various populations of T cells. As the immune system matures, the points that Debray sees as important may act via a perturbation of the DHEA–cortisol balance which disrupts immune activity.

This does not mean that a problem in symbolizing a conflict or an experience will lead to illness, and certainly not to any one illness in particular. But we should be alert to challenges to the processes of symbolization and representation. These may occur at the moment of a loss, but also at any time in life when a position must be taken, like an important act (a marriage, a birth), a decision (a job, a contract), a judgement (legal or personal), or having to say something in a formal context (a speech, a complaint, the acceptance of an honour). All of these moments are distinguished from the continuity of everyday existence. They introduce not only a discontinuity, but also accentuate the symbolic or ritual dimension in human life. It's not just any old speech or decision, but one that matters. They are moments when life changes. And it is precisely this taking on of a new position which in some cases cannot be symbolized or processed.

Wouldn't this explain the fact that sometimes people fall ill after events which actually seem positive or good for them? As we saw in Chapter 3, one of the perplexing features of the scales of life changes which aim to quantify the stress value of events like marriage, divorce and bereavement is that positive events rub shoulders with negative ones. At such moments, a person may be left facing an enigma. With no possibility of symbolizing and elaborating the situation mentally, it simply inscribes itself – perhaps like a holophrase – on the body. This idea could be tested cross-culturally by seeing if there is indeed any correspondence between peaks in the curves of certain illnesses and the ages at which social, symbolic rites of passage would be expected to take place.

We should thus distinguish the commonsense idea that events are traumatic because they flood us with an excess of emotion from the notion that there may be a *basic, structural problem in representation.* Think of the case we mentioned in Chapter 3 in which a diabetic man experienced a hypoglycaemic episode when talking about his son's Communion celebration. Asked if anything untoward or upsetting had happened, he said 'No', yet after detailed questioning, the therapist found that his father had chosen not to attend this important event. While it might seem obvious to argue that, unable to access his mental state of sadness and anger, the split-off feelings were rerouted to produce the dangerous drop in blood glucose, we could also explain it using these ideas about representation.

The Communion celebration, after all, accentuated his place as father. Perhaps it was this idea of paternity that he was unable to symbolize, and it was this that caused the changes in his blood sugar. *The illness became exacerbated at exactly this moment where he was forced to take on a symbolic place.* And indeed, he had become diabetic at the time of the birth of his second child, with a hypoglycaemic episode occurring at the moment of birth itself. Why, we could then ask, had he not fallen ill when he had first become a father? The patient had found a particular solution here. He could have a family, he said, but only on condition it was an exact replica of his own: father, mother and son. The duplication of the image of his own family thus shielded him from the traumatic dimension of becoming a father himself. When the second child was born, this was no longer possible.

It is interesting to note how this question about paternity had an effect on the actual management of the diabetes. At weekends, the patient would spend all his time working flat out on restoring a country house. He would systematically neglect to modify his insulin dosage, although he knew full well that this would be necessary given the physical exertions he was subjecting himself to. The result was frequent hypoglycaemic episodes as well as diabetic comas, occurring almost always at weekends. His wife and daughter would be left to revive him. Now, this echoes in a peculiar way his own childhood situation. His father would be away most of the week, and on his return at weekends would want to be left alone. Isn't this image of an absent father played out in the hypoglycaemic episodes and comas? He becomes himself the father who is *there but not there*, physically present but removed and distant. Unable to take on the symbolic position of father, he would play out the *image* of his own father using the mechanisms of his illness.

Taking on a symbolic place is thus a crucial factor in our lives. Although events like divorce, bereavement, separation and accident may really be 'too much' for us to take in many cases, they also confront us directly with this problem of how to register symbolically what has happened. Which mechanisms will be available to give meaning to the experience? And will it be able to become connected to unconscious mental life? Will the person be able to compare what has happened to previous experiences of themself and others? Focusing exclusively on questions of emotional expressivity, as is so often the case in psychosomatic research, runs the risk of neglecting these crucial issues.

Our focus on problems of symbolization and mental elaboration might also allow us to deepen our understanding of onset situations. For example, Debray believes that the sexual aetiology in juvenile-onset diabetes is combined with genetic disposition to generate the disease, after a failure to integrate the sexual elements. But why not see it as a *symbolic dimension* that is missing in such cases, and hence the problem will have nowhere else to be registered than in the body? In the Swedish studies of diabetes we mentioned in Chapter 10, it was argued that increased demand on insulin-producing beta cells was sometimes linked with stressful situations for a mother, such as giving birth to a child outside of one's native country. This, we are told, might be perceived as 'extra-stressful' since becoming a parent is a major life transition that awakens thoughts about one's own origin.

Our argument is that it is not a stress overload that is so crucial here but the fact that the moment of transition cannot be symbolically processed. It is a symbolization problem rather than simply a stress problem. And when one system of symbolic registration cannot function, other systems may take over. This might help to make sense of the link noted by innumerable authors between the kind of mechanisms at work in somatization and those characteristic of psychosis, such as extreme dissociation and splitting – in which the world can only be experienced in terms of rigid polarities, such as good and evil, benevolent and malign – and the necessity for many of these subjects – unable to internalize certain forms of symbolic structure – to have friends, partners or relatives present all the time.

It is easy to see how this might lead to the fallacy that external events are a *cause* of diabetes. External events, on the contrary, may become important precisely because of failures of psychical integration and symbolic processing. They are not linked to symbolic frameworks at an unconscious level. And this means that experiences and events are seen as things that happen to us, rather than as aspects of our lives which we are actively involved in. The result is a stimulus-based view of reality: external events become understood according to the model of bacterial infection. And this may be exactly what we find in some cases of physical illness.

14. Does Therapy Work?

Will any of this help in treating illness? If there are deep-rooted mechanisms which serve to distance us from unconscious processes, can therapy really make any difference? Almost everyone who has studied this question seriously has agreed that there are many cases where talking cures are of little use. Early studies of therapy found that somatizing patients responded less well than those who seemed able to articulate their emotions. And we have seen why this might be so. The very mechanisms involved in somatizing imply, in some cases, a difficulty or even impossibility in elaborating problems through speech.

Historically, this meant that many researchers lost hope in the psychosomatic approach. As the optimism of the early days of this research began to wane, a range of new medical treatments became available which provided relief from symptoms. The introduction of the drug cimetidine and other H2-receptor blockers was good for peptic ulcer, and later advances in medication made many illnesses easier to manage than before. At the same time, fewer medical specialists kept up their interest in psychoanalysis. The late 1940s and '50s saw a separation of American and British psychoanalysis from the exciting developments of Freud's thought taking place on the Continent. And with the poor response of somatically ill patients to traditional psychoanalytic therapy, it seemed to many that psychoanalysis had little to offer.

On the other hand, we have seen how in some cases speaking and words can crucially affect the course of a serious illness: think of the woman we discussed in Chapter 4 who recovered from multiple sclerosis or the man whose analysis allowed him to overcome his ulcerative colitis. It is worth remembering here how the old-fashioned approach of talking therapies is very different from the one adopted today by many analytic practitioners. The traditional method would often involve directly confronting the patient with an interpretation, as if an explanation of their mental situation could be immediately assimilated and thought through. They would be told, for example, that their physical symptom was caused by a conflict with their parents, yet we have seen in the previous chapter why this style of therapy is ill-starred. It neglects the very problem of symbolization that may lie at the root of the illness.

The more modern approach, used for example by Lacanian psychoanalysts, dispenses by and large with such appeals to insight. In the case of physical illness, problems of symbolization are taken very seriously and will affect the way that the analyst works with the patient. Rather than trying to explain the symptoms, they will help the patient to construct their biography, and this process will hopefully set the stage for links to be made between the illness and the details of their life. Such links are never forced on the patient, and there is an emphasis on words as the most powerful instrument of change. When we consider the question of the efficacy of talking therapies here, it is worth remembering how different many of them are today from the varieties most popular at the time of the older research.

We must also take care here to distinguish between causality and treatment: if psychological factors play a part in someone becoming ill, this does not mean that they will necessarily be the only thing to make them well again. One of the great failures of so many psychological approaches to organic illness has been to ignore this apparent paradox. However obvious the role of psychological factors in illness might seem, this doesn't give the *exclusive* recipe for a cure. Or at least it doesn't all the time. A somatic problem more often than not requires a medical treatment, and in some cases is so far developed that little can be done to remove it. But it is vital to recognize that there is always a psychological factor, which must be weighed up in each individual case. Likewise, we have seen how the way in which medical treatments are administered may have powerful effects on an organic process. The advantage of psychosomatics here is that it is about an *approach* to a problem, seeing how psychological factors are involved without claiming that they provide an exclusive route to a cure.

What can psychotherapy achieve, and what else can be done when this proves unhelpful? Researchers have come up with a number of ways to try to tackle the impasse here. They have spoken of operational thinking, alexithymia, foreclosure and holophrase to describe the mechanisms which might be at play in those people who have no interest in, or ability to speak about, their situation. While psychotherapy may be helpful in many cases, even the least experienced therapist knows that in others there may be no inclination or desire to engage in a talking cure – hence, as we've seen, the apparent mental 'health' of some, though by no means all, unwell people.

Today, non-psychoanalytic therapies flourish in many health-service settings. Cognitive-behavioural therapies, stress-management courses and a diverse range of brief therapies have all been taking ground fast. Behavioural therapies like relaxation training, biofeedback, meditation and guided mental imagery are available to somatically ill people in some places, although there is a real geographical lottery here as to what is on offer through one's local health service. Short-term use of these therapies has been claimed to be beneficial in a wide range of illnesses, from coronary heart disease to hypertension, cancer, asthma, peptic ulcer, diabetes and arthritis.

Do these therapies really work? And if so, how? Before entering these rather dangerous waters, we would do well to reflect for a moment on what, in fact, we are asking. Enquiring whether a therapy works could be compared to the question 'Does aspirin work?' How we answer this depends on our idea of what aspirin *is supposed to be doing*. Do we mean aspirin as a remedy for mild headaches, or as an agent for thinning the blood or as a drug to reduce inflammation, so reducing some of the risks of heart disease? We need to say what we expect from aspirin to say if it works. And the same goes for all forms of therapy.

Let's take an example here by asking the question 'Does acupuncture work?' A man is rushed to hospital after collapsing in an art gallery. The doctors are very worried about him, and perform a variety of tests. Despite medication, his anxiety levels are high and he continues to suffer palpitations, chest pains and shortness of breath. He is convinced that he is about to die of heart failure, and undertakes several different treatments recommended by his doctors and by his own research. Nothing changes until he has acupuncture. His symptoms disappear, his anxiety is dissipated, and he enthusiastically recommends acupuncture now to all his friends and colleagues.

Surely we could say here that acupuncture worked? But let's look at the case a bit more closely. The man had kept certain details from his doctors about the circumstances of the initial attack. He had been having an affair for some time, meeting his lover regularly in a discreet location. That week it had not been possible to meet her in the usual place and she had suggested the gallery as a rendezvous. When he arrived there he was slightly nervous as it was more public than he had expected. As he embraced her, he thought he noticed a woman some distance away glancing at him. Her face reminded him of someone who happened to be a friend of his wife. Then he collapsed.

This sheds some light on the context of the incident, but still doesn't tell us about the efficacy of the acupuncture. Describing the tests and subsequent treatments, he complained of how fruitless they seemed. Nothing worked. But when he started talking about the acupuncture, he suddenly became animated, repeating several times how painful it had been: 'It was like torture, like a terrible punishment.' The fact that he kept on saying how much like a punishment it was can hardly fail to evoke the spectre of guilt that marked the whole episode. There he was, cheating on his wife, imagining he saw one of her friends, collapsing, and then describing the only treatment that had worked as a punishment.

This does not mean that the acupuncture didn't work. But it does suggest that how a treatment works will involve several factors that could not realistically be revealed by a medical questionnaire. How could the detail of this man's clandestine life be factored into an assessment of the efficacy of acupuncture? Many other people may benefit from acupuncture and have no feelings of guilt which need to be assuaged by punishment. This is not to adopt a completely relativistic approach where 'anything goes'. Rather, it is to attend to the complexity at play in each individual case.

This situation is not made any easier by the fact that therapists and patients may have different ideas here about what a treatment actually aims at. A therapist might expect their work to involve the ventilating of bottled-up emotions, while a patient might expect it to allow the voicing of a complaint, the opportunity to meet other people in a similar situation or simply the pursuit of an activity they have *chosen* rather than been forced into. If we define therapy exclusively in terms of results, even a physical examination of the body can count as psychotherapy since in many cases it will greatly relieve a patient's anxiety. The only way to assess these questions is through a detailed exploration of each patient's participation in the form of therapy they are engaged in. It is only then that one can begin to reply to the question of whether a therapy works.

Even so, the role of a therapy *may change* for the patient during the actual course of treatment. In the case of traditional psychotherapy, someone may visit a therapist for years without actually doing a therapy. Up until a certain point, they may not really be engaged with what they are saying. The words used or the themes discussed may be 'emotional' or 'painful' if viewed on paper, yet the speaker may bring them up in a detached and distant way and have no desire at all to explore them. This will make evaluating therapy rather difficult: how is the researcher conducting an external study to know if a patient has become involved with an active exploration of their own life? Going to therapy and doing therapy are two completely different things.

In some cases, a therapist might find a particular treatment effective, assuming that the patient has engaged with unconscious processes and linked them to their current life situation. But scrutiny of the treatment may reveal that its efficacy was not due to any kind of insight, but rather to the image provided by the therapist, their constant presence and attention, or even the routine provided by the cycle of appointments. These very simple examples show that any questioning of whether a therapy works must be examined from several angles.

Many of the therapies aimed at somatically ill patients involve group work, and it is worth noting how many obstacles there have been in the past to this kind of practice despite the obvious economic benefits: more patients treated for less money. But group work was initially discouraged. In the US, the only formal psychological support in the postwar years was through the American Cancer Society's visitor programmes, where patients who had already undergone a distressing procedure were encouraged to speak with those about to undergo a similar treatment. These projects gradually expanded, but there was much resistance from medical staff and refusal to recognize their value. It was frequently considered improper for patients to communicate with each other, as if this might somehow get in the way of conventional medical treatment. Presumably this meant get in the way of clear, uncluttered, positive feelings towards the doctor giving the treatment.

In this sense, groups can be dangerous. Patients can learn each other's stories and form new transferences – emotionally charged bonds which usually have one's early relations with a parent as their template – to other members of the group as opposed to the treating physicians. The more people there are, the more opportunities, after all, for the patient to project their split-off feelings, and so doctors, and sometimes others in the group, can become identified with malign persecutors or beneficial helpers. Medical staff are very aware of the fact that the responses they get from a patient will not necessarily be determined by how well or poorly they have served them. Powerful forces are at work here, which can inflect the relation of patient to doctor, and vice versa, with great rapidity.

Group work comes in many forms, and the different practices and goals should be distinguished. Some of these aim to analyse the unconscious processes going on in the group, where others specifically aim to avoid this. Some involve the focused discussion of medical treatments, some are left quite open. Some involve relaxation techniques, others don't. Some aim at control of emotions, others at release. Yet even the therapies which simply bring a group of sufferers from some complaint together seem to produce real results on occasion, and this may be the case for even the most serious forms of organic illness.

Heart disease patients have been shown in particular to respond to forms of therapy which focus on relaxation and reducing their sense of time urgency and hostility. In the Recurrent Coronary Prevention Project, 1,013 subjects who had suffered myocardial infarction were assigned into groups to receive either cardiac counselling, cardiac counselling combined with a form of counselling designed to help with Type A behaviour, or no counselling. Over a three-year period, the Type A group showed significant decrease in their Type A behaviour, and the average annual recurrence rate proved to be 44 per cent lower than that of the other group which had received just cardiac counselling. Subsequent follow-ups confirmed these results over a longer period.

Other studies have claimed even higher rates of reduction in recurrence, and there seems to be an agreement that behaviour-style therapies are beneficial here. Working at a time when bypasses and angioplasties often had to be redone relatively soon after the first operation, Dean Ornish used group work, with diet, relaxation, aerobics and meditation to aim at unclogging coronary arteries. The groups would meet three times a week for a year, with very impressive results. Ornish claimed that, in some of his subjects, arterial blockage was actually reversed, and this without medication. Scans showed that blood flow to the heart was indeed improved.

In another well-known project, Jon Kabat-Zinn at the University of Massachusetts Medical Center introduced group programmes involving discussion, meditation and body techniques. These were correlated in some groups of patients with reduced use of medication and fewer symptomatic episodes. Many researchers have looked to support such findings by a better understanding of the physiological mechanisms involved. The neuroscientist Richard Davidson and his colleagues, for example, have studied the effects on the brain and immune system of 'mindfulness meditation'. After an eight-week training programme in meditation, 25 subjects were vaccinated with flu vaccine. Four weeks later the average immune response was found to be significantly greater in this group compared with immune response in a control group. Anxiety levels were reduced too. Davidson suggests that an important factor here is a shift in the frontal regions of the brain to greater left-hemisphere activation, which he associates with positive affects. The meditation group did indeed show significant increases in such activity, and this work tallies with a host of other research suggesting the larger role played by the left hemisphere in cell-mediated immunity.

In one of the most famous and ground-breaking projects, David Spiegel from Stanford Medical School formed a series of support groups for women suffering from breast cancer in 1976. They would meet each week for a year, talking about their treatments, fears and experiences. Some relaxation exercises were used, and Spiegel's hope was that these meetings and the bonds established through them would help improve the patients' quality of life. But he found something much stronger had taken place: the group work actually seemed to have an effect on the cancers themselves. Ten years later, it was found that the women who had participated in the groups had double the life expectancy of the women who had not. They lived for an average of eighteen months longer. Although this might not seem a lot, it would be newsworthy if a drug had been correlated with the same result.

In a similar study, Fawzy Fawzy from the UCLA School of Medicine organized groups for patients suffering from malignant melanoma. Six months into the project, those who had participated in the psychiatric intervention groups had not only better coping skills and reduced psychological distress but much better NK-cell activity, and the rate of tumour recurrence was lower than in those who received only conventional treatment. Although these studies have received some criticism of their methodology, the accumulation of results suggesting the benefits of group work in conditions ranging from heart disease to cancer has been growing steadily. In many cases, however, the statistical style of the research can turn powerful effects into modest ones. In a recent study conducted across a number of hospitals in the Netherlands, Gieta van der Pompe and her colleagues looked at the effects of group therapy on early-stage breast cancer sufferers. They found that the therapy patients had lower levels of cortisol and responded better to challenges to the immune system. Like similar studies, the published results are quite modest, yet an accurate picture may be obscured by the absence of material on individual cases.

Strong responses to therapy get lost when they become averaged out with the results for those with little or no response. To give one example among many, a recent project aimed to assess the effects of therapy for depression on cardiac outcomes in nearly 2,500 patients with myocardial infarction. Yet its rather negative findings become meaningless due to its failure to distinguish between those in the group who had responded positively to treatment and those who hadn't. So many variables can get lost in this statistical approach to group studies that detailed histories of individual patients are vital. If ten people in a group did badly, why did the other two do so well? Surely it is attention to each of their unique stories that matters here? One might hope that it is exactly the two exceptional cases that may offer some clues to further research, and it is in this direction that some current research projects are moving.

Studies at the Ontario Cancer Institute, for example, are focusing on the individual responses to therapeutic treatment, rather than simply aiming at statistics that average out results. Each patient is tracked in detail over time, using material from several interviews, as well as patients' written accounts and notes from therapy sessions. Uniqueness and individuality are privileged here over personality profiles, although such specificity is slightly sabotaged by the researchers' decision to paraphrase and summarize the interviews, even if some sections are later chosen for verbatim transcription. The emphasis on individual responses, rather than calculations which average out the responders and the non-responders, is clearly a move in the right direction.

But how do these treatments work? A fundamental starting point here is to recognize the difference between registers of human experience. Language and social structures form a symbolic order, and we saw in Chapter 10 how our emotional investments and attachments will be regulated primarily by this network. It introduces systems of naming, classifying and symbolizing to our lives, as well as establishing limits and prohibitions. As the body is taken up into symbolic structures, mental and physical excitations can be channelled and regulated. These can form symptoms – as we saw with conversion – but also protect us from symptoms, by providing a structure for our experience and a means for articulating distress. Symbolic, linguistic organization establishes a template for making sense of our interactions and environment.

This supposes a process of internalizing symbolic structures, which occurs during our infancy and childhood. From biological organisms, we become social, speaking beings who operate according to the codes and sign systems that make up our symbolic environment. But what happens if the process of internalization fails? This may be due either to the unavailability of the symbolic dimension, if the caregiver cannot transmit any notion of a register beyond themselves and the child, or to the child's rejection of it. In many cases, when these structures have not been internalized, the person may try to find them outside the body: literally in reality. There may be a gravitation towards procedures and practices that seem to impose symbolic structures on to the body from an external source. The person might subject themselves to a carefully constructed regime of gym visits or spend a great deal of their time at the computer. What matters is finding a differentiated symbolic system. The body can then be plugged into it, whether in the form of a ritual like gym visits or diet or the system of a computer software program.

Another response to the failure of internalization is an appeal to the dimension of the image. Lacking an internalized symbolic structure, the person may use the image of other people as their guide. Other people's physical presence becomes vital here, as if their image compensated for the missing symbolic dimension. This is one reason why we often see such close, almost adhesive links between certain people: if one of them isn't there, it's as if the other is lost. Images function to organize and regulate our libidinal investments. This is especially the case in the absence of a symbolic structure, since now the image takes on a new importance. It provides an anchoring point at exactly the place that the symbolic order failed to do so. Think, for example, of the diabetic patient discussed in the last chapter who had to preserve the image of his own nuclear family as a way of compensating for the impossibility of assuming the symbolic role of father.

We often see these alternatives at work in psychosis. To achieve some form of stabilization, a psychotic subject may appeal either to the register of the image – copying the appearance and behaviour of a friend or acquaintance – or to the external embodiment of a symbolic structure: computer circuitry, a field of scientific research, genealogy and other abstract systems. Although the two approaches don't rule each other out, the emphasis is often on one or the other of these forms of solution, suggesting that they may constitute important routes for avoiding collapse. Looking back to the film *Castaway*, which we discussed earlier, we can see this at work. As we saw, the character played by Tom Hanks manages to survive by hanging on to the abstract position that the Fedex package confers on him: as a reminder of his role, it gives him a place in the symbolic universe. But as well as this, Hanks has another means of maintaining his identity: the visual image that he creates of a human counterpart – the volleyball with a face drawn on it.

It follows that treatments that work with language and images may have potential powers. The question of identification is once again important here. We have seen in previous chapters how identifying with other people can have real effects on the body. The roommates with synchronized periods or the illnesses that emerge at the same date

as those of another person show how identifying with someone can impact directly on the endocrine, immune and other
body systems we have discussed. Given the power of these
processes, it seems likely that participating in a group may
provide a new arena for such identificatory processes to
unfold. Many are based, after all, on the explicit idea that
since members suffer from the same condition, they share
something in common. There is of course the open question of whether this may encourage the patient not only to
get well but, in some cases, to become more unwell. But the
image of another person in the same situation can often have
beneficial effects. An image can become an anchoring point.

Research into the effects of unconscious identifications on
the body can help us to understand how some treatments
work. Group work can establish and sustain identifications,
and also allow the opportunity to develop the role identifications we discussed earlier. In these cases, the patient has
structured their life around an unconscious formula – for
example, 'X helps Y' – in which they can occupy either the
first or the second of the two places. They will create situations at home, at work or in their social environment in which
they are in the place of the one helping someone else or being
helped, for example. If illness ensues when the formula breaks
down, for reasons specific to the details of each particular case,
treatment in a group can sometimes be just as effective as
individual therapy in re-establishing a role.

In the most general sense, a group can help to give someone a place. We have seen already the importance of the
question 'How is my existence registered?' for human life.
This will matter in an individual's relation to the family as
well as in the wider context of society. Illness never fails to
reactivate this question about our existence: what value do
we have? What do we mean for others? Hence it is all the

more vital that the question is not left unanswered in an atmosphere of neglect and isolation, the patient waiting for hours unattended in a hospital cubicle, left on a waiting list or, more generally, excluded from the possibility of human dialogue. When participating in a group benefits health, it may be due to this basic form of registering existence, maintaining a dialogue and establishing a role for oneself.

This provision of a kind of personal point of reference may occur in other ways. Group work can allow new forms of management and control of oneself. A sense of order is established, involving ritualized procedures like diet, exercise and meetings: one has to be at a certain place at a certain time, eat certain foods and not others, or do certain exercises. And this in itself can have significant benefits. It allows a framework of rules and programmes to be applied to the body. In other words, a prosthetic form of symbolic order is being introduced. The power of these processes is often obscured by conflating the activity and *the frame* that the activity provides. Exercise might be good for you, but the ritual involved in exercise might, in some cases, be even better. The symbolic, structural dimension in human life should never be underestimated.

This structural dimension is also fundamental to the question of choice. Is there not something inhuman in the outcry at patients being conned into ineffective regimes? Whether it is a cardiologist who can't really take seriously the patient's belief that a new diet will help unclog their arteries, or the advice of the oncologist to break off a time-consuming and expensive alternative therapy, what value do such attitudes really have? Couldn't the fact that the patient has made a choice be of value in itself *as a human act*?

There is a very basic and profound question here of the *human right to hold false beliefs*. This is surely a fundamental right, yet many alternative treatments for illness are actively discouraged by health professionals. If they are not seen as damaging the person's health, what reason could there be to discourage them, apart from the physician's own belief system? It is interesting to compare this with the medical profession's attitude to religious beliefs. Religious beliefs tend to be tolerated if they are not deemed harmful to society, yet a patient's belief in some forms of complementary medicine may be openly attacked even if it is not physically harmful. This raises some significant problems, especially given the fact that several studies have claimed that religious faith is good for one's health.

It will obviously be helpful here to develop and explore theories of how belief systems function, and to make certain simple but significant distinctions which will allow a greater sensitivity when exploring a patient's choices. Human culture is built up of symbolic structures, involving language, social laws and ritualized practices. Burial rites, for example, signify that a body is human and not animal. These rites may have little meaning in themselves, but they count precisely because they indicate that a formal, ritualized action is taking place. As we have seen, growing up involves the absorption of social and linguistic structures into the very fabric of the body.

These structures have an effect on bodily rhythms. As infants, we cry less as we learn to speak. Our sleeping patterns become more stable, and every parent knows the calming effect reading a story to a child at bedtime may have. The more we are taken up into symbolic, linguistic structures, the more the experience of the body in pain can be mediated. We can talk about it, ask for help, give a meaning to it, and so on. The symbolic dimension can have pacifying effects on pain, and will play its part in structuring bodily experience. Given the fact that many therapies involve the introduction of a grid or plan to the body, through diet, exercise, and so on, isn't there a benefit in the very framework they impose?

Couldn't the investment of the body image provided by such techniques compensate in some cases for the perturbations and disorientation that the person has experienced prior to and during an illness? Even if it 'just' gives the patient the sense of control – however illusory some medical practitioners might believe this to be – this in itself might be vitally significant to them. If one of the key factors in our development as human beings is the effort to separate from our caregivers, this may suggest that formulating aspects of one's own treatment plan will be of the utmost value.

How, after all, does a child show its independence, its very subjectivity, if not through refusals? Refusal to look where the parent wants them to look, to eat what the parent wants them to eat or do what the parent wants them to do. Through these painful moments of refusal, the child asserts its autonomy. Later in life, illness and the necessity of relying on medical intervention put the patient in a situation of dependency which will evoke that of infancy. So what place will there be here for refusal? This situation will reactivate the question of what our existence means, and of how we are registered by others. Perhaps sometimes this can take the form of the decision to follow a therapy of one's own choice, or even the refusal to comply with a recommended medical treatment. The question of refusal should not be put down to caprice or provocation, but taken as a serious dimension of human rights. In some cases, non-compliance will contribute to health.

This is movingly described by René Allendy in his *Diary of a Sick Doctor*, published in 1944. As well as being a physician, Allendy was one of the first analysts in France, and he kept a candid diary of his thoughts during the six-month-long illness that was to end with his death. As well as describing how he felt his illness involved an identification with his own father, who had suffered from respiratory disease throughout his life, Allendy experienced a strong desire to revolt against the medical advice he was receiving. Refusing, he says, would be the only thing he could do to maintain his freedom. In a state of complete helplessness and unable to move because of his physical condition, saying 'No' was crucial to restore to him his dignity as a human being. With characteristic frankness, he also acknowledged a 'dark jealousy' of his doctor, who now had power over him and whom he thus wished to prove wrong.

Refusal may be a personal necessity in some cases. Techniques like biofeedback, which hook the body up to a machine to 'feed back' information about physiological activity, may work in some cases for precisely this reason. They represent the choice of the patient, and give them a sense of control and mastery rather than helplessness. As they are wired up to a machine, they can see how their body is affecting readings, and introduce changes through acts of conscious control. Consciously trying to relax, for example, may produce a reduction in blood pressure visible on the machine's monitor. As well as a sense of control, this may help to provide a representation of internal processes. The inside of the body is registered through the readings. It is thus a way of building a body image which is not confined to the body surface as in a mirror.

Studies have claimed that even blood flow can be influenced by these methods. Given the need for tumours to divert blood supply towards themselves, such control is potentially significant. One study has claimed to use biofeedback techniques to increase blood flow to the middle cerebral artery, and so prevent migraine headaches. Another has shown how temperature increases of 3–6 degrees Celsius can be produced in the hand using this process. As a patient becomes more familiar with the practice, the body may be experienced as being linked to an external machine. This can allow a new investment of the body and its functions, and help to modify patterns of bodily experience. The machine itself can even be felt, in some cases, to be embodying the symbolic dimension absent in the patient's life, like a registration or processing device outside the body. We can find an extreme example of this in some cases of psychosis, where a machine outside the body becomes the centre of the patient's world.

And this introduces some other possibilities. If we take seriously the idea that there are mechanisms which foreclose ideas and feelings, and that this may contribute to somatic illness, what should we infer about treatment? One view would be that these feelings and ideas have to be reintegrated by the person, and the work of therapy would consist in this painful process. The therapist would tactfully present the patient with hypotheses about their early life, traumatic experiences or suppressed emotions. But, if the defence mechanisms are so extreme, *couldn't a treatment be used to work with them rather than against them*? For example, rather than trying to reverse the mechanism, why not try to actually reinforce the idea of illness as a foreign body, which could then be modelled or embodied by such techniques as the external machine of biofeedback or by using 'clay therapy'? Here the tumour is constructed and externalized through the form of sculpture or, in other practices, through mental imagery. This may or may not be helpful for the individual patient, but it does suggest that techniques focusing on externalization may be more effective in some cases than those based on the idea of reintegration. We could recall here that many instances of shamanistic practice gave a special place to dramatizations of removing some object from the body.

These different pathways illuminate the effects of many therapies. The body can be realigned or resituated in a structure, as if to provide the patient with a kind of prosthetic symbolic order, as well as reinvested through techniques linked to the body image. Subjectivity can be not only respected but actively affirmed through a recognition of the rights of refusal and a place or role gained by participation in a group. Ideally, a therapy should also allow pathways to emerge for the articulation of distress, but if the mechanisms at play in a patient render this task unlikely or impossible, the identifications offered by group work or the regulations of biofeedback and other techniques may prove useful and matter enormously to the patient. They offer unique opportunities to reinvest the body. As the patient is encouraged to focus on and give meaning to their body in a novel way, it may encourage the construction of a mental image of the body and a new framework for bodily sensations and processes.

When should these therapies become available? Although it might seem a rather obvious question, timing is frequently neglected when discussing types of treatment. Yet anyone who becomes a patient should be alert to the importance of danger periods. While most therapies won't be available anyway, given poor resources and waiting lists, certain high-risk periods may escape both the patient's and the doctor's scrutiny. One example here would be the post-operative period for transplant patients and, indeed, anyone admitted for a surgical procedure. Several studies show a marked increase in depressive symptoms following bypass surgery, and these may emerge quite some time after the operation itself. It has even been estimated that, however hidden at first, post-operative psychosis appears in between 30 and 60 per cent of cardiac patients. If post-operative delusions occur, they are known to emerge quite swiftly after most forms of surgery, but depression often becomes established several weeks or months later, and so is less noticeable. Potency problems that may have no biological link to the effects of the surgery are also often encountered.

Given what is known about the effect of depression on the body's functioning, it would be odd to see this as a separate and isolated problem with no link to the course of medical procedures. The evidence here is particularly impressive in cardiovascular disease. The need for intervention may be crucial, and it has been demonstrated that even in the short term social intervention will impact on surgery patients, with decrease of blood loss, speedier return to gastric motility, faster wound healing, less need for painkillers, and shorter hospital stays. Back in the 1930s and '40s, doctors recommended that post-operative therapy be immediately available to a patient, however successful the surgical procedure itself.

Lacan worked for several years in pre-operative consultation, and he suggested that, as well as paying careful attention to a patient's history, particular care should be taken to learn something about how they had reacted to *symbolic* moments in their lives. Patients should be encouraged to talk about how moments of transition had been experienced: a new job, a promotion, becoming a parent, and so on. Since it would be likely that an operation would be registered at some level as a symbolic event, it was all the more important to have an idea of how they had coped in the past and what their self-image consisted of. Post-operative care, likewise, would ideally not be limited to those cases with poor medical results. A real danger period is the time when patients have finished a course of treatment, however successful it has been. Moments of *punctuation* – 'You're well now', 'At last you're back on your feet' – can be very fragile, and may precipitate depression and other severe physical symptoms. These are not just 'real' moments when the efficacy of a treatment can be confirmed, but symbolic ones, indicating a moment of transition or change.

If such symbolic moments are of special importance, we should also not neglect the times which seem to be their exact opposite: the uninterrupted periods of *waiting* which constitute much of hospital existence. In a troubling and moving book, the psychiatrist and psychoanalyst Diane Chauvelot recounts the further stays in hospital which followed some incompetent surgery on her shoulder. It was waiting, she writes, that formed the central part of her experience, and this produced feelings of frustration, fury and abandonment. Such feelings in a patient may then revive childhood agonies, in which being kept waiting (perhaps for the breast or the mother's presence) can be felt as vengeful neglect or a deliberate attack. Indeed, it is difficult not to conclude that *any* period of waiting in a hospital will have adverse effects on one's health. And it is not surprising to learn that assaults on staff are more frequent in accident and emergency wards than they are in psychiatric ones.

These temporal factors are highly significant. Another example would be the symbolic moment of retirement. Medically speaking, retirement can be less a sought-after dream than a minefield. A job may have maintained a role for someone throughout their life, and given them a symbolic place. In that sense, it provided an answer to the question 'How is my existence registered?' which we have seen to be so important. So how will this be dealt with on retirement?

What will happen if alternative mechanisms are not in place?

If one's own personal history has led one to a particular profession or activity, losing it may be catastrophic. It may seem as if one no longer has a place in the world: identity is fractured. If in the best of cases we have been able to find a profession that fits with our unconscious interests, stopping work will have consequences at several levels. If work has been the main conduit for libidinal investment, what will happen to the libido on retirement? Will the libido retire as well? The responses of giving in and being given up described by Engel may emerge here, and the libido may swing back to be invested in the body. Once again, an intensification of hypochondriacal fears is often seen after retirement, as well as real organic illness. Unable to sustain their desire through work, the individual searches unconsciously for new points of investment. When desire cannot be maintained in something, the individual is always in danger, and all the risk factors inherent in a given case may be mobilized once the person is decompensated by the loss of their professional activity. The loss of desire, often called 'depression', is a major factor in the propensity to ill-health.

If therapy can matter here, it doesn't necessarily mean psychotherapy, but simply the possibility of speaking with someone, if the patient so wishes. It should be obvious that anyone admitted to a hospital should have a contact person to speak to, and ideally one sensitive to these factors, although it would perhaps be over-optimistic to hope for this kind of support in today's medical climate. A Healthcare Commission survey found recently that out of 4,000 cardiac patients studied, nearly half did not benefit from proper outpatient care. They were not briefed on vital lifestyle changes, and 40 per cent of the smokers received no advice on giving up. Given this lack of resources, what can realistically be hoped for?

Psychotherapy would presumably take a back seat here, despite the fact that it has so much to offer.

Ideally, the contact person would be alert to the dynamics of an individual's unconscious mental life, but there is little reason why any exploration of this should be *forced* on the patient. Psychotherapy cannot be administered like a drug. Rather, a setting can be established which encourages the patient to speak if they wish to. But contact with others is crucial here in a much more general sense. It is less insight into unconscious processes that can be hoped for than the possibilities of identification and recognition, reinvestment of the body and an opening of the pathways of speech and dialogue.

Would it be naive to hope that every patient should receive an open-ended interview on their first medical visit or when hospitalized? No hospitalized patient should be deprived of the opportunity to speak about themself. Such work requires skill and sensitivity, yet there are just not enough posts or staff available to do this. An ever-increasing problem, which will only compound the difficulty of change, is the contemporary assumption that human beings can be rotated and replaced in the hospital setting provided their skills and experience levels are equal. This allows the rotation of housemen and registrars, for example, and it is creeping further and further from the hospital into GP practices. Patients may find it difficult to see the same GP, especially in busy city practices.

Given the fact that people feel disappointment even when their bank tellers change, it is a sad fact that so often contact with the same person proves impossible, be it a GP, a midwife, a nurse or a counsellor. In a random sample of hospital patients in England and Wales, it was found that 64 per cent had no named nurse in charge of their care, with 22 per cent having in addition no named doctor. The methodology of this survey, together with anecdotal evidence, leads one to suspect that the actual rates of these shortcomings may in reality be far greater. Britain currently has fewer doctors per head of population than almost any other European country, and there are fears that by 2025 there may be a shortfall of around 25,000 doctors.

If relationships – and the unconscious mechanisms involved in them – are so important, and if these will shape how the patient articulates their distress, it is surely unwise to substitute one person for another so casually. How our existence is registered is a crucial aspect of all our lives, and any situation which brings it into focus will involve powerful emotional reactions which may well affect the body. A series of anonymous helpers is bound to exacerbate the feeling of being an object, and this will work against the efficacy of any treatment. Everything suggests that this will compromise the self-healing mechanisms of the body.

When psychological factors are invoked by medicine in the context of organic disease, it is more likely to be in terms of the emotional reactions to being ill and the failure to take the prescribed medications, yet this should be seen as a symptom in itself of other problems. Individual relations are central to human interaction and they play a part in all medical transactions. These psychological factors are all too often ignored, as we have seen in previous chapters. Taking them into account cannot be easy for hard-pressed, overworked medical staff, yet they must be explored in order to explain the often enigmatic cycles of falling ill and recovery observable in patients, and to provide the best treatment possible. The power of listening cannot be overemphasized here, together with the establishment of some form of *dialogue* with the sick person.

Dialogue, after all, is what so many alternative therapies offer. It is the principal way of recognizing someone else's existence. We are not advocating the usurping of medical procedures and medication by speech. Far from it. But these practices may be most fruitfully conducted within the broader context of a dialogue. The fragmentation and alienation imposed on patients in the current medical climate work against this. Yet life itself, it has been said, is a dialogue. And when the dimension of dialogue is obliterated, an individual's life is always put at risk.

15. What Do Doctors Want?

What of the physician's own desire? Is the role of the doctor always unambiguous? And should medicine always aim at the removal of symptoms? If illness is seen as an objective process unfolding along a predetermined route in a human body, there may well be reasons to favour this choice. But if the life and history of the patient have been included, this may be less obvious. Psychosomatic researchers noted very early on that, in many cases, the removal of an organic symptom precipitated a psychosis. The successful medical treatment of, say, a metabolic disorder would be followed by the outbreak of a paranoia. Advances in medical treatments could remove someone's symptoms, but at times something much worse would be triggered. Medical literature is full of such reports.

Although there are several ways to understand this, early theorists took what could be called an *economic* approach. If an illness was at the centre of someone's life, removing it could risk upsetting a vital balance. It would obviously require a great deal of time and skill on the physician's part to be able to assess the place the illness occupied for the individual patient, but this could be of the utmost importance. Successful drug treatments have been known to lead to the triggering of a psychosis or to the emergence of somatic symptoms just as serious as the original ones. Hence the care required in the approach to organic symptoms. If there are indeed cases where a person is ill precisely because they don't want to − or can't − know anything about their thought processes or feelings, what would be the consequences of a medical cure?

These situations often evade medical scrutiny. If the problems start to appear sometime after the treatment, there is a good chance they will not be noted by those initially involved. If new symptoms emerge in different parts of the body, different doctors will probably be consulted. If there is not an obvious physiological thread linking them, the relations between these disparate sets of symptoms can go unnoticed. Dementia, for example, sometimes develops in elderly people after operations under general anaesthetic or the experience of shock during the course of serious illness. The physician concerned with the patient's liver, kidneys or heart may be less interested in or alert to these aspects. And it may well be a different physician who attends to the symptoms of dementia.

The doctor is in a difficult position here. Can they really be expected to weigh up the pros and cons of medical treatment, factoring in what they predict about the effects on the patient's mental equilibrium? And yet this was exactly the advice given to doctors by Michael Balint, whose meeting groups for GPs still operate in many parts of the world today. Balint encouraged doctors to discuss their own personal responses to patients with each other in small groups, and to question their own aims in each case. Whether the doctor believed exclusively in organic or psychological causation was irrelevant here, as Balint thought that both approaches should be actively questioned. While we hear today of so many GPs expressing dissatisfaction with their jobs, a recent study found that those who participated in Balint groups benefited enormously from these encounters.

Sceptical of both an exclusively biomedical and an exclusively psychological approach, Balint pointed to the dangers of making a beeline for the supposed psychological source of a patient's somatic illness. The doctor here is aiming to take something away from the patient (the organic symptoms) and at the same time forcing them to face up to the problems causing it (the psychological source). Yet what justifies this manoeuvre? And what kind of an exchange is involved? The patient is being pressured to give up a limited physical symptom and transform it into the vast mental suffering that had been avoided precisely by the flight into what might be the more bearable form of physical suffering. Balint thought that this could be seen as a violation of the patient's rights – what we could call the *patient's right to fall ill*.

If it is true that there are some cases where a physical symptom protects the patient from some other area of unbearable suffering, what right does anyone have to try to remove it? 'There is a danger,' Balint wrote, 'not only in missing a physical symptom, but also in finding one.' Similarly, what would happen if a physical symptom had come to satisfy an unconscious demand for self-punishment? Would its disappearance result in a state of terrible anxiety? And how long would it be before another symptom replaced it? Techniques to evaluate different treatments and therapies tend to overlook this important factor, so that on paper it looks as if the results have been good: the symptoms are gone, so the treatment worked. But what if very different symptoms then emerged a month later, to fill the void left by the initial cure?

So-called 'alternative symptoms' have been extensively explored by psychoanalysis but little by medicine. The fact that terrible headaches could disappear during episodes of bleeding or diarrhoea in colitis patients and then reappear afterwards suggested that the same psychological pressures were being directed down different somatic paths. Symptom-shifts from one part of the body to another are very frequent, and the fact that different specialists may be consulted for each ailment makes it difficult to keep track of their evolution and displacement.

In a bizarre experiment, the American psychiatrist Philip Seitz took this idea so seriously that he tried not to relieve his patient of her symptoms but to replace them with alternative ones. The 49-year-old woman had developed muscular spasms, a jerking of her trunk and limbs, when her younger son had left to serve in the armed forces. These had disappeared on his return, but they reappeared after his tragic death in a motorbike accident. She now developed a facial grimacing, a jerking of the hands to the chest, and a 'salaam' gesture. Seitz found under hypnosis that the patient had quarrelled with her son just before he rode off on his fatal trip. And so it seemed natural to interpret her symptoms as articulating guilty feelings: she was blaming and punishing herself for the whole world to see. So what were the therapeutic options?

Seitz used hypnosis in a first attempt, and her limbs indeed stopped jerking but the facial grimace became much more severe. When he then suggested to her in a hypnotic state that she not jerk at all, she held her arms firmly behind her back. When he told her in the next hypnosis session not to hold her arms in this way, she would comply, but a new muscular spasm would take its place. In a series of subsequent 'experiments' Seitz proceeded to see if he could find a more bearable substitute symptom. He managed to replace the jerking by a facial blush, but discontinued this for fear of her developing the chronic skin disorder rosacea. Two experiments followed in which he used hypnosis to induce first anaesthesia of the scalp, and then itching of the ankles, but this did not succeed in removing the jerking. However, when she was allowed to scratch her ankles, her original symptom disappeared. After a month, however, she reverted to her old symptom, so she was told under hypnosis that she would become itchy, this time on the forearm, and this new state was maintained by weekly hypnosis.

Within a month dermatitis had developed in the part of her body she was scratching, followed by a severe skin disorder over her entire trunk and limbs. Seitz then hypnotized her again, telling her to return to the original jerking, and continued his search for more acceptable symptoms to impose. He tried almost everything. In the hypnotism sessions, he would tell her to come back next time with sweating of the palms, or to develop warts, or alopecia, or the skin disease urticaria. These commands met with varying degrees of success. With some, she would develop the new symptom but *still retain the old one* (the muscular jerking). The only two replacement symptoms which succeeded in getting rid of the initial symptom were those involving itching, when she was told under hypnosis that she was allowed to scratch, and facial blushing. For Seitz, this suggested that the initial symptom could disappear only if it were replaced by one that involved both self-punishment and some degree of exhibitionism. Or, we could say, exposure of her self-punishment to an audience.

In the final experiment, it was suggested to her under hypnosis that a blister-like rash the size of a five-cent piece would appear on the back of her right hand. When she entered Seitz's office a week later for her appointment, she wore a bandage on the designated zone of her hand. Asked how she had injured herself, she explained that 'the weirdest accident that ever happened to me' had occurred. She had been washing up when a fruit-punch, used to extract the core of a grapefruit, had slipped out of her grip. She'd grabbed it and, as she did so, sustained a 'punch' on the back of her hand. 'Isn't that the craziest thing you ever heard?' she added.

However instructive we might find this experiment, it is amazing that there is no question of the psychiatrist's own inclusion in the merry-go-round of symptoms and hypnotic sessions. In particular, there is no question for Seitz of his own desire. What did he want by manipulating the patient in this way? One might even interpret the apparent compliance and continuation of the meetings as playing out the self-punishment the patient supposedly suffered from. She kept returning, after all, to be symbolically punished by a doctor. There must have been the question for her of *what Seitz wanted* in all this. And the case raises the whole question of the doctor's desire to influence and have power over a woman's body.

It is curious why traditional psychotherapy was not used here. Instead, we find the treatment perpetuating the unconscious structure of the symptom. If this symptom was her way of showing her guilt, why remove the symptom rather than work on the guilt? Balint's ideas about illness bring such problems into focus. And they raise a number of other questions. What if the guilt, in this case, could not be treated with traditional therapy? If, in some cases, a somatic symptom emerges where something simply can't be thought about, trying to force the patient to 'work through' or 'confront' some unsymbolizable event or loss might trigger dangerous behaviour. As the doctor or therapist insists that the patient engage with what they are supposed to be pushing out of their mind, the material in question might return *but not in the form of thought or memory*. Unable to gain symbolization, it might be forced to appear through a dangerous compulsive act or even in some cases a hallucination. If the psychiatrist in the above case had insisted that the woman confront her guilt, there is a possibility that, unable to work it through, she would be left with no choice but to *show it*: perhaps even through a suicidal act to join her son.

Once again, many of the early psychosomaticists were aware of this problem. In one case, a man in his fifties was suffering from congestive heart failure. There were clear links between exacerbations in his condition and his fury at a former lover who had left him, and his rage was progressively threatening to immobilize him. The treating physician noted that the relation with his ex-lover played out relations and scenes from his childhood between him and his mother, aunt and sister, and that this was tightly bound up with the present problems. Yet, perhaps very sensibly, the physician made no attempt to interpret these things directly to the patient. Rather, he was encouraged to deal with the intense emotions elicited by the helplessness in which he found himself physically. The physician agreed with the apparent correctness of the patient's views on his situation, telling him that these were past history and need no longer stir up the storm that was damaging his health.

This strategy, it seems, proved effective, and the course of the disease was much improved **through a strengthening** rather than **through an analysis** of the patient's defences. The physician noted that the emotionally distant cardiologist who worked with him on the case was able, precisely by his detached manner, to allay many of the patient's worst fears about his health. This example is particularly relevant as it shows that each case must be considered on an individual basis, rather than blindly applying some rule such as the imposition of a talking therapy. What mattered here was that the physician knew enough about psychoanalysis and took the time to learn more about his patient. He was then in a better position to decide on treatment, and he chose not to pursue an analytic path. He felt that the patient's precon-scious assumptions – perhaps his belief in medical knowledge or in the authoritative male doctor – could be used to improve his condition more successfully than any kind of insight into his childhood.

We are seeing here how there is no one rule for an approach to somatic symptoms. Sometimes aiming to remove them is risky. Interestingly, a similar argument has been made regard-ing so-called mental illness. A vast amount of research exists studying the coexistence of symptoms of classic organic illness and psychiatric illness. Researchers have tried again and again to see if certain mental illnesses accompany or exclude certain physical ones. Innumerable projects have tried to find corre-lations here: do paranoiacs, for example, get cancer less than anyone else? Or do schizophrenics develop fewer auto-immune disorders? Some French researchers have argued that, if indeed psychiatric symptoms can protect people from organic ones, there is a certain risk in curing psychiatric symptoms. If the 'mental' symptoms are defence mechanisms, contemporary efforts to socialize the 'mentally ill' through drugs may increase the risk of somatic illness in people who are protected against it.

　　The common symptom of anxiety, for example, may be relieved by modern drugs, but at what price? If anxiety is a kind of *psychical signal* which will mobilize defence mech-anisms, won't drugs that numb anxiety sometimes risk producing somatic symptoms by blocking these pathways? If the usual defence mechanisms can't be activated here, other symptoms – sometimes physical ones – may occur to respond to traumatic events or situations. In one case, an elderly woman was hospitalized for serious eczema on her back. An only child, she had lost her mother early and found herself living alone with her father, whose gaze was intolerable to her. After her second marriage, she had a hysterectomy and fell into a depression. The neurologist she went to see said to her, 'Madame, the older you get, the more trapped you will be,' and sure enough she found herself living with her husband in a small flat in the provinces after their retirement. Isolated and caring for her now sick husband, she began to experience the feeling of being stared at from behind. Her doctor prescribed tranquillizers to alleviate her anxiety, and they worked most effectively. But now that her subjective experience of anxiety was gone, it was replaced by an area of eczema on her back at the point she felt she was being looked at. If the anxiety was her response to the situation, once she was deprived of it the intrusive gaze of her father was simply inscribed on her body in the form of the eczema.

Such examples suggest that the treating doctor question their own attitudes to the patient's symptoms. Which isn't to say that this will be a simple process. And it might involve a basic questioning of *why they had decided to become a doctor in the first place.* The *Devil's Dictionary* definition of a doctor is 'One upon whom we set our hopes when ill, and our dogs when well', but despite this warning, we would do well to ask this question. Is it really feasible that the unconscious motivations which push someone to become a doctor can have no influence at all on their style of practice? Or, on the contrary, should we expect medical training to purify its subjects of any of the darker threads which had drawn them there in the first place?

When we discussed alexithymia – a rigid inability to connect with one's emotional life, to elaborate fantasies and a focusing on concrete details – we saw how one characteristic of this way of thinking was the explanation of somatic symptoms in terms of somatic causes. The idea of psychological causation was anathema. Alexithymia has indeed been defined precisely as the difficulty in distinguishing feelings and the bodily sensations of emotional arousal. Now, for the purposes of argument, suppose that some people who become doctors are in fact alexithymic themselves. Alexithymics, after all, are supposed to have a stimulus-based appreciation of reality, in which causes are reduced to external agents like bacteria or 'stress'. Couldn't this be one of the many reasons why such people became doctors in the first place? If that were true, what consequences would it have?

There would be no real exploration of emotional life because it would be precisely the detachment from this that allowed the person to become a doctor. The very same mechanisms that permitted witnessing people's suffering and pain and the examination of their unwell bodies would be those that made emotions and unconscious factors both inaccessible and irrelevant. Rosine Debray noted with surprise how not a single one of the consultants who had referred diabetic subjects to her bothered to check on their progress or familiarize themselves with her findings. And one of our colleagues reported recently the experience of being asked to teach a course on emotional literacy to medical students: although they duly attended class, it was as if nothing could be registered. There was just no interest, and not even enough rebellion to skip the class. Yet we should not forget that in the case of congestive heart failure we discussed, it was precisely the cardiologist's detachment that helped the patient. Indeed, as the psychiatrist Karl Menninger once observed, many of the most successful surgeons have been 'the least noted for the tenderness of their clinical approach'.

Research on the psychology of doctors has revealed many disturbing facts. One study found that 70 per cent of medical students expressed a desire for psychiatric help, although only 27 per cent actually sought it. Levels of psychiatric illness are greater in the medical profession than in the general population, ranging from 25 per cent in an Italian study to up to 30 per cent in an English one. One study found that a third of physicians reported depersonalization in relation to their patients, together with a low sense of personal accomplishment. Drug addiction, suicide and alcoholism are also at much higher levels than in many other professions, with the suicide rate especially pronounced for female doctors, approximately four times higher than that for other professional women. After pub owners and bar staff, doctors are the professional group most likely to die of alcohol-related liver disease. Interestingly, none of these statistical studies bothered to ask the question *why these people had chosen to become physicians*.

It is usually assumed, in fact, that any problems doctors have are a result of the stresses their jobs impose. Busy schedules, bureaucracy, hospital pressures and troublesome patients all add up to a difficult routine. Helen Flanders Dunbar observed in *Emotions and Bodily Changes* that it is important to know not only what the doctor does to the patient, but what the patient does to the doctor. And yet this should not mean that we ignore the questions of continuity between the physician's life before and after their medical training. It would be far-fetched to attribute all problems to the pressures of the job. And indeed, recent work has shown that each person's methods of responding to difficulty and pressure are more or less the same *before* and *after* medical school.

Freud thought that the popular childhood game of playing doctor meant repeating in an active way what one had been subjected to. The child becomes almighty and all-powerful, a master of the situation in which they had once been passive. His colleague Ernst Simmel looked at the link between the doctor game and the future vocation for the job itself and found many clear correlations. Interestingly, although few doctors would consciously subscribe to the Freudian idea of all-powerfulness and mastery, realizing that the daily routine of a GP's surgery might involve quite the opposite, it is not unlikely that they might still believe in this omnipotence, but they'd situate it somewhere else: in a consultant, for example.

Other studies have also made some curious observations. The doctor's first patient, after all, is a corpse. And this cadaver is seen as a *prototype* of a human being, not as an individual. François Magendie, the great early-nineteenth-century French physician, protested against the use of anaesthesia for that reason: he'd never let a patient be reduced to the inanimate state of a corpse. The American psychoanalyst Bertram Lewin found that doctors (we assume mostly male ones) could be divided into those who treated their patients as dead and those who saw their patients as alive. A dead patient in many ways is the optimal one: no answering back, no lip, no resistance to medication, no recurrent visits. Many doctors will work best with the compliant patient, like a surgeon with an anaesthetized subject. Lewin thought that these attitudes might even explain the physicians' take on the mind–body problem: those with a preference for the dead patient would admit only organic factors in the causation of illness, while those who opted for the live patient would favour the psychological.

Other physicians function well if the patient is helpless, as a result of acute illness. Although we should be wary of such generalizations, it is quite likely that each physician will have her or his individual, unconscious preference here, and an exploration of their history and fantasy life is necessary to have a more precise idea. Simmel reports the case of a physician who was able to practise only on condition that he performed a particular ritual every morning before work. He would pace rapidly up and down his surgery, insulting the patients he would be seeing later on that day with every obscenity he could think of. Only then would he be able to see them with the politeness and patience that his profession required.

Equally fascinating is the choice of medical speciality. A doctor who chooses to devote their time to one particular organ or system of the body is not dissimilar to a fetishist who accords greater importance to a single body part or an inanimate object than to the rest of their partner. Specializing is perhaps a socially sanctioned form of fetishism, and it would be prudish to deny the sexual currents implicit in medical interests. The speciality allows the active engagement with the body part in question without fear of arrest or shame. Ideally, it will also be of benefit to the patient, and so a kind of equilibrium is maintained.

This combination of factors is contained in the very wish to be a doctor. It represents a brilliant solution for a child: on the one hand, it satisfies the exigencies of society, the respected profession functioning as an ideal; and on the other, it allows a pursuit of precisely those infantile interests that society prohibits – exploring the body, nakedness, urine and excrement, and so on. It is difficult not to notice how in those early childhood games the apparatus of stethoscope, syringe and surgeon's knife are used to play out rather crude enactments of sexual scenarios, involving the penetration and mutilation of bodies. The underlying conception of sexual relations between the parents being acted out here explains why so many children are happy to play not just the 'doctor' but also the 'patient'.

The idea of a happy balance between childhood interests and professional activity is no doubt rather idealized. There will clearly be cases where a specialist's choice no longer 'works' for them, just as there will be many cases where outside pressures, from a health service or from colleagues, start to block the particular way the specialist had elaborated their interest in an organ or system of the body. The increasing restructuring of modern health services along managerial and legalistic lines involves the risk that isolated and individualistic practices may be challenged, although one might suspect that the fragmentation of the body encouraged by medicine today actually works at another level in its favour.

There is also the very obvious fact that specialists will often disagree about a particular case, in ways that indicate the direction of their own unconscious interests. A world authority on gynaecology recently remarked, after a few drinks, that she simply couldn't understand why any woman would want to have a vaginal birth. All births, she thought, should be Caesarean. One wonders how much this inner conviction is linked to her own fantasies and how much it would actually influence the advice and opinion she would give to patients and colleagues professionally.

Could medical education influence the fantasy life of doctors? This is doubtful, since unconscious attitudes cannot be changed in a classroom. Someone can attend hundreds of classes and parrot all the right views, but this will have no connection at all with unconscious fantasies and convictions. These can be changed only by the exploration of *the routes which led to the formation* of these fantasies in the first place, which means years of analysis. So should we be pessimistic here? In a sense, we can still hope for changes in the *background of medicine*, and we would agree with Engel that the basic step is to challenge the thesis that the disciplines basic to medicine are physics and chemistry. Would it be so absurd to suggest that literature and philosophy would make better candidates, as they encourage the study of human beings living in a world of meaning?

This might encourage wider uses of the medical encounter. Many of the demands made on health services come from people who are experiencing psychological problems in their daily lives. When they complain to a doctor about their symptoms, they may well be sent on endless rounds of consultations until some abnormality is found. Given the complexity of the human body, how many of us, after all, will be 'normal' on all bodily parameters? It has been observed that, if enough bodily functions and processes are measured, one in twenty of them will be abnormal. When some fault is found, this can then be proposed as the cause of their complaint, and often a period of peace will follow. The patient might feel a bit better or relieved at the least. But what if the complaint were seen as an opportunity to explore what is not working in the patient's life in a larger context? As Balint pointed out, the medical solution here would in fact just be a way of refusing the patient's implicit offer to talk, even if this offer might not prove fruitful in every case.

This is where listening matters. In a discussion of the relation of psychoanalysis to medicine, Lacan made the point that medicine is above all about responding to demand. When a patient asks for something or complains, the doctor must try to have a sense of *what is really being asked*. The patient might actually be ill, in the sense of displaying the signs of some named illness, but essential to their appeal could be the demand to be *authenticated* as ill. This is not the same thing as being ill, although it is perfectly possible that the patient is both ill and in need of being authenticated as ill. This demand to be recognized might conceal unconscious desire or guilt, as we saw in the case of conversion symptoms. Or, it may involve the search for a way of registering some event or experience that cannot be processed or thought about. Lacan remarked that, as a careful process of listening and then using this listening to judge how best to respond, psychoanalysis is, in fact, the last relic of traditional medicine.

Analysis, after all, is based on careful listening, and allows the patient to discern what is being said beyond their manifest complaint. It aims to distinguish between a person's conscious demands and the unconscious desires that lie hidden beyond them. It is also time-consuming, and it would be difficult to think of a current medical practice that involves meeting a patient for up to an hour a day, five days a week, over a period lasting several years. But it will allow a degree of intimacy to be built up as well as a knowledge about the particularity of that unique person.

If the traditional place of the doctor in some societies involved the process of attentive listening and a detailed knowledge of the patient, the advent of scientific medicine with its host of bureaucracies, technologies and scales has dramatically changed this. With the doctor no longer in the position of someone to whom a suffering human being can truly address themself, it is inevitable that people will turn to and create new forms of listener. Modern medicine is sadly not about listening, and it is not about trying to unravel what is being articulated beyond the manifest symptoms of an illness. As the doctor's place in society is so radically transformed, could psychoanalysis, Lacan asked, be the only practice that allows the doctor to retain something of the originality of their position?

Afterword

We have seen how many aspects of conventional Western medicine are poorly suited to respond to human illness. As the body has become more and more fragmented, and health services reduced to local applications of intervention and expertise, the individual has been lost in a vast maze of conflicting interests and misguided techniques. This has led, quite naturally, to an appeal to alternative forms of medicine that take the time to listen and to respect the particularity of the patient. Rather than let this split widen, it would seem logical, if not imperative, for conventional medicine to learn from such trends and rethink some of its own procedures and practices.

A stumbling block for so many of those concerned with these questions, both as patients and as health workers, is the stance taken on the causality of illness and the relation of mind to body. An insistence on either the one or the other will most likely discourage dialogue with proponents of the opposite view. And yet we have seen throughout this book how illness will involve a variety of factors which can rarely be reduced to either agency of mind or body. If we choose, for example, to name some bodily process in the genesis of an illness, we may well find that the biology itself involves autonomic, endocrine or immunological factors that will be partly affected by subjective experience and unconscious mental life.

How much this will be so is clearly a question for research into each individual case. We have seen how the idea that a single cause is responsible for a single illness is both wrong and unhelpful. Most illnesses are complex processes that involve many different contributing causal factors. In one case, a psychological situation may be especially important, and even in the same case the factors that matter the most may change from one moment to the next. Likewise, the factors that predispose one to an illness will not necessarily be the same as those that sustain it or, indeed, those that initiate it. The presence of a whole cluster of predisposing factors may never result in illness in one person, yet be fatal for another. All of this moves us away from simple single-cause models that are nonetheless so attractive to common-sense thinking.

Even the psychological factors most widely acknowledged as contributing to physical illness may fail to produce any symptoms. Depression may increase the likelihood of becoming unwell in some situations, but not everyone who is depressed will also develop a physical illness like coronary heart disease. Those who are unable to express emotion may be found among cancer sufferers, but being unable to express emotion doesn't mean one is going to get cancer. Life changes like separation, bereavement, job loss and long-term relationship difficulties may have an impact on health, but what matters is how they are interpreted and processed by an individual according to their unique history. Actual, imagined or threatened separations may well affect autonomic, endocrine and immune functions, but how this is dealt with and what course it takes cannot be predicted with any certainty.

This should not encourage anyone to give up psychologically minded research. On the contrary, it should simply warn us of the dangers of pursuing inappropriate methods – those sadly that are currently dominant in our culture. What we need are long, detailed, book-length studies of individual patients and their histories – and the time to read them. It is no accident that there are more narratives of illness in our bookshops than ever before, yet they are authored not by doctors but by novelists and those affected directly or indirectly by illness. The very fact of this imbalance should be taken as a warning by medicine, and encourage the publication of case studies rich in detail and context.

The conflict here is perhaps a structural one. The health services and bureaucracies of contemporary society are based on a rejection of the very dimension of human narrative. We can have personality traits and stress scores and all manner of statistics, but not the stories and details of a human life. And this, perhaps, is why it is left to the novelists and other writers to bring back the dimension of narrative. Even in the field of psychoanalysis, the days of the long case history are over. What we find instead are brief vignettes and compressed cases where the direct speech of the patient is increasingly neglected and unreported.

As patients and potential patients, we are faced with the difficult task of inscribing our own narratives within medical systems that are not equipped to deal with them. We can do a number of things here. As well as actively researching theories and treatments of illness, we can insist on the importance of dialogue and explore the possibilities of articulating our own individual histories. This supposes, of course, that there are people willing to listen. And here we knock up against a fundamental problem in medical training. How long will it be, we can ask, before it is acknowledged that the natural sciences do not necessarily constitute the optimum background for work as a GP? Surely a solid formation in the arts of listening and interpreting would serve doctors just as well, if not better, than the scientific studies they have pursued prior to medical school?

Could it be possible that the pendulum will one day swing back the other way? It is true that social conditions have historically made the detailed scrutiny of cases less likely at some times than at others. When the great seventeenth-century physician Thomas Sydenham was writing not long after the last plague in London, he may have had less interest in multi-causal models of illness. Yet today's landscape of chronic disease suggests that it is precisely multi-causal models that will do most justice to the phenomena. Will the impasses generated by the management of such diseases produce a renewed interest in the psychosomatic approach? Or will their complexity simply spawn an endless multiplication of causes that risks making us lose sight of those factors that may at times be of much more importance than others?

But here again we return to the problem. Whether the model is single or multi-causal, the old prejudices and beliefs about the respective role of mind and body will emerge. People tend to be rigid and set in their opinions. Yet as we have explored the issues thoroughout the book, the conclusion is almost forced on us that the split between mind and body is in fact itself *a defence mechanism against recognizing how disturbing, excessive or unprocessable ideas affect us*. We have seen again and again how bodily signs are understood without any reference to their meaning, as if the whole question of mental life had to be split off. In the language of the alexithymia theorists, there is a failure to link thoughts and feelings with the bodily sensations of emotional response and arousal.

This means that bodily sensations, symptoms and complaints will be explained exclusively in terms of bodily processes. And this attitude will fit most medical frameworks very well. Illness is caused by a problem in the body and it needs a bodily cure. But if, in many cases, *the intellectual split between mind and body is itself a defence mechanism*, the medical solution that relies on this simply replicates the defensive structure of the patient. As the British psycho-analyst Donald Winnicott once pointed out, 'The doctor's own dissociations need to be considered along with the dissociations in the personalities of the patients.' Where the patient dissociates mind and body, so may the doctor and so may a culture. Splitting them may allow the patient to adapt to social reality, but how much will it further an under-standing of human illness? And at what price?

Endnotes

Introduction

p. 1   *American Psychosomatic Society brochure*: Dennis Novack, 'Realizing Engel's Vision: Psychosomatic Medicine and the Education of Physician-Healers', *Psychosomatic Medicine*, 65 (2003), pp. 925–30.

p. 2   *Three out of every four people in the UK and the US*: Gordon Asmundson, Steven Taylor and Brian Cox, *Health Anxiety* (Wiley, Chichester, 2001), and Wayne Katon, Richard Ries and Arthur Kleinman, 'The Prevalence of Somatisation in Primary Care', *Comprehensive Psychiatry*, 25 (1984), pp. 208–15.

p. 5   *Psychosomatic medicine would not be a speciality*: Franz Alexander, 'Psychological Aspects of Medicine', *Psychosomatic Medicine*, 1 (1939), pp. 7–19; Z. Lipowski, 'Review of Consultation Psychiatry and Psychosomatic Medicine', *Psychosomatic Medicine*, 30 (1968), pp. 395–422; Roy Grinker, *Psychosomatic Research* (Grove Press, New York, 1953).

p. 10   *the studies funded by industry*: 'Medical Journals are an Extension of the Marketing Arm of Pharmaceutical Companies', *PloS Medicine*, 2(5) (May 2005), pp. 364–6, and the report 'Pharmaceuticals Companies Accused of Manipulating Drug Trials for Profit', *Independent*, 23 April 2004, pp. 6–7.

1. What Causes Illness?

p. 15   *Most people will have 2–5 colds a year*: Sheldon Cohen et al., 'Emotional Style and Susceptibility to the Common Cold',

Psychosomatic Medicine, 65 (2003), pp. 652–7, and Cohen et al., 'Types of Stressors that Increase Susceptibility to the Common Cold in Healthy Adults', *Health Psychology*, 17 (1998), pp. 214–23.

p. 16 *the idea that one unique entity*: Herbert Weiner and Fawzy Fawzy, 'An Integrative Model of Health, Disease and Illness', in Stanley Cheren (ed.), *Psychosomatic Medicine: Theory, Physiology and Practice*, vol. 1 (International Universities Press, Madison, 1989), pp. 9–44.

p. 17 *only 3.5 per cent of the decline in mortality*: J. and S. McKinlay, 'The Questionable Contribution of Medical Measures to the Decline of Mortality in the United States in the Twentieth Century', *Millbank Memorial Fund Quarterly*, 55 (1997), pp. 405–28.

p. 18 *Malaria, likewise, is caused by a parasite*: Daniel Funkenstein, 'Tertian Malaria and Anxiety', *Psychosomatic Medicine*, 11 (1949), pp. 158–9.

p. 19 *an estimated 24 million homes*: Jimmie Holland, 'History of Psycho-Oncology: Overcoming Attitudinal and Conceptual Barriers', *Psychosomatic Medicine*, 64 (2002), pp. 206–21.

p. 19 *Ulcers were caused by the presence of Helicobacter pylori*: Peter Strang, 'Gastrointestinal Disorders', in Stanley Cheren (ed.), *Psychosomatic Medicine: Theory, Physiology and Practice*, vol. 2 (International Universities Press, Madison, 1989), pp. 427–501, and Robert Sapolsky, *Why Zebras Don't Get Ulcers: An Updated Guide to Stress, Stress-related Diseases, and Coping* (W. H. Freeman, New York, 1998).

p. 20 *the suicide rate goes up*: D. P. Phillips, 'The Influence of Suggestion on Suicide: Substantive and Theoretical Implications of the Werther Effect', *American Sociological Review*, 39 (1974), pp. 340–54.

p. 20 Alberto Seguin, 'The Concept of Disease', *Psychosomatic Medicine*, 8 (1946), pp. 252–7.

p. 21 D. J. Weatherall, 'How Much has Genetics Helped?', *The Times Literary Supplement*, 30 January 1998, pp. 4–5.

p. 22 *there is a growing literature*: Anna Feissel-Lebovici, *Le Gène et son génie: patient, médecin, psychanalyste face à l'hérédité et au cancer* (Erès, Paris, 2001).

p. 25 *secretion of high levels of hydrochloric acid and pepsin*: K. G. Wormsley and M. I. Grossman, 'Maximal Histalog Test in Control Subjects and Patients with Peptic Ulcer', *Gut*, 6 (1965), pp. 427–35.

p. 25 *supposedly homogeneous diseases*: Herbert Weiner, 'The Illusion of Simplicity: The Medical Model Revisited', *American Journal of Psychiatry*, 135 (1978), pp. 27–33.

p. 25 *different mechanisms may produce the same lesions*: Herbert Weiner, 'Psychobiological Markers of Disease', *Psychiatric Clinics of North America*, 2 (1979), pp. 227–42.

p. 26 *a strong psychological factor in one case*: David Kissen, 'The Significance of Syndrome Shift and Late Syndrome Association in Psychosomatic Medicine', *Journal of Nervous and Mental Disease*, 136 (1963), pp. 34–41.

p. 26 *conversation . . . with the philosopher Willard Quine*: Ronna Burger (ed.), *Seth Bernadete, Encounters and Reflections* (University of Chicago Press, Chicago, 2002).

p. 27 *obstacles in the path of future discoveries*: Franz Alexander, 'Psychological Aspects of Medicine', *Psychosomatic Medicine*, 1 (1939), p. 9.

p. 27 *it is estimated that almost 100 million people*: A. A. Rothman and E. H. Wagner, 'Chronic Illness Management: What is the Role of Primary Care?', *Annals of Internal Medicine*, 138 (2003), pp. 256–61.

p. 27 *over 5,000 residents of the town of Framington*: Robert Aronowitz, *Making Sense of Illness, Science, Society and Disease* (Cambridge University Press, Cambridge, 1998).

p. 28 *up to 50 per cent of the commonest causes of death*: J. M. McGinnis and W. H. Foege, 'Actual Causes of Death in the United States', *Journal of the American Medical Association*, 270 (1993), pp. 2207–12.

p. 28 *out of the seven to eight thousand hours of training*: Dennis Novack, 'Realizing Engel's Vision: Psychosomatic Medicine and the Education of Physician-Healers', *Psychosomatic Medicine*, 65 (2003), pp. 925–30.

p. 29 *several studies have shown the high rate of non-compliance*: Brigitta Bunzel and Kurt Laederach-Hofmann, 'Solid Organ Transplantation: Are there Predictors for Post-transplant Noncompliance? A Literature Overview', *Transplantation*, 70 (2000), pp. 711–16.

p. 30 *diabetic girl*: Albert Danan, 'Diabète et maladies auto-immunes', in M. Sami-Ali et al. (eds.), *Identité et psychosomatique* (Recherche en Psychosomatique, EDK, Paris, 2003), pp. 107–22.

p. 31 E. Weiss and O. S. English, *Psychosomatic Medicine* (WB Saunders Co., Philadelphia, 1943).

p. 31 *Procter & Gamble's decision*: George Lundberg, 'Resolved: Psychosocial Interventions Can Improve Clinical Outcomes in Organic Disease – Discussant Comments', *Psychosomatic Medicine*, 64 (2002), pp. 568–70.

2. Why Listening Matters

p. 33 *hospital patients were less satisfied*: C. R. Joyce, 'The Issue of Communication within Medicine', *Psychiatry in Medicine*, 3 (1972), pp. 357–63.

p. 33 *the average time a patient is allowed to speak*: M. K. Marvel, 'Soliciting the Patient's Agenda: Have We Improved?', *Journal of the American Medical Association*, 281 (1999), pp. 283–7.

p. 34 *in 50 per cent of medical encounters*: see M. Simpson et al., 'The Toronto Consensus Statement', *British Medical Journal*, 303 (1991), pp. 1385–7.

p. 34 *'a mosaic of specialities'*: Helen Flanders Dunbar, *Emotions and Bodily Changes*, 3rd edn (Columbia University Press, New York, 1946).

p. 34 Stefan Zweig, *Mental Healers* (1932) (Cassell, London, 1933).

p. 34   *In America the number of visits to alternative practitioners*: D. M. Eisenberg et al., 'Trends in Alternative Medicine Use in the United States, 1990–1997', *Journal of the American Medical Association*, 280 (1998), pp. 1569–75.

p. 34   *best-selling textbook*: Parveen Kumar and Michael Clark, *Clinical Medicine*, 5th edn (Saunders, London, 2004).

p. 38   On the psychological factors in dentistry, see Edward Ryan, *Psychobiologic Foundations of Dentistry* (Charles Thomas, Springfield, 1946); Marvin Burstone, 'The Psychosomatic Aspects of Dental Problems', *Journal of the American Dental Association*, 33 (1946), pp. 862–71; A. W. Gill, 'Psychology of Mouth and Teeth', *British Dental Record*, 61 (1941), pp. 175–84.

p. 39   *between 40 and 100 per cent of recorded eye disorders*: Carl Zimet and Allan Berger, 'Emotional Factors in Primary Glaucoma', *Psychosomatic Medicine*, 22, 1960, pp. 391–9.

p. 40   T. F. Schlaegel and M. Hoyt, *Psychosomatic Ophthalmology* (Williams and Wilkins, Baltimore, 1957).

p. 40   *a man consulted an opthalmologist*: William Inman, 'Clinical Observations on Morbid Periodicity', *British Journal of Medical Psychology*, 21 (1948), pp. 254–62, and 'Emotional Factors in Diseases of the Cornea', *British Journal of Medical Psychology*, 38 (1965), pp. 277–87.

p. 41   *the 'aversion'*: Richard Rahe, 'Life Change Measurement Clarification', *Psychosomatic Medicine*, 40 (1978), pp. 95–8.

p. 42   *Swiss conference proceedings*: 'Le Point sur le mouvement des idées en psychosomatique', *Actualités Psychosomatiques*, 7 (2004).

p. 42   *the popular topic of pain research*: Francis Keefe et al., 'Changing Face of Pain: Evolution of Pain Research in "Psychosomatic Medicine"', *Psychosomatic Medicine*, 64 (2002), pp. 921–38.

p. 42   *'one patient (0.7 per cent) . . .'*: S. Zipfel et al., 'Effects of Depressive Symptoms on Survival', *Psychosomatic Medicine*, 64 (2002), pp. 740–47.

p. 43   *one study found that 54 per cent of city dwellers*: M. Landolt et al., 'Living Anonymous Kidney Donors', *Transplantation*, 71 (2001), pp. 1690–96.

p. 44   *subjects were shown film footage*: Boris Cyrulnik, *Les Nourritures affectives* (Odile Jacob, Paris, 1993).

3. Is Stress the Culprit?

p. 47   Oliver Wendell Holmes, 'Opening Speech', *Boston Medical and Surgery Journal*, 1883, pp. 361–8.

p. 48   *a 36-year-old journalist*: Avery Wiseman, 'The Doctor–Patient Relationship: Its Role in Therapy', in Henry Miles, Stanley Cobb and Harley Shands (eds.), *Case Histories in Psychosomatic Medicine* (Norton, New York, 1952), pp. 22–40.

p. 51   *medical forms leave only enough space for a single word*: James Gordon, *Manifesto for a New Medicine* (Perseus Books, Reading, 1996).

p. 52   *a woman develops Raynaud's disease*: George Engel and Arthur Schmale, 'Psychoanalytic Theory of Psychosomatic Disorder', *Journal of the American Psychoanalytic Association*, 15 (1967), pp. 344–65.

p. 54   *The concept of stress*: Walter Cannon, *Bodily Changes in Pain, Hunger, Fear and Rage* (Appleton, New York, 1929).

p. 55   *general adaptation syndrome*: Hans Selye, *The Physiology and Pathology of Stress* (Acta, Montreal, 1950). On the context of stress research, see Pascal-Henri Keller, *La Médecine psychosomatique en question* (Odile Jacob, Paris, 1997).

p. 57   James Lynch, *The Broken Heart: The Medical Consequences of Loneliness* (Basic Books, New York, 1977).

p. 58   On stressors, see Herbert Weiner, 'Some Psychological Factors Related to Cardiovascular Responses: A Logical and Empirical Analysis', in Robert Roessler and Norman Greenfield (eds.), *Physiological Correlates of Psychological Disorder* (University of Wisconsin Press, Madison, 1962), pp. 115–41.

p. 59   *those who obeyed orders displayed fewer stress symptoms*: B. E. Eleftheriou and J. P. Scott (eds.), *The Physiology of Aggression and Defeat* (Plenum, New York, 1971).

p. 59   *absence of stress could only really occur after death*: Hans Selye, *Stress Without Distress* (Hodder & Stoughton, London, 1974).

p. 60   *a consensus could be found on what constituted life stress*: Richard Rahe, 'Subjects' Life Changes and their Near-Future Illness Susceptibility', *Advances in Psychosomatic Medicine*, 8 (1972), pp. 2–19, and Rahe 'Subjects' Recent Life Changes and their Near-Future Illness Reports', *Annals of Clinical Research*, 4 (1972), pp. 250–65.

p. 61   *the case of a transvestite*: Graeme Taylor, *Psychosomatic Medicine and Contemporary Psychoanalysis* (International Universities Press, Madison, 1987), p. 265.

p. 64   *scale of choice could be 'contaminated'*: Richard Rahe, 'Life Change Measurement Clarification', *Psychosomatic Medicine*, 40 (1978), pp. 95–8.

p. 64   *no place . . . for the individual narratives*: Alasdair MacIntyre, *After Virtue* (University of Notre Dame Press, Chicago, 1983), ch. 15.

p. 64   *parents consistently misreport health*: S. A. Mednick and J. B. P. Shaffer, 'Mothers' Retrospective Reports in Childrearing Research', *American Journal of Orthopsychiatry*, 33 (1963), p. 457, and Charles Wenar, 'The Reliability of Developmental Histories', *Psychosomatic Medicine*, 25 (1963), pp. 505–9.

p. 65   *One study of 463 patients*: Stanley Cheren and Peter Knapp, 'Gastrointestinal Disorders', in H. I. Kaplan et al., *Comprehensive Textbook of Psychiatry*, vol. 3 (Williams & Wilkins, Baltimore, 1980), pp. 1862–72. See also J. J. Feldman, 'The Household Interview Survey as a Technique for the Collection of Morbidity Data', *Journal of Chronic Disease*, 11 (1960), pp. 535–57.

p. 65   *a 22-year-old man*: See George Engel, 'How Much Longer Must Medicine's Science be Bound by a Seventeenth Century World View?', *Psychotherapy and Psychosomatics*, 57 (1992), pp. 3–16.

p. 67   *diabetic man*: Rosine Debray, *L'Equilibre psychosomatique: organisation mentale des diabétiques* (Dunod, Paris, 1983).

4. The Timing of Illness

p. 69   *significant times*: D. P. Phillips and D. G. Smith, 'Postponement of Death Until Symbolically Meaningful Occasions', *Journal of the American Medical Association*, 263 (1990), pp. 1947–51. The Harvest Moon and Passover research has been critiqued recently by Gary Smith, 'Asian-American Deaths Near the Harvest Moon Festival', *Psychosomatic Medicine*, 66 (2004), pp. 378–81, but note that, with the Millennium, more than 20,700 British people died in the first week of January, a 65 per cent rise on the last week of December. The same imbalance occurred in New York, where 50 per cent more people than usual died in January.

p. 69   *the single most likely time to die*: D. R. Thompson, J. E. F. Pohl and T. W. Sutton, 'Acute Myocardial Infarction and Day of the Week', *American Journal of Cardiology*, 69 (1992), pp. 266–7.

p. 70   On voodoo or sudden death, see Walter Cannon, '"Voodoo" Death', *Psychosomatic Medicine*, 19 (1957), pp. 182–90. See also George Engel, 'Sudden and Rapid Death During Psychological Stress: Folklore or Folk Wisdom?', *Annals of Internal Medicine*, 74 (1971), pp. 771–82, and Efrain Gomez, 'Voodoo and Sudden Death: The Effects of Expectations on Health', *Transcultural Psychiatric Research Review*, 19 (1982), pp. 75–92.

p. 70   *some 25 per cent of all fatalities*: Engel, 'Sudden and Rapid Death', op. cit.

p. 71   *patients who are sure they will die during surgery*: A. D. Weisman and T. P Hackett, 'Predilection to Death', *Psychosomatic Medicine*, 23 (1961), pp. 232–56, and Dean Kilpatrick et al., 'The Use of Psychological Test Data to Predict Open-Heart Surgery Outcome: A Prospective Study', *Psychosomatic Medicine*, 37 (1975), pp. 62–73.

p. 71   *pre-operative depression in patients*: S. Zipfel et al., 'Effects of Depressive Symptoms on Survival', *Psychosomatic Medicine*, 64 (2002), pp. 740–47.

p. 71   *which patients would die during open-heart surgery*: Kilpatrick et al., 'The Use of Psychological Test Data', op. cit.

p. 72   *military recruits*: Herbert Weiner, Morton Resier and Arthur Mirsky, 'Etiology of Duodenal Ulcer', *Psychosomatic Medicine*, 19 (1957), pp. 1–10.

p. 72   *twenty cases of perforated ulcer*: Pietro Castelnuovo-Tedesco, 'Emotional Antecedents of Perforation of Ulcers of the Stomach and Duodenum' (1962), in *Dynamic Psychiatry: Explorations in Psychotherapy, Psychoanalysis and Psychosomatic Medicine* (International Universities Press, Madison, 1991), pp. 267–90.

p. 73   On the risk after relaxing, see J. Overmier, R. Murison and H. Ursin, 'The Ulcerogenic Effect of a Rest Period after Exposure to Water-restraint Stress', *Behavioral and Neural Biology*, 46 (1986), pp. 372–82, and J. Isenberg et al., 'Impaired Proximal Duodenal Mucosal Bicarbonate Secretion in Duodenal Ulcer Patients', *New England Journal of Medicine*, 316 (1987), pp. 374–9.

p. 73   *onset situation*: Castelnuovo-Tedesco, 'Emotional Antecedents of Perforation of Ulcers', op. cit.

p. 73   *polio patients*: Lawrence Kubie, 'Influence of Symbolic Processes on the Role of Instincts in Human Behavior', *Psychosomatic Medicine*, 18 (1956), pp. 189–208.

p. 74   *links between the onset of diseases*: George Daniels, 'The Role of Emotion in the Onset of Diabetes', *Psychosomatic Medicine*, 10 (1948), pp. 288–90.

p. 74   *diabetic girl*: Albert Danan, 'Diabète et maladies auto-immunes', in M. Sami-Ali et al. (eds.), *Identité et psychosomatique* (Recherche en Psychosomatique, EDK, Paris, 2003), pp. 107–22.

p. 76   *Whitehall civil servants*: M. Kumari et al., 'Prospective Study of Social and Other Risk Factors for Incidence of Type 2 Diabetes in the Whitehall II Study', *Archives of Internal Medicine*, 164 (2004), pp. 1873–80.

p. 76   *Estimates for the percentage of patients with psychological factors*: Herbert Weiner, *Psychobiology and Human Disease* (Elsevier, New York, 1977).

p. 77   *nearly 90 per cent of patients experienced heightening of symptoms*: G. S. Philippopoulos, Eric Wittkower and A. Cousineau, 'The Etiologic Significance of Emotional Factors in Onset and Exacerbations of Multiple Sclerosis', *Psychosomatic Medicine*, 20 (1958), pp. 458–74.

p. 78   *'infantile medical theories'*: S. D. Kipman, *L'Enfant et les sortilèges de la maladie* (Stock, Paris, 1981).

p. 78   *rewriting the apparent facts involved*: Micheline Glicenstein and André Lehmann, 'Cancer et histoire: comment le sujet ré-écrit son histoire', *Psychosomatique*, 9 (1987), pp. 27–32.

p. 78   *eight-year-old girl*: Pascale Bertagne, 'Le Diabète ou l'autre en soi à l'adolescence', *Revue Française de Psychosomatique*, 24 (1990), pp. 41–56.

p. 79   *a woman . . . experienced a knife-like pain*: Françoise Dolto, *L'Image inconsciente du corps* (Seuil, Paris, 1984).

p. 80   *deceased women*: Gabor Mate, *When the Body Says No* (Wiley, New Jersey, 2003).

p. 80   *the death of a loved one has a stronger correlation with mortality*: K. F. Rowland, 'Environmental Events Predicting Death for the Elderly', *Psychological Bulletin*, 84 (1977), pp. 349–72.

p. 81   *75 out of 87 patients had suffered a bereavement*: E. Lindemann, 'Symptomatology and Management of Acute Grief', *American Journal of Psychiatry*, 101 (1944), pp. 141–7.

p. 81   *95,647 people*: Jaako Kaprio, Markku Koskenvuo and Heli Rita, 'Mortality after Bereavement: A Prospective Study of 95,647 Widowed Persons', *American Journal of Public Health*, 77 (1987), pp. 283–7.

p. 81   *mortality was highest in the six months following bereavement*:

Colin Parkes, 'The First Year of Bereavement: A Longitudinal Study of the Reaction of London Widows to the Death of Their Husbands', *Psychiatry*, 33 (1970), pp. 444–67; Parkes, 'Effects of Bereavement on Physical and Mental Health: A Study of the Medical Records of Widows', *British Medical Journal*, 2 (1964), pp. 274–9; Paula Clayton, 'The Sequelae and Nonsequelae of Conjugal Bereavement', *American Journal of Psychiatry*, 136 (1979), pp. 1530–34.

p. 81   *women under sixty-five who had experienced the death of a significant other*: Eric Cottington et al., 'Environmental Events Preceding Sudden Death in Women', *Psychosomatic Medicine*, 42 (1980), pp. 567–74.

p. 81   *relatives of a person who died had a much higher mortality rate*: W. D. Rees and S. G. Lutkins, 'Mortality of Bereavement', *British Medical Journal*, 4 (1967), pp. 13–16.

p. 82   *a tenfold reduction in lymphocyte function*: R. W. Bartrop et al., 'Depressed Lymphocyte Function after Bereavements', *Lancet*, 8016 (1977), pp. 834–6. See also Myron Hoffer et al., 'A Psycho-endocrine Study of Bereavement', parts 1 and 2, *Psychosomatic Medicine*, 34 (1972), pp. 481–504.

p. 83   *how often his patients had become ill*: William Inman, 'Clinical Observations on Morbid Periodicity', *British Journal of Medical Psychology*, 21 (1948), pp. 254–62.

p. 83   *the case of a man whose family had been murdered*: Varda Mei-Tal, Sandford Meyrowitz and George Engel, 'The Role of Psychological Process in a Somatic Disorder: Multiple Sclerosis', *Psychosomatic Medicine*, 32 (1970), pp. 67–86.

p. 83   *'anniversary reactions'*: Sandor Ferenczi, 'Sunday Neuroses', *Further Contributions to the Theory and Technique of Psychoanalysis* (Basic Books, New York, 1926), pp. 174–7.

p. 84   *men often fell ill on the anniversary of . . . their father*: George Pollock, 'Anniversary Reactions, Trauma and Mourning', *Psychoanalytic Quarterly*, 39 (1970), pp. 347–71.

p. 84   *the anniversaries of . . . his father and twin brother.* George Engel, 'The Death of a Twin: Mourning and Anniversary Reactions: Fragments of 10 Years of Self-Analysis', *International Journal of Psychoanalysis*, 56 (1975), pp. 23–40.

p. 85   *a 45-year-old female patient*: Graeme Taylor, *Psychosomatic Medicine and Contemporary Psychoanalysis* (International Universities Press, Madison, 1987), pp. 48–9.

p. 85   *the weakening of heart muscle*: April Witt, 'How Do You Cure a Broken Heart?', *Washington Post* magazine, 29 May 2005, pp. 10–15.

5. Words and Beliefs

p. 94   Helen Flanders Dunbar, *Emotions and Bodily Changes*, 3rd edn (Columbia University Press, New York, 1946).

p. 94   Sigmund Freud, *Psychical (or Mental) Treatment* (1905), Standard Edition, vol. 7 (Hogarth Press, London, 1953), pp. 283–302.

p. 95   *contact dermatitis*: Y. Ikemi and S. Nakagawa, 'A Psychosomatic Study of Contagious Dermatitis', *Kyoshu Journal of Medical Science*, 13 (1962), pp. 335–50.

p. 95   *patients who had undergone painful tooth extraction*: I. Hashish et al., 'Reduction of Postoperative Pain and Swelling by Ultrasound Treatment: A Placebo Effect', *Pain*, 33 (1988), pp. 303–11.

p. 96   *asthmatic subjects*: T. J. Luparello et al., 'Influences of Suggestion on Airway Reactivity in Asthmatic Subjects', *Psychosomatic Medicine*, 30 (1968), pp. 819–25, and Luparello et al., 'The Interaction of Psychologic Stimuli and Pharmacologic Agents on Airway Reactivity in Asthmatic Subjects', *Psychosomatic Medicine*, 32 (1970), pp. 509–13. See also the inhaler experiments by M. Castes et al., 'Immunologic Changes Associated with Clinical Improvement of Asthmatic Children Subjected to Psychosocial Intervention', *Brain, Behavior and Immunity*, 13 (1999), pp. 1–13.

p. 97   *hexed to die before she reached the age of twenty-three*: George

Engel, 'Sudden and Rapid Death during Psychological Stress', *Annals of Internal Medicine*, 74 (1971), pp. 771–82.

p. 97   *a more personal kind of hex*: James Mathis, 'A Sophisticated Version of Voodoo Death', *Psychosomatic Medicine*, 26 (1964), pp. 104–7.

p. 99   For the lupus case, see R. Dantzer, *L'Illusion psychosomatique* (Odile Jacob, Paris, 1989).

p. 100   *hypnotic suggestion not only worked*: A. H. Sinclair-Gieben and Derek Chalmers, 'Evaluation of Treatment of Warts by Hypnosis', *Lancet*, 3 October 1959, pp. 480–82. See also Hermann Vollmer, 'Treatment of Warts by Suggestion', *Psychosomatic Medicine*, 8 (1946), pp. 138–42, and, more recently, R. B. Noll, 'Hypnotherapy of a Child with Warts', *Journal of Developmental and Behavioral Pediatrics*, 9 (1988), pp. 89–91.

p. 101   *patients recovering from heart attacks*: K. A. Jarvinen, 'Can Ward Rounds be a Danger to Patients with Myocardial Infarction?', *British Medical Journal*, 4909 (1955), pp. 318–20.

p. 102   *metal bending*: R. Wiseman and E. Greening, '"It's Still Bending": Verbal Suggestion and Alleged Psychokinetic Ability', *British Journal of Psychology*, 96 (2005), pp. 115–29.

p. 103   *women in eighteenth-century Saxony*: Barbara Duden, 'The Woman Beneath the Skin: A Doctor's Patients in Eighteenth Century Germany', trans. Thomas Dunlap (Harvard University Press, Cambridge, MA, 1991).

p. 104   *recurrent laryngitis*: Leon Kreisler, *La Psychosomatique de l'enfant* (PUF, Paris, 1976).

p. 105   *the most frequently used 'drug' in medical practice*: Michael Balint, *The Doctor, His Patient and the Illness*, revised edn (International Universities Press, Madison, 1964), p. 199.

p. 105   *a few words from the anaesthetist prior to surgery*: Lawrence Egbert et al., 'Reduction of Postoperative Pain by Encouragement and Instruction of Patients', *New England Journal of Medicine*, 270 (1964), pp. 825–7.

p. 107   *effectiveness rates*: Anne Harrington (ed.), *The Placebo Effect* (Harvard University Press, Cambridge, MA, 1997).

p. 108   *government official*: Sigmund Freud, *Notes Upon a Case of Obsessional Neurosis* (1909), Standard Edition, vol. 10 (Hogarth Press, London, 1955), pp. 197–8.

p. 109   *an ill-advised sentence*: Roy Grinker and Fred Robbins, *Psychosomatic Case Book* (Blakiston, New York, 1954), p. 305.

p. 110   *as recently as 1961*: Jimmie Holland, 'History of Psycho-Oncology: Overcoming Attitudinal and Conceptual Barriers', *Psychosomatic Medicine*, 64 (2002), pp. 206–21.

p. 110   *downward spiral*: Robert Hahn, 'The Nocebo Phenomenon: Scope and Foundations', in Harrington, *The Placebo Effect*, op. cit., pp. 56–76.

p. 110   *diagnosis becomes a cause of death*: G. W. Milton, 'Self-willed Death or the Bone-pointing Syndrome', *Lancet*, 7817 (1973), pp. 1435–6.

p. 112   *the case of an engineer in his seventies*: Robert Aronowitz, *Making Sense of Illness, Science, Society and Disease* (Cambridge University Press, Cambridge, 1998).

p. 113   *What was once a risk is now an illness*: ibid.

p. 114   *emotional weeping would one day be reclassified*: Francis Crookshank, 'Organ-Jargon', *British Journal of Medical Psychology*, 10 (1931), pp. 295–332.

p. 114   On labelling, see David Healy, *The Antidepressant Era* (Harvard University Press, Cambridge, MA, 1997).

p. 115   *cases where the sex of an infant is ambiguous*: Suzanne Kessler, 'The Medical Construction of Gender: Case Management of Intersexed Infants', in Barbara Laslett (ed.), *Gender and Scientific Authority* (University of Chicago Press, Chicago, 1996), pp. 340–63.

p. 116   *only 2–3 per cent of the surgical interventions*: James Gordon, Dennis Jaffe and David Bresler, *Mind, Body and Health, Toward an Integral Medicine* (Human Sciences Press, New York, 1984), pp. 4–5.

p. 117   *Pain . . . a necessary part of the procedure*: Editorial, *New York Journal of Medicine*, 9 (1847), pp. 1223–5.

6. Can Illness have a Meaning?

p. 118   *coded expressions of unconscious fantasies*: Sigmund Freud, *Studies on Hysteria* (1895), Standard Edition, vol. 2, and *Three Essays on the Theory of Sexuality* (1905), Standard Edition, vol. 7 (Hogarth Press, London, 1955 and 1953); Felix Deutsch, *On the Mysterious Leap from the Mind to the Body* (International Universities Press, Madison, 1959). See also Roy Grinker and Fred Robbins, *Psychosomatic Case Book* (Blakiston, New York, 1954).

p. 123   *the case of a 24-year-old woman*: Jose Barchilon and George Engel, 'Dermatitis: An Hysterical Conversion Symptom in a Young Woman', *Psychosomatic Medicine*, 14 (1952), pp. 295–305.

p. 126   *imagine there is an unstressed, relaxed fellow*: M. Friedman and V. Price, 'Alteration of Type A Behavior and Reduction in Cardiac Recurrences in Post-Myocardial Infarction Subjects', paper presented at the 15th European Conference on Psychosomatic Research, reported in Taylor, *Psychosomatic Medicine and Contemporary Psychoanalysis* (International Universities Press, Madison, 1987), p. 304.

p. 127   For Freud on feelings, see Sigmund Freud, *Psychical (or Mental) Treatment* (1905), Standard Edition, vol. 7 (Hogarth Press, London, 1953), p. 287.

p. 127   *'there is no symbolism in the symptom'*: Roy Grinker, in Grinker and Robbins, *Psychosomatic Case Book*, op. cit.

p. 127   Franz Alexander, *Psychosomatic Medicine* (Norton, New York, 1950). On Alexander and his influence, see Chase Patterson Kimball, 'Conceptual Developments in Psychosomatic Medicine: 1939–1969', *Annals of Internal Medicine*, 73 (1970), pp. 307–16, and Harold and Helen Kaplan, 'An Historical Survey of Psychosomatic Medicine', *Journal of Nervous and Mental Diseases*, 124 (1956), pp. 546–68. The volume edited by Alexander, Thomas French and George Pollock, *Psychosomatic Specificity* (University of Chicago Press, Chicago, 1968), published after Alexander's death, gives a good idea of how his approach had changed. The legacy of Alexander's scientific work can perhaps best be judged by reading the 650-page study by Herbert Weiner, *Psychobiology and Human Disease* (Elsevier, New York, 1977), a labour of love that compares the Chicago research with later developments in medicine. This exemplary work finds both for and against, and stands out for its careful and non-reductive readings of the earlier research.

p. 129   On conversion mechanisms, see George Engel and Arthur Schmale, 'Psychoanalytic Theory of Somatic Disorder', *Journal of the American Psychoanalytic Association*, 15 (1967), pp. 344–65, and Engel, 'A Reconsideration of the Role of Conversion in Somatic Disease', *Comprehensive Psychiatry*, 9 (1968), pp. 316–25. See also Max Schur, 'Comments on the Metapsychology of Somatization', *Psychoanalytic Study of the Child*, 10 (1955), pp. 119–64.

p. 130   *a twenty-year-old soldier*. Engel, 'A Reconsideration of the Role of Conversion', op. cit., pp. 322–3.

p. 132   On skin disorders, see Eric Wittkower and Brian Russell, *Emotional Factors in Skin Diseases* (Hoeber, New York, 1953).

7. When the Body Replies

p. 134   For the ulcerative colitis case, see Jeanine Jafferali, 'Le Phénomène psychosomatique: un appel au nom du père?', *Zig Zag*, 6 (1997), pp. 19–25. See also Alexandre Stevens, 'Phénomènes psychosomatiques et symptomes de conversion', *Zig Zag*, 6 (1997), pp. 11–18, and the collected papers in 'Le Phénomène psychosomatique et la psychanalyse', *Analytica* (Navarin, Paris, 1986).

p. 136   George Engel, 'Studies of Ulcerative Colitis': I *Psychosomatic Medicine*, 16(6) (1954), pp. 496–501; II *American Journal of Medicine*, 16(3) (1954), pp. 416–33; III *American Journal of Medicine*,

19(2) (1955), pp. 231–56; IV *Psychosomatic Medicine*, 18(4) (1956), pp. 334–46; (V) *American Journal of Digestive Diseases*, 3(4) (1958), pp. 315–37.

p. 139 *a woman discovered a lump*: Richard Renneker et al., 'Psychoanalytical Explorations of Emotional Correlates of Cancer of the Breast', *Psychosomatic Medicine*, 25 (1963), pp. 106–23.

p. 139 *case of eczema*: Gérard Szwec, 'Devenir d'une depression de la première enfance génératrice de somatisations et consequences psychosomatiques de la maltraitance', in Gérard Le Goues and Georges Pragier (eds.), *Cliniques psychosomatiques* (PUF, Paris, 1997), pp. 67–90.

p. 140 On pleasure in scratching, see Max Schur, 'Comments on the Metapsychology of Somatization', *Psychoanalytic Study of the Child*, 10 (1955), pp. 119–64.

p. 142 For McDougall on conversion symptoms, see Joyce McDougall, *Theatres of the Body* (Free Association Books, London, 1989).

8. The Heart

p. 145 *Cambodian refugees*: Devon Hinton et al., 'The Khmer "Weak Heart" Syndrome: Fear of Death from Palpitations', *Transcultural Psychiatry*, 39 (2002), pp. 323–44.

p. 146 Statistics from the British Heart Foundation (www.heartstats.org) and American Heart Association (www.americanheart.org).

p. 148 *A study of male health professionals*: I. Kawachi et al., 'A Prospective Study of Phobic Anxiety and Risk of Coronary Disease in Men', *Circulation*, 89 (1994), pp. 1192–7.

p. 149 On the myth of the upholstery, see Robert Sapolsky, *Why Zebras Don't Get Ulcers: An Updated Guide to Stress, Stress-related Diseases, and Coping* (W. H. Freeman, New York, 1998).

p. 150 *'unlimited number of relatively poorly defined . . .'*: Meyer Friedman and Ray Rosenman, *Type A Behavior and Your Heart*

(Knopf, New York, 1974). For more on the Type A concept, see B. Kent Houston and C. R. Snyder (eds.), *Type A Behavior Pattern: Research, Theory and Intervention* (Wiley, New York, 1988), and John Gallacher et al., 'Is Type A Behavior Really a Trigger for Coronary Heart Disease Events?', *Psychosomatic Medicine*, 65 (2003), pp. 339–46.

p. 150   '*Widespread reduction of such behaviour . . .*': Glen Elliott, 'Stress and Illness', in Stanley Cheren (ed.), *Psychosomatic Medicine: Theory, Physiology and Practice*, vol. 1 (International Universities Press, Madison, 1989), pp. 45–90.

p. 150   *whether hard work gave people heart attacks*: Dean Ornish, in Bill Moyers, *Healing and the Mind* (Broadway, New York, 1993), p. 101.

p. 151   *review of Type A studies*: S. Booth-Kewley and H. S. Friedman, 'Psychological Predictors of Heart Disease', *Psychological Bulletin*, 101 (1987), pp. 343–62.

p. 152   *so-called Type Ds were at a five-fold greater risk*: S. S. Pedersen et al., 'Type D Personality is Associated with Increased Anxiety and Depressive Symptoms in Patients with an Implantable Cardioverter Defibrillator and their Partners', *Psychosomatic Medicine*, 66 (2004), pp. 714–19.

p. 152   *1,800 middle-aged men*: R. B. Shekelle et al., 'Hostility, Risk of Coronary Disease, and Mortality', *Psychosomatic Medicine*, 45 (1983), pp. 219–28.

p. 152   *coronary-artery calcification*: C. Iribarren et al., 'Association of Hostility with Coronary Artery Calcification in Young Adults: The CARDIA Study', *Journal of the American Medical Association*, 283 (2000), pp. 2,546–51.

p. 153   '*Negative affectivity*': Ernest Harburg et al., 'Expressive/Suppressive Anger-Coping Responses, Gender and Types of Mortality: A 17-year Follow-up', *Psychosomatic Medicine*, 65 (2003), pp. 588–97.

p. 153   On the mechanisms of psychological impact, see James

Januzzi et al., 'The Influence of Anxiety and Depression on Outcomes of Patients with Coronary Artery Disease', *Archives of Internal Medicine*, 160 (2000), pp. 1913–21, and L. Wulsin and B. Singal, 'Do Depressive Symptoms Increase the Risk for the Onset of Coronary Disease?', *Psychosomatic Medicine*, 65 (2003), pp. 201–10. See also J. C. Barefoot, 'Depression and Coronary Heart Disease', *Cardiologia*, 42 (1997), pp. 1245–50.

p. 153 *the patient's cholesterol*: P. Libby 'Inflammation in Athero-sclerosis', *Nature*, 420 (2002), pp. 868–74.

p. 154 On the function of the endothelium, see C. B. Nemeroff and D. L. Musselman, 'Are Platelets the Link Between Depression and Ischemic Heart Disease?', *American Heart Journal*, 140 (2000), pp. 57–62.

p. 155 *support from a spouse was crucial*: B. Bunzel, *Herztransplantation: Psychsoziale Grundlagen und Forshungsergebnisse zur Lebensqualität* (Thieme Verlag, New York, 1993).

p. 155 On the importance of social bonds, see James Lynch, *The Broken Heart: The Medical Consequences of Loneliness* (Basic Books, New York, 1977); James House, Karl Landis and Debra Umberson, 'Social Relationships and Health', *Science*, 241 (1988), pp. 540–45; R. B. Williams et al., 'Prognostic Importance of Social and Economic Resources among Medically Treated Patients with Angiographi-cally Documented Coronary Artery Disease', *Journal of the American Medical Association*, 267 (1992), pp. 520–24; T. Rutledge et al., 'Social Networks and Marital Status Predict Mortality in Older Women', *Psychosomatic Medicine*, 65 (2003), pp. 688–94.

p. 155 *Roseto study*: J. G. Bruhn and S. Wolf, *The Roseto Story: An Anatomy of Health* (University of Oklahoma Press, Norman, 1979), and J. G. Bruhn, 'An Epidemiological Study of Myocardial Infarc-tion in an Italian-American Community', *Journal of Chronic Diseases*, 18 (1965), pp. 352–65.

p. 156 *Rates of heart disease in Japan*: Michael Marmot and Leonard Syme, 'Acculturation and Coronary Heart Disease in Japanese-Americans', *American Journal of Epidemiology*, 104 (1976), pp. 225–47.

p. 156   *matched menstrual cycles in roommates*: C. A. Graham and W. C. McGrew, 'Menstrual Synchrony in Female Undergraduates Living on a Co-educational Campus', *Psychoneuroendocrinology*, 5 (1980), pp. 245–52.

p. 156   *the reaction of squirrel monkeys placed under stress*: C. Gonzalez et al., 'Cortisol Responses under Different Housing Conditions in Female Squirrel Monkeys', *Psychoneuroendocrinology*, 7 (1982), pp. 209–16. See also L. Sklar and H. Anisman, 'Social Stress Influences Tumor Growth', *Psychosomatic Medicine*, 42 (1980), pp. 347–65.

p. 157   *Alameda County*: L. F. Berkman and S. L. Syme, 'Social Networks, Host Resistance and Mortality: A 9-year Follow-up of Alameda County Residents', *American Journal of Epidemiology*, 109 (1979), pp. 186–204.

p. 157   On the Michigan study, see J. S. House, C. Robbins and H. M. Metzner, 'The Association of Social Relationships and Activities with Mortality: Prospective Evidence on the Tecumseh Community Health Study', *American Journal of Epidemiology*, 116 (1982), pp. 123–40.

p. 157   *patients with myocardial infarcts were treated*: H. G. Mather et al., 'Acute Myocardial Infarction: Home and Hospital Treatment', *British Medical Journal*, 3 (1971), pp. 334–8.

p. 157   *cardiac arrythmias*: H. Leigh et al., 'A Psychological Comparison of Patients in "Open" and "Closed" Coronary Care Units', *Journal of Psychosomatic Research*, 16 (1972), pp. 449–57.

p. 157   *story of a canny medical student*: George Engel, 'Physician-Scientists and Scientific Physicians: Resolving the Humanism-Science Dichotomy', *American Journal of Medicine*, 82 (1987), pp. 107–11.

p. 158   For an overview of research on culture and the heart, see William Dressler, 'Social and Cultural Influences in Cardiovascular Disease: A Review', *Transcultural Psychiatry Research Review*, 21 (1984), pp. 5–42.

p. 158 *Studies of the elderly*: Jean Carney and Bertram Cohler, 'Developmental Continuities and Adjustment in Adulthood: Social Relations, Morale and the Transformation from Middle to Late Life', in George Pollock and Stanley Greenspan (eds.), *The Course of Life*, vol. 6 (International Universities Press, Madison, 1993), pp. 199–226.

p. 159 For Lacan on the psychosocial factors in hypertension, see Jacques Lacan, 'Les Facteurs psychiques: essai sur les réactions psychiques de l'hypertendu', in Sylvain Blondin, A. Weiss, Claude Rouvillois and Lacan (eds.), *Le Traitement chirurgical de l'hypertension artérielle*, 51ème Congrès Français de Chirurgie (Paris, 1948), pp. 171–6. See also 'Interventions à l'SPP', 1933–1953', *Ornicar?*, 31 (1984), pp. 7–27, and 'A propos de la communication de M. J. Gosset sur les problèmes psychosomatiques en chirurgie générale', *Mémoires de l'Académie de Chirurgie*, 16/17 (1947), pp. 370–73. For context, see Carl Binger et al., *Personality in Arterial Hypertension* (American Society for Research in Psychosomatic Problems, New York, 1945). See also Darian Leader, 'Psychanalyse et psychosomatique', *Savoirs et Clinique*, 7 (2007).

p. 160 *cycle of rivalries*: Jacob Arlow, 'Identification Mechanisms in Coronary Occlusion', *Psychosomatic Medicine*, 7 (1945), pp. 195–209.

p. 162 *a 'rival' attitude had a higher risk factor for mortality than smoking*: A. Skrabski, M. Kopp and I. Kawachi, 'Social Capital and Collective Efficacy in Hungary', *Journal of Epidemiology and Community Health*, 57 (2003), pp. 114–19.

9. Two Bodies or One?

p. 164 *Research into the relation of mother and foetus*: Alan Husband and Maree Gleeson, 'Ontogeny of Mucosal Immunity: Environmental and Behavioral Influences', *Brain, Behavior and Immunity*, 10 (1996), pp. 188–204.

p. 165 *a kind of dialogue between foetus and mother*: Joseph Jaffe et al., 'Rhythms of Dialogue in Infancy', *Monographs of the Society for Research in Child Development*, 66 (2001).

p. 166   *Attunements*: Daniel Stern et al., 'Affect Attunement: The Sharing of Feeling States between Mother and Infant by Means of Intermodal Fluency', in Tiffany Field and Nathan Fox (eds.), *Social Perception in Infants* (Ablex, Norwood, 1985), pp. 249–68.

p. 166   On sound being out of synch, see B. Dodd, 'Lip Reading in Infants: Attention to Speech Presented In and Out of Synchrony', *Cognitive Psychology*, 11 (1979), pp. 478–84.

p. 166   *only 13 per cent of attunements*: Daniel Stern, *The Interpersonal World of the Infant* (Basic Books, New York, 1985).

p. 167   On cycles of exchange, see Colwyn Trevarthen, 'Communication and Cooperation in Early Infancy: A Description of Primary Intersubjectivity', in Margaret Bullowa (ed.), *Before Speech: The Beginnings of Human Communication* (Cambridge University Press, Cambridge, 1979), and Trevarthen, 'The Self Born in Intersubjectivity: The Psychology of an Infant Communicating', in U. Neisser (ed.), *Ecological and Interpersonal Knowledge of the Self* (Cambridge University Press, Cambridge, 1993).

p. 167   *differently textured dummies*: P. E. Bryant and I. Raz, 'Visual and Tactual Perception of Shape by Young Children', *Developmental Psychology*, 11 (1975), pp. 525–6.

p. 167   *limb movements*: Bullowa, *Before Speech*, op. cit., p. 141.

p. 169   *human dialogue*: ibid., p. 195.

p. 170   *research on infants who had been abandoned*: René Spitz, 'Hospitalism: An Inquiry into the Genesis of Psychiatric Conditions in Early Childhood', *Psychoanalytic Study of the Child*, 1 (1945), pp. 53–74, and Spitz, *The First Year of Life* (International Universities Press, Madison, 1965). For a critique of Spitz, see Diane Eyer, *Mother–Infant Bonding: A Scientific Fiction* (Yale University Press, New Haven, CT, 1992).

p. 171   For Lacan on the mother–child relation, see Jacques Lacan, *La Relation d'objet* (1956–7), ed. J.-A. Miller (Seuil, Paris, 1994).

p. 172   *'an organic filiation'*: Jean Guir, 'Réflexions sur les phéno-mènes psychosomatiques', *Analytiques*, 1 (1978), pp. 89–91.

p. 173   *we have too much choice here*: Jerome Kagan, *Three Seductive Ideas* (Harvard University Press, Cambridge, MA, 1998), p. 188.

p. 174   *a number of studies in the 1950s*: Harry Harlow, 'The Nature of Love', *American Psychologist*, 13 (1958), pp. 673–85.

p. 174   *bodies of the mammalian mother and her offspring are enmeshed*: M. A. Hofer, 'Relationships as Regulators', *Psychosomatic Medicine*, 46 (1984), pp. 183–97.

p. 176   On the absence of grief, see Helene Deutsch, 'Absence of Grief' (1937), *Neuroses and Character Types* (International Universities Press, Madison, 1965), pp. 226–36.

p. 178   *Monica study*: George Engel and F. Reichsman, 'Spontaneous and Experimentally Induced Depressions in an Infant with Gastric Fistula: A Contribution to the Problem of Depression', *Journal of the American Psychoanalytic Association*, 4 (1956), pp. 428–52, and Engel, 'Selection of Clinical Material in Psychosomatic Medicine: The Need for a New Physiology', *Psychosomatic Medicine*, 16 (1954), pp. 368–73. See also Graeme Taylor, 'Mind–Body Environment: George Engel's Psychoanalytic Approach to Psychosomatic Medicine', *Australian and New Zealand Journal of Psychiatry*, 36 (2002), pp. 449–67.

p. 178   *Growth-hormone disorders are quite rare*: G. F. Powell, J. A. Brasel and R. M. Blizzard, 'Emotional Deprivation and Growth Retardation Simulating Idiopathic Hypopituitarism', *New England Journal of Medicine*, 276 (1967), pp. 1271–83, and Leon Kreisler, *La Psychosomatique de l'enfant*, 3rd edn (PUF, Paris, 1989), p. 73.

p. 178   *children allergic to household dust*: J. Lamont, 'Psychosomatic Study of Asthma', *American Journal of Psychology*, 114 (1958), pp. 890–99.

p. 179   *cases of leukaemia and lymphoma in children*: William Greene: 'Disease Response to Life Stress', *Journal of the American Medical Women's Association*, 20 (1965), pp. 133–40; 'Psychological Factors and Reticuloendothelial Disease: 1. Preliminary Observations on a Group of Males with Lymphomas and Leukemias', *Psychosomatic Medicine*, 16 (1954), pp. 220–30; 'Psychological Factors and Reticuloendothelial Disease: 1. Observations on a Group of Women with Lymphomas and Leukemias', *Psychosomatic Medicine*, 18 (1956), pp. 284–303; Greene and G. Miller, 'Psychological Factors and Reticuloendothelial Disease: 1. Observations on a Group of Children and Adolescents with Leukemia', *Psychosomatic Medicine*, 20 (1958), pp. 124–44.

p. 180   On the child as an object of projection, see William Greene, 'Role of a Vicarious Object in the Adaptation to Object Loss', *Psychosomatic Medicine*, 21 (1959), p. 438–47, and John Adamson and Arthur Schmale, 'Object Loss, Giving Up, and the Onset of Psychiatric Disease', *Psychosomatic Medicine*, 27 (1965), pp. 557–76.

p. 180   *loss and grief*: Arthur Schmale, 'Relationship of Separation to Disease and Death', *Psychosomatic Medicine*, 20 (1958), pp. 259–77, and Schmale, 'Giving Up as a Final Common Pathway to Changes in Health', *Advances in Psychosomatic Medicine*, 8 (1972), pp. 21–40.

p. 180   *helplessness would affect the biological systems*: George Engel, 'A Life Setting Conducive to Illness: The Giving Up–Given Up Complex', *Annals of Internal Medicine*, 69 (1968), pp. 293–300,

p. 181   *Several studies of rheumatoid arthritis in women*: See Adelaide Johnson, Louis Shapiro and Franz Alexander, 'Preliminary Report on a Psychosomatic Study of Rheumatoid Arthritis', *Psychosomatic Medicine*, 9 (1947), pp. 295–300, and the review in Herbert Weiner, *Psychobiology and Human Disease* (Elsevier, New York, 1977).

p. 184   *the response of incubator babies to human care*: Catherine Mathelin, *Le Sourire de la Joconde: clinique psychanalytique avec les bébés prématurés* (Desnoel, Paris, 1998).

10. Identification

p. 187   *when a child is left by someone they love*: René Spitz, *The*

First Year of Life (International Universities Press, Madison, 1965).

p. 187   On the problems of rumination, see R. Gaddini, 'The Pathology of the Self as a Basis of Psychosomatic Disorders', *Psychotherapy and Psychosomatics*, 28 (1977), pp. 260–71.

p. 189   On the mirror phase, see Jacques Lacan, *Ecrits*, trans. Bruce Fink (Norton, New York, 2006), pp. 75–81, and Guy le Gaufey, *Le Lasso spéculaire* (Epel, Paris, 1997).

p. 189   For Freud on identification, see *Group Psychology and the Analysis of the Ego* (1920), Standard Edition, vol. 18 (Hogarth Press, London, 1955).

p. 190   *'couvade'*: Laurence Kirmayer, 'Culture, Affect and Somatization', part 2, *Transcultural Psychiatric Research Review*, 21 (1984), pp. 237–62.

p. 191   *yawning is contagious*: M. Schurmann et al., 'Yearning to Yawn: The Neural Basis of Contagious Yawning', *NeuroImage*, 24 (2005), pp. 1260–64, and S. Platek et al., 'Contagious Yawning and the Brain', *Cognitive Brain Research*, 23 (2005), pp. 448–52.

p. 192   *female roommates . . . can synchronize their periods*: C. A. Graham and W. C. McGrew, 'Menstrual Synchrony in Female Undergraduates Living on a Co-educational Campus', *Psychoneuroendocrinology*, 5 (1980), pp. 245–52.

p. 193   *The image of the deceased has engulfed their own ego*: Sigmund Freud, *Mourning and Melancholia* (1916), Standard Edition, vol. 14 (Hogarth Press, London, 1957), pp. 243–58.

p. 194   *a recent study of heart disturbances*: Ilan Wittstein et al., 'Neurohumoral Features of Myocardial Stunning Due to Sudden Emotional Stress', *New England Journal of Medicine*, 352 (2005), pp. 539–48.

p. 196   *a man felt persecuted by his transplanted kidney*: P. H. L. Muslin, 'On Acquiring a Kidney', *American Journal of Psychiatry*, 127 (1971), pp. 1185–8; S. H. Basch, 'The Intrapsychic Integration of a New Organ', *Psychoanalytic Quarterly*, 52 (1973), pp. 364–84; R. M. Eisendrath, 'The Role of Grief and Fear in the Death of Kidney

Transplant Patients', *American Journal of Psychiatry*, 126 (1969), pp. 381–7.

p. 197   *depressions in the mother will have an effect on the sugar metabolism*: Magda Liakopoulou et al., 'Maternal Expressed Emotion and Metabolic Control of Children and Adolescents with Diabetes Mellitus', *Psychotherapy and Psychosomatics*, 70 (2001), pp. 78–85.

p. 198   For the blood and lineage case, see Hélène Buquet, 'Le "Sang-Sucre" du diabétique', *Revue de Médecine Psychosomatique*, 17/18 (1989), pp. 147–62.

p. 198   *Paediatricians*: Leon Kreisler, Michel Fain and Michel Soule, *L'Enfant et son corps* (1974) (PUF, Paris, 6th edn, 1999).

p. 198   On the bodies of mother and child, see Joyce McDougall, *Theatres of the Body* and *Theatres of the Mind* (Free Association Books, London, 1989 and 1985).

p. 199   Karin Stephen, *Psychoanalysis and Medicine: The Wish to Fall Ill* (Cambridge University Press, Cambridge, 1933).

p. 202   On role identifications: isn't this what Alexander noticed in his theories of mental conflict? His explanations always seem so confusing: is the person supposed to want to dominate or be dominated? Do they want to separate from the mother or stay close to her? Why not read these apparent confusions as clues: they show how the person can function as long as they have one of the two roles in the formula. Someone may lose their place as loving father to a son, yet then stabilize by becoming the beloved 'son' of a new boss at work, for example. What matters in this case will be to keep the formula 'a father loves a son' going. See Geneviève Morel, *Sexual Ambiguities* (Karnac Books, London, 2007).

11. The Immune System

p. 211   *mixed a drug that suppressed immune responses*: Robert Ader, David Felten and Nicholas Cohen (eds.), *Psychoneuroimmunology*

(Academic Press, San Diego, 2001), 2 vols.

p. 212   For a review, see Robert Ader, 'On the Development of Psychoneuroimmunology', *European Journal of Pharmacology*, 405 (2000), pp. 167–76.

p. 212   *immunology was reductionistic*: Robert Ader, 'Psychosomatic and Psychoimmunological Research', *Psychosomatic Medicine*, 42 (1980), pp. 307–21.

p. 213   *higher incidence of breast cancer among female night-shift workers*: S. Davis et al., 'Night Shift Work, Light at Night, and the Risk of Breast Cancer', *Journal of the National Cancer Institute*, 93 (2001), pp. 1557–62.

p. 214   *Subjects kept alone in a room where a light came on at the same time*: S. Elmore et al., 'Light, Social Zeitgebers, and the Sleep–Wake Cycle in the Entrainment of Human Circadian Rhythms', *Research in Nursing and Health*, 17 (1994), pp. 471–8.

p. 215   *mice injected with pneumococci*: Herbert Weiner, 'The Prospects for Psychosomatic Medicine', *Psychosomatic Medicine*, 44 (1982), pp. 491–517.

p. 215   *chronomodulation*: F. Levi, 'From Circadian Rhythms to Cancer Chronotherapeutics', *Chronobiology International*, 19 (2002), pp. 1–19.

p. 215   *dysregulation of the HPA axis via cortisol*: G. Chrousos and P. Gold, 'A Healthy Body in a Healthy Mind – and Vice Versa: The Damaging Power of "Uncontrollable Stress"', *Journal of Clinical Endocrinology and Metabolism*, 83 (1998), pp. 1842–6, and M. Ockenfels et al., 'Effect of Chronic Stress Associated with Unemployment on Salivary Cortisol', *Psychosomatic Medicine*, 57 (1995), pp. 460–67.

p. 215   *immune system may be affected . . . by our experiences*: Janice Kiecolt-Glaser, 'Stress, Personal Relationships and Immune Function: Health Implications', *Brain, Behavior, and Immunity*, 13 (1999), pp. 61–72, and Miranda Olff, 'Stress, Depression, Immunity: The Role of Defense and Coping Styles', *Psychiatry Research*, 85 (1999), pp. 7–15.

p. 216   *depression in mothers and increased cortisol in their infants*:
G. Spangler and K. Grossman, 'Biobehavioral Organization in
Securely and Insecurely Attached Arousal', *Child Development*, 64
(1993), pp. 1439–50, and Deborah Lott, 'Brain Development,
Attachment and Impact on Psychic Vulnerability', *Psychiatric Times*,
15 (1998), pp. 1–5. See also R. Huot et al., 'Negative Affect in
Offspring of Depressed Mothers is Predicted by Infant Cortisol
Levels at Six Months and Maternal Depression during Pregnancy
but not Postpartum', *Annals of New York Academy of Science*, 1032
(2004), pp. 234–6.

p. 216   *asthma results*: L. J. Warner et al., 'Health Effects of Written Emotional Disclosure in Adolescents with Asthma', *Journal of
Pediatric Psychology*, 31 (2006), pp. 557–68.

p. 216   *diseases would be seen as varieties of inflammation*: Michael
Balint, 'Two Notes on the Erotic Component of the Ego-Instincts'
(1933), in *Primary Love and Psychoanalytic Technique* (Hogarth Press,
London, 1952), pp. 42–8. Balint's observation is worth quoting in
full: 'Inflammation is the central problem of present-day pathology; with a little exaggeration it can be said: pathology is the
theory of inflammation. It is worth noting that it is still not settled
whether the several pathological processes – hyperaemia, stasis,
oedema, atrophy, degeneration, metaplasia, hypertrophy, tumours,
etc. – are truly independent phenomena or only extreme cases of
inflammation which, only for the sake of systematisation and teaching, have been described as independent . . . The various diseases
– according to this idea – are differentiated less by the essence of
the illness than by its localisation; and so our diagnosis too is
primarily localisatory. If this is so, then most diseases are basically
inflammations – and thus inseparably linked with erotisation.'

p. 218   *A recent series of studies in Sweden*: Anneli Sepa et al.,
'Psychological Stress May Induce Diabetes-related Autoimmunity
in Infancy', *Diabetes Care*, 28 (2005), pp. 290–95; Sepa et al.,

'Mothers' Experiences of Serious Life Events Increase the Risk of Diabetes-related Autoimmunity in their Children', *Diabetes Care*, 28 (2005), pp. 2394–9; B. Hagglof et al., 'The Swedish Childhood Diabetes Study: Indications of Severe Psychological Stress as a Risk Factor for Type 1 (Insulin-Dependent) Diabetes Mellitus in Childhood', *Diabetologia*, 34 (1991), pp. 579–83.

p. 219   *Prolonged steroid use appears to shift the Th1/Th2 balance*: P. Evans, F. Hucklebridge, A. Clow, *Mind, Immunity and Health: The Science of Psychoneuroimmunology* (Free Association Books, London, 2000).

p. 220   On interrelations of the immune, endocrine and nervous systems, see Helga Susanne Haas and Konrad Schauenstein, 'Neuroimmunomodulation via Limbic Structures: The Neuroanatomy of Psychoimmunology', *Progress in Neurobiology*, 51 (1997), pp. 195–222.

p. 220   *facial herpes*: A. Buske-Kirschbaum et al., 'Preliminary Evidence for Herpes Labialis Recurrence Following Experimentally Induced Disgust', *Psychotherapy and Psychosomatics*, 70 (2001), pp. 86–91.

p. 222   *wounds of Alzheimer's carers took nine days longer to heal*: J. Kiecolt-Glaser et al., 'Slowing of Wound Healing by Psychological Stress', *Lancet*, 346 (1995), pp. 1194–6.

p. 223   *Tape recordings of their speech*: S. Sabat, 'Facilitating Conversation with an Alzheimer's Disease Sufferer through the Use of Indirect Repair', in H. Hamilton (ed.), *Language and Communication in Old Age: Multidisciplinary Perspectives*, Garland Press, 1999, pp. 115–31.

p. 223   On the language of immunology, see Anne-Marie Moulin and Alberto Cambrosio (eds.), *Singular Selves: Historical Issues and Contemporary Debates in Immunology* (Elsevier, New York, 2001). In order to avoid the vocabulary of 'self' and 'non-self', some immunologists have adopted what is known as the 'danger theory', according to which immune cells are responding to self-cells which behave abnormally rather than 'foreign' bodies. Rather than confusing 'self' and 'other', they are just helping self-cells that seem to be in distress. The idea that this danger theory should replace the self/non-self framework is doubtful since it replaces the self/non-self language with a more technical but equally dualistic vocabulary. Such metaphors seem to have a tight grip over some areas of medical thinking. Progress just consists in the replacement of one simplistic metaphor by another. See Russell Vance, 'Cutting Edge Commentary: A Copernican Revolution? Doubts about the Danger Theory', *Journal of Immunology*, 165 (2000), pp. 1725–8.

p. 225   *illness frequently may follow*: Marie-Claire Célérier, 'Maladies auto-immunes, événements de la vie et personnalités psycho-pathologiques', *Revue de Médecine Psychosomatique*, 6 (1987).

p. 225   *a patient suffering from the autoimmune disorder lupus*: Sylviane Bertolus, 'Lupus et psychosomatique', in *Identité et psychosomatique* (EDK, Paris, 2003), pp. 15–28.

p. 225   *handedness*: This is likely to be due to many different factors. Possible determinants include birth stress, genes relating also to hair-twirl direction, placental levels of testosterone, ultrasound tests, and many others.

12. Cancer

p 229   James Paget, *Surgical Pathology* (Longmans Green, London, 1870).

p. 229   Walter Walshe, *The Nature and Treatment of Cancer* (Taylor and Walton, London, 1846).

p. 230   *several research teams had tried to find evidence*: Lawrence LeShan and Richard Worthington, 'Personality as a Factor in the Pathogenesis of Cancer: A Review of the Literature', *British Journal of Medical Psychology*, 29 (1956), pp. 49–57; LeShan, 'Some Psychologic Correlates of Neoplastic Disease: A Preliminary

Report', *Journal of Clinical and Experimental Psychopathology*, 16 (1955), p. 281; E. Blumberg et al., 'A Possible Relationship between Psychological Factors and Human Cancer', *Psychosomatic Medicine*, 16 (1954), pp. 277–86.

p. 230   *the health of 1,337 medical students*: C. B. Thomas and K. R. Duszynski, 'Closeness to Parents and the Family Constellation in Five Disease States', *Johns Hopkins Medical Journal*, 134 (1974), pp. 251–70. See also Thomas, Duszynski and J. W. Shaffer, 'Family Attitudes Reported in Youth as Potential Predictors of Cancer', *Psychosomatic Medicine*, 41 (1979), pp. 287–302.

p. 231   *Psychological risk factors were just as significant*: R. L. Horne and R. S. Picard, 'Psychosocial Risk Factors for Lung Cancer', *Psychosomatic Medicine*, 41 (1979), pp. 503–14.

p. 231   *emotional inexpressivity . . . and survival time*: S. Greer and Tina Morris, 'Psychological Attributes of Women who Develop Breast Cancer: A Controlled Study', *Journal of Psychosomatic Research*, 19 (1975), pp. 147–53.

p. 232   *University of Illinois study*: V. W. Persky, 'Personality and Risk of Cancer: A 20-year Follow-up of the Western Electric Study', *Psychosomatic Medicine*, 49 (1987), pp. 435–49.

p. 232   *depression levels for 4,825 people*: B. Penninx et al., 'Chronically Depressed Mood and Cancer Risk in Older Persons', *Journal of the National Cancer Institute*, 90 (1998), pp. 888–93.

p. 232   *patients with fighting spirit or denial*: S. Greer, T. Morris and K. W. Pettingale, 'Psychological Response to Breast Cancer: Effect on Outcome', *Lancet*, 13 October 1979, pp. 785–7. See also M. Watson et al., 'Influence of Psychological Response on Survival in Breast Cancer: A Population-based Cohort Study', *Lancet*, 354 (1999), pp. 1331–6.

p. 233   *women with malignant melanoma*: R. J. DiClemente and L. Temoshok, 'Psychological Adjustment to having Cutaneous Malignant Melanoma as a Predictor of Follow-up Clinical Status', *Psychosomatic Medicine*, 47 (1985), p. 81, and Temoshok, 'Biopsychosocial Studies on Cutaneous Malignant Melanoma', *Social Science and Medicine*, 20 (1985), pp. 833–40.

p. 233   On Type C, see L. Temoshok, 'Personality, Coping Style, Emotion and Cancer: Towards an Integrative Model', *Cancer Survival*, 6 (1987), pp. 545–67, and S. Greer and M. Watson, 'Towards a Psychobiological Model of Cancer: Psychological Considerations', *Social Science Medicine*, 20 (1985), pp. 773–7.

p. 234   *women were interviewed prior to biopsy*: M. Wirsching et al., 'Psychological Identification of Breast Cancer Patients before Biopsy', *Journal of Psychosomatic Research*, 26 (1982), pp. 1–10.

p. 234   *A similar British project screened 2,000 women*: C. L. Cooper and E. B. Faragher, 'Psychosocial Stress and Breast Cancer', *Psychological Medicine*, 23 (1993), pp. 653–62. See also Janine Giese-Davis and David Spiegel, 'Suppression, Repressive-Defensiveness, Restraint, and Distress in Metastatic Breast Cancer: Separable or Inseparable Constructs?', *Journal of Personality*, 69 (2001), pp. 417–49.

p. 237   *medical students during exam periods*: L. Tomei et al., 'Psychological Stress and Phorbol Ester Inhibition of Radiation-induced Apoptosis in Human Peripheral Blood Leukocytes', *Psychiatric Research*, 33 (1990), pp. 59–71.

p. 237   *methyltransferase*: R. Glaser et al., 'Effects of Stress on Methyltransferase Synthesis', *Health Psychology*, 4 (1985), pp. 403–12.

p. 238   *inflammation, which has been found to play a vital role*: L. Coussens and Z. Werb, 'Inflammation and Cancer', *Nature*, 420 (2002), pp. 860–67.

p. 239   *holes were punched in the roof of the mouths*: J. Kiecolt-Glaser et al., 'Slowing of Wound Healing by Psychological Stress', *Lancet* 346 (1995), pp. 1194–6.

p. 239   On the examiner's gaze, see Gabor Mate, *When the Body Says No* (Wiley, New Jersey, 2003).

p. 239   *Mice showed a poorer ability to rid themselves of sarcomas*: A. Amkraut and G. F. Solomon, 'Stress and Murine Sarcoma

Virus (Moloney)-induced Tumors', *Cancer Research*, 32 (1972), pp. 1428–33.

p. 240 *the rhythm of immune functioning has been disturbed*: S. Sephton et al., 'Diurnal Cortisol Rhythm as a Predictor of Breast Cancer Survival', *Journal of the National Cancer Institute*, 92 (2000), pp. 994–1000, and M. Mormont and F. Levi, 'Circadian-system Alterations During Cancer Processes: A Review', *International Journal of Cancer*, 70 (1997), pp. 241–7.

p. 240 On tumour cells and glucose, see J. Turner-Cobb et al., 'Psychosocial Effects on Immune Function and Disease Progression in Cancer: Human Studies', in Robert Ader, David Felten and Nicholas Cohen, *Psychoneuroimmunology* (Academic Press, San Diego, 2001), vol. 1, pp. 565–82.

p. 241 *High DHEA levels*: G. B. Gordon et al., 'Relationship of Serum Levels of Dehydroepiandrosterone and Dehydroepiandrosterone Sulfate to the Risk of Developing Postmenopausal Breast Cancer', *Cancer Research*, 50 (1990), pp. 3859–62.

p. 242 On 'life force', see Arthur Kleinman, *Patients and Healers in the Context of Culture* (University of California Press, Berkeley, 1980), and Kleinman, *The Illness Narratives: Suffering, Healing and the Human Condition* (Basic Books, New York, 1988).

p. 242 *giving up . . . giving in*: Joyce McDougall, *Theatres of the Body* (Free Association Books, London, 1989).

p. 243 *cancer . . . as an enemy*: Patrick Ben Soussan, *Le Cancer est un combat* (Erès, Paris, 2004).

13. Health Risks of being Normal

p. 247 On emotions, see C. Izard (ed.), *Measuring Emotions in Infants and Children* (Cambridge University Press, Cambridge, 1982); Richard Davidson, Klaus Scherer and Hill Goldsmith, *Handbook of Affective Sciences* (Oxford University Press, Oxford, 2004); Catherine Lutz, *Unnatural Emotions: Everyday Sentiments on a*

Micronesian Atoll and Their Challenge to Western Theory (University of Chicago Press, Chicago, 1988).

p. 248   For Rebecca West, see Victoria Glendinning, *Rebecca West: A Life* (Knopf, New York, 1987).

p. 249   *bottling up*: M. Julius et al., 'Anger-coping Types, Blood Pressure, and All-cause Mortality: A Follow-up in Tecumeh, Michigan (1971–1983)', *American Journal of Epidemiology*, 124 (1986), pp. 220–33.

p. 251   *operative thinking*: Pierre Marty and Michel de M'Uzan, 'La Pensée opératoire', *Revue Française de Psychanalyse*, 27 (1963), pp. 345–56, and Marty, de M'Uzan and Christian David, *L'Investigation psychosomatique* (PUF, Paris, 1963). Earlier in the 1940s and '50s, researchers like Paul MacLean and Jurgen Ruesch were already suggesting that there might be a link between somatic illness and difficulties in accessing emotional states. MacLean argued that there might be feelings that, rather than being relayed to the neocortex, travelled from the limbic system via autonomic pathways to bodily organs. The idea here was that it is good for one's mental health, and subsequently physical health, to have the limbic system – which was thought to be the archaic emotional centre of the brain – thoroughly integrated with the higher regions of the brain, the neocortex, where symbolic elaboration could take place. Without these outlets to process emotional mental activity, bodily organs would bear the brunt of an unbuffered nervous system. See Paul MacLean, 'Psychosomatic Disease and the "Visceral Brain"', *Psychosomatic Medicine*, 11 (1949), pp. 338–53, and Jurgen Ruesch, 'The Infantile Personality: The Core Problem of Psychosomatic Medicine', *Psychosomatic Medicine*, 10 (1948), pp. 134–44. These ideas are very popular today, and have led to a great deal of research, yet they tend to rely on a simplistic idea of the relation between thoughts and feelings. Talk of the 'emotional brain' and the 'thinking brain', coupled with hypotheses about the role of the amygdala and limbic system, usually fail to factor in the difference between instincts and drives, between unconscious and preconscious processes, between emotions and passions, and between observable behaviour and subjectivity. Interestingly, much of this research goes hand in glove with modern treatments like cognitive behavioural therapy: both rely on a pedagogical model whereby one party – the 'emotional' brain or the patient – must be educated by another, more mature party – the 'thinking' brain or the therapist.

p. 252   For the McDougall vignettes, see Joyce McDougall, *Theatres of the Mind* (Free Association Books, London, 1985), p. 23. See also McDougall, 'The Psychosoma and the Psychoanalytic Process', *International Journal of Psychoanalysis*, 55 (1974), pp. 437–59.

p. 255   *alexithymia . . . was introduced by the Boston analysts*: J. C. Nemiah, H. Freyberger and P. Sifneos, 'Alexithymia: A View of the Psychosomatic Process', in O. Hill (ed.), *Modern Trends in Psychosomatic Medicine* (Butterworth, London, 1976), pp. 430–39.

p. 255   On alexithymia, see Fernando Lolas and Michael Von Rad, 'Alexithymia', in Stanley Cheren (ed.), *Psychosomatic Medicine: Theory, Physiology and Practice*, vol. 1 (International Universities Press, Madison, 1989), pp. 189–237, and Graeme Taylor, R. Bagby and J. Parker, *Disorders of Affect Regulation: Alexithymia in Medical and Psychiatric Illness* (Cambridge University Press, Cambridge, 1997).

p. 255   *work with diabetic patients*: Rosine Debray, *L'Equilibre psychosomatique: organisation mentale des diabétiques* (Dunod, Paris, 1983).

p. 257   *Developing these ideas*: McDougall, *Theatres of the Mind*, op. cit., and Michel Fain, 'Prélude à la vie fantasmatique', *Revue Française de Psychanalyse*, 35 (1971), pp. 291–364.

p. 258   *'essential depression'*: Pierre Marty, *L'Ordre psychosomatique* (Payot, Paris, 1980).

p. 258   For Szwec on depression, see Gérard Szwec, 'Devenir d'une dépression de la première enfance génératrice de somatisations et consequences psychosomatiques de la maltraitance', in Gérard Le

Goues and Georges Pragier (eds.), *Cliniques psychosomatiques* (PUF, Paris, 1997), pp. 67–90.

p. 262 '*Foreclosure*': This is a concept developed by Lacan and it is surprising that nowhere, to our knowledge, does McDougall acknowledge her debt to him for this important part of her theoretical apparatus. Curiously, it seems as if McDougall has done to Lacan's name exactly what these patients supposedly do to their affects.

p. 262 *inscription*: The idea of somatic illness arising through direct inscription may also shed some light on the relation of sleep and dreams to health. One way of understanding the function of dreams is to see them as filters that work to connect our everyday experiences with unconscious trains of thought. If something happens in the day that concerns us, the dream can help to make sense of this by registering it in the unconscious, linking it to previous experiences and to childhood desires, fantasies and fears. Dreams thus have a protective role, allowing us to inscribe the events of our lives in a framework. That's why, for example, it is often a positive sign if someone who has been severely traumatized starts to dream. The dreams are making sense of the trauma, connecting the unknown, unpredicted event with what is already structured and represented. We saw in Chapter 11 how sleep problems could impact negatively on immune functioning, and this disturbance to dreamlife may have equally serious consequences. Disturbances to sleep, which block the dreaming process, may mean that events are unable to find a place in the unconscious. Cut off from chains of unconscious representations, they are once again isolated and unbound to networks of meaning and mental elaboration. If sleep and hence dreamlife are disrupted, this may then make bodily illness more likely.

p. 263 *book on psychosomatic illness*: Marty, de M'Uzan and David, *L'Investigation psychosomatique*, op. cit.

p. 263 *holophrase*: Alexandre Stevens, 'L'Holophrase, entre psychose et psychosomatique', *Ornicar?*, 42 (1987), pp. 45–79.

p. 263   *single words or phrases used by a child*: Alison Elliot, *Child Language* (Cambridge University Press, Cambridge, 1981), pp. 90–93, and John Dore, 'Holophrases, Speech Acts and Language Universals', *Journal of Child Language*, 2 (1975), pp. 21–40.

p. 265   For the haemophilia case, see Robert Chilcote and Robert Baehner, 'Atypical Bleeding in Hemophilia: Application of the Conversion Model to the Case Study of a Child', *Psychosomatic Medicine*, 42 (1980), pp. 221–30.

p. 266   Vincent Sheean, *Lead, Kindly Light* (Cassell, London, 1950), pp. 216–17.

p. 271   *rates of somatic illness are reduced*: Geoffrey Gorer, *Death, Grief, and Mourning* (Doubleday, New York, 1965), and J. Yamamoto, K. Okonogi and T. Iwasaki, 'Object Loss Prior to Medical Admissions in Japan', *Psychosomatics*, 10 (1969), pp. 46–50.

p. 271   On non-integration, see Debray, *L'Equilibre psychosomatique*, op. cit. See also Veronique Mead, 'A New Model for Understanding the Role of Environmental Factors in the Origins of Chronic Illness: A Case Study of Type 1 Diabetes Mellitus', *Medical Hypotheses*, 63 (2004), pp. 1035–46.

14. Does Therapy Work?

p. 283   *group work was initially discouraged*: Jimmie Holland, 'History of Psycho-Oncology: Overcoming Attitudinal and Conceptual Barriers', *Psychosomatic Medicine*, 64 (2002), pp. 206–21.

p. 284   *In the Recurrent Coronary Prevention Project, 1,013 subjects*: M. Friedman et al., 'Alteration of Type A Behaviour and Reduction in Cardiac Recurrences in Post-Myocardial Infarction Patients', *American Heart Journal*, 108 (1984), pp. 237–48.

p. 285   For the work of Dean Ornish and Jon Kabat-Zinn, see Kabat-Zinn et al., 'Influence of a Mindfulness-based Stress Reduction Intervention on Rates of Skin Clearing in Patients with

Moderate to Severe Psoriasis', *Psychosomatic Medicine*, 60 (1998), pp. 625–32.

p. 285   *'mindfulness meditation'*: Richard Davidson et al., 'Alterations in Brain and Immune Function Produced by Mindfulness Meditation', *Psychosomatic Medicine*, 65 (2003), pp. 564–70.

p. 285   *support groups for women*: David Spiegel et al., 'Effect of Psychosocial Treatment on Survival of Patients with Metastatic Breast Cancer', *Lancet*, 8668 (1989), pp. 888–91. For an opposing view, see P. J. Goodwin et al., 'The Effect of Group Psychosocial Support on Survival in Metastatic Breast Cancer', *New England Journal of Medicine*, 345 (2001), pp. 1719–26.

p. 286   Fawzy Fawzy et al., 'Malignant Melanoma: Effects of an Early Structured Psychiatric Intervention, Coping, and Affective State on Recurrence and Survival 6 Years Later', *Archives of General Psychiatry*, 50 (1993), pp. 681–9. See also Fawzy Fawzy and Nancy Fawzy, 'Malignant Melanoma: Effects of a Brief, Structured Psychiatric Intervention on Survival and Recurrence at 10-year Follow-up', *Archives of General Psychiatry*, 60 (2003), pp. 100–103, and the review by T. Meyer and M. Mark, 'Effects of Psychosocial Interventions with Adult Cancer Patients: A Meta-Analysis of Randomized Experiments', *Health Psychology*, 14 (1995), pp. 101–8. Not all the data from replication studies for the Fawzy and Spiegel work is currently available, yet the results published so far are balanced between positive and negative assessments. Fawzy's recent re-evaluation is less optimistic than the initial study. The follow-up found that the survival benefits were much weaker than previously assumed, although not entirely absent.

It is remarkable that, despite the level of funding and sophisticated techniques used in this study, no one seems to have noticed the absurdity of studying the effects years later of group work that took place once a week for one and a half hours over six weeks. To do a proper study, the group work should have been ongoing, or lasted significantly longer. What, we might ask, could get done in six weeks? The Spiegel study has also been criticized with the argument that in fact statistically the control group died earlier than they should have given mortality rates in the general population. A further problem is that data on coping and distress will depend a great deal on the language used by the patients, yet this language may have actually been learned in the group work. People might pick up new ways of speaking about their emotions and well-being which are more a surface veneer than a reflection of their deeper psychology. Remember how the descriptions of operative thinking had emphasized the ease with which other people's language would be appropriated. It is a pity that high-profile studies like Fawzy's open themselves to so many methodological criticisms which could well have been avoided. Enough studies exist to show the benefits of long-term group work that manages to avoid such pitfalls. Critics raise other methodological problems. Differences between control and non-control groups in terms of diet, lifestyle and compliance with treatments are not always clear, and nor are the frequency and content of further medical interventions. Similarly, there are many questions raised by changes in survival rate after certain time periods during follow-up. But could these problems be clues as well as obstacles? When critics complain that they prevent us from seeing the direct effect of treatment on survival, this implies that we are dealing with a single-cause model – which is, of course, exactly what so much of this research is contesting. The whole point is to move away from the idea of the direct effect of a single agent on the illness.

p. 286   Gieta van der Pompe et al., 'Effectiveness of a Short-term Group Psychotherapy Program on Endocrine and Immune Function in Breast Cancer Patients: An Exploratory Study', *Journal of Psychosomatic Research*, 42 (1997), pp. 453–66.

p. 286   *2,500 patients*: L. F. Berkman et al., 'Effects of Treating Depression and Low Perceived Social Support on Cardiac Events after Myocardial Infarction: The Enhancing Recovery in Coronary

Heart Disease Patients (ENRICHD) Randomized Trial', *Journal of the American Medical Association*, 289 (2003), pp. 3106–16.

p. 287   *individual responses to . . . treatment*: Alastair Cunningham and Kimberley Watson, 'How Psychological Therapy May Prolong Survival in Cancer Patients: New Evidence and a Simple Theory', *Integrative Cancer Care Therapies*, 3 (2004), pp. 214–29.

p. 289   *synchronized periods*: M. McClintock, 'Menstrual Synchrony and Suppression', *Nature*, 229 (1971), pp. 244–5.

p. 293   René Allendy, *Journal d'un médecin malade* (Denoel, Paris, 1944).

p. 294   *biofeedback techniques*: A. Wauquier et al., 'Changes in Cerebral Blood Flow Velocity Associated with Biofeedback-assisted Relaxation Treatment of Migraine Headaches as Specific for the Middle Cerebral Artery', *Headache*, 35 (1995), pp. 358–62.

p. 296   *depressive symptoms*: Matthew Berg et al., 'Presurgical Depression Predicts Medical Morbidity 6 Months after Coronary Bypass Graft Surgery', *Psychosomatic Medicine*, 65 (2003), pp. 111–18, and G. McKhann et al., 'Depression and Cognitive Decline after Coronary Artery Bypass Grafting', *Lancet*, 9061 (1997), pp. 1282–4.

p. 297   *post-operative delusions*: Harry Abram, 'Therapeutic Consultation with the Surgical Patient', in Eric Wittkower and Hector Warnes (eds.), *Psychosomatic Medicine: Its Clinical Applications* (Harper & Row, Maryland, 1977), pp. 42–8; R. M. Morse and E. M. Littin, 'Postoperative Delirium: A Study of Etiologic Factors', *American Journal of Psychiatry*, 126 (1969), pp. 388–95; Helene Deutsch, 'Some Psychoanalytic Observations on Surgery' (1942), in *Neuroses and Character Types: Clinical Psychoanalytic Studies* (International Universities Press, Madison, 1965), pp. 282–304.

p. 297   *painkillers, and shorter hospital stays*: H. Dreher, 'Mind–Body Interventions for Surgery: Evidence and Exigency', *Advances in Mind–Body Medicine*, 14 (1998), pp. 207–22.

p. 297   *how they had reacted to symbolic moments in their lives*: Jacques Lacan, 'A propos de la communication de M. J. Gosset sur les problèmes psycho-somatiques en chirurgie générale', *Mémoires de l'Académie de Chirurgie*, 16/17 (1947), pp. 370–73.

p. 298   On end of treatment, see Kenneth Cohn, 'Chemotherapy from an Insider's Perspective', *Lancet*, 319(8279) (1982), p. 1006–9.

p. 298   Diane Chauvelot, *L'Hôpital se moque de la charité* (Erès, Paris, 2004).

p. 299   *Healthcare Commission survey: The Times*, 14 June 2005.

p. 300   *no named nurse*: S. Bruster et al., 'National Survey of Patients', *British Medical Journal*, 309 (1994), pp. 1542–9.

p. 301   *Britain currently has fewer doctors: The Times*, 17 January 2005.

15. What Do Doctors Want?

p. 303   On the dangers of removing symptoms, see Smith Ely Jelliffe, *Sketches in Psychosomatic Medicine* (Nervous and Mental Disease Monographs, New York, 1939); Melitta Sperling, 'Psychosis and Psychosomatic Illness', *International Journal of Psychoanalysis*, 36 (1955), pp. 320–27; Karl Menninger, 'Polysurgery and Polysurgical Addiction', *Psychoanalytic Quarterly*, 3 (1934), pp. 173–99; Jesse Appel and Samuel Richard Rosen, 'Psychotic Factors in Psychosomatic Illness', *Psychosomatic Medicine*, 12 (1950), pp. 237–43; Pierre Marty and Rosine Debray, 'Current Concepts of Character Disturbance', in Stanley Cheren (ed.), *Psychosomatic Medicine: Theory, Physiology and Practice*, vol. 1 (International Universities Press, 1989), pp. 159–88.

p. 304   *Balint groups*: D. Kjeldmand et al., 'Balint Training Makes GPs Thrive Better in Their Job', *Patient Education and Counseling*, 55 (2004), pp. 230–35.

p. 304   Michael Balint, *The Doctor, His Patient and the Illness* (1957), revised edn (International Universities Press, Madison, 1964), p. 208.

p. 306   For Seitz's experiment, see P. Seitz, 'Symbolism and Organ Choice in Conversion Reactions: An Experimental Approach', *Psychosomatic Medicine*, 13 (1951), pp. 254–59.

p. 309   On the congestive heart failure case, see Roy Grinker and Fred Robbins, *Psychosomatic Case Book* (Blakiston, New York, 1954), p. 312.

p. 311   On the woman hospitalized, see Alain Merlet, 'Psychosomatique', *Carnets Cliniques de Strasbourg*, 2 (2000), p. 65.

p. 312   *stimulus-based appreciation of reality*: J. G. Flannery, 'Alexithymia: 1. The Communication of Physical Symptoms', *Psychotherapy and Psychosomatics*, 28 (1977), pp. 133–40.

p. 313   *70 per cent of medical students*: S. M. Woods, J. Natterson and J. Silverman, 'Medical Students' Disease: Hypochondriasis in Medical Education', *Journal of Medical Education*, 41 (1966), pp. 785–90.

p. 313   On the problems experienced by doctors, see Luigi Grassi and Katia Magnani, 'Psychiatric Morbidity and Burnout in the Medical Profession', *Psychotherapy and Psychosomatics*, 69 (2000), pp. 329–34; John Duffy and Edward Litin, *The Emotional Health of Physicians* (Charles Thomas, Springfield, 1967); Eric Wittkower and Hector Warnes (eds.), *Psychosomatic Medicine: Its Clinical Applications* (Harper & Row, Maryland, 1977), p. 5.

p. 313   *suicide rate*: K. Hawton, A. Malmberg and S. Simkin, 'Suicide in Doctors', *Journal of Psychosomatic Research*, 57 (2004), pp. 1–4.

p. 314   *doctor game*: Sigmund Freud, *Beyond the Pleasure Principle* (1920), Standard Edition (Hogarth Press, London, 1955), pp. 7–64.

p. 314   *future vocation*: Ernst Simmel, 'The "Doctor-Game", Illness and the Profession of Medicine', *International Journal of Psychoanalysis*, 7 (1926), pp. 470–83.

p. 314   Bertram Lewin, 'Counter-Transference in the Technique of Medical Practice', *Psychosomatic Medicine*, 8 (1946), pp. 195–9.

p. 317   *disciplines basic to medicine*: George Engel, 'Enduring Attributes of Medicine Relevant for the Education of the Physician', *Annals of Internal Medicine*, 78 (1973), pp. 587–93.

p. 317   *one in twenty*: Arnold Relman and Marcia Angell, 'Resolved: Psychosocial Interventions Can Improve Clinical Outcomes in Organic Disease (Con)', *Psychosomatic Medicine*, 64 (2002), pp. 558–63.

p. 317   Balint, *The Doctor, His Patient and the Illness*, op. cit.

p. 317   Jacques Lacan, 'Psychanalyse et médecine', unpublished transcription (1966).

Afterword

p. 324   D. W. Winnicott, 'Psycho-Somatic Illness in Its Positive and Negative Aspects', *International Journal of Psychoanalysis*, 47 (1966), pp. 510–16.

Index